78.6043

Building Access™ 2 Applications

Building Access™ 2 Applications

Using Point-and-Click Programming

John S. Dranchak

Joseph R. LaCroce

JOHN WILEY & SONS, INC.

New York • Chichester • Brisbane • Toronto • Singapore

Publisher: Katherine Schowalter
Editor: Tim Ryan
Assistant Managing Editor: Angela Murphy
Text Design and Composition: SunCliff Graphic Productions

Designations used by companies to distinguish their products are often claimed as trademarks. In all instances where John Wiley & Sons, Inc. is aware of a claim, the product names appear in Initial Capital or all CAPITAL letters. Readers, however, should contact the appropriate companies for more complete information regarding trademarks and registration.

This text is printed on acid-free paper.

This publication is designed to provide accurate and authoritative information in regard to the subject matter covered. It is sold with the understanding that the publisher is not engaged in rendering legal, accounting, or other professional service. If legal advice or other expert assistance is required, the services of a competent professional person should be sought.

Library of Congress Cataloging-in-Publication Data

Dranchak, John
　　Building Access 2 Applications: using point-and-click programming / John Dranchak
　　　　p.　　cm.
　　Includes index
　　ISBN 0-471-30361-5 (paper : acid-free paper)
　　1. Database management.　　2. Microsoft Access.　　3. Application software.　　I. Title.
QA76.9.D3D73　　　1995
005.75'65—dc20　　　　　　　　　　　　　　　　　　　　　　　　　　　93-39731

Printed in the United States of America
10　9　8　7　6　5　4　3　2　1

This book is dedicated to my mother, Mary Lorraine Dranchak.

John S. Dranchak

This book is dedicated to my daughter Marilyn as an example that diverse opportunities present themselves to you every day. J.L.

Joseph R. LaCroce

Contents

Chapter 3   Windows Design Basics — 47

Chapter 4   Information Modeling — 83

Part II Applications with No Code

Part III   Enhancing Your Application with Macros

Chapter 9   Macros   329

Chapter 10   Using Macros to Modify the User Interface   365

Acknowledgments

First of all, I'd like to thank Joseph R. LaCroce for making this project fun—hopefully this is the first of many books we will work on together; Alice C. Mack for encouraging me to finish this book when the responsibilities and commitments of Logic Control seemed overwhelming; Tim Ryan for having the vision to publish this book, and for being patient with the delivery of the manuscript; Teri LaCroce for all of her support; Mary C. Doyle for always being a great friend; Ed Ross, of MediaMorphosis, for designing the graphics at the end of this book; Carlos Santos for designing the Logic Control logo; Pete Thompson, of Microsoft, for his perpetual enthusiasm; Natash and Ginger for endless love and eternal smiles.

John S. Dranchak

Thank you to my wife Teri, for being the driving force behind the successes I've had in my life, and for her encouragement, love, understanding, and editing skills throughout this project. I'd also like to thank my parents Lou and Jeannine LaCroce for their efforts to expose me to new interests and pursuits. To Joe Jackson, Pete Roberts, Karen LaGarde, Lynn Colligan, and Roma Blanchet for your positive thoughts and influences when I needed them most. To Bob DeMichiell, Ph.D., for being my mentor and friend since college. Finally, to John S. Dranchak, thank you for the opportunity and the last ten years of good times.

Joseph R. LaCroce

Production Environment

This book was produced using Microsoft Word 6.0, running on a variety of different platforms at various points in time, including beta versions of Windows 95, Windows 3.1, Windows for Workgroups 3.11, Windows NT Workstation 3.5, and Windows NT Server 3.5. All screen shots were performed and cataloged with Halcyon Software's DoDot—an indespensable tool on a project of this scope. For more information on DoDot, contact Halcyon Software at 408-378-9898.

Introduction

Who This Book Is For

Microsoft Access 2.0 is a powerful, yet deceivingly simple to use database management system. Many Access users never fully exploit its capabilities to easily build graphical database applications. While they master some of the components that Access uses (i.e. tables and queries), they never master the art of putting these pieces together to build a complete application. This does not occur because it is a difficult process, but because there is not a clear roadmap of how to put these components together, or because the object-based, event-driven paradigm that Access uses is not familiar enough to them. *Building Access 2 Applications* is your roadmap to working with this paradigm, which will show you how to quickly and easily put all of the pieces together.

This book is targeted at both professional developers and end users who face the responsibility of building complete applications, using Microsoft Access 2.0. This book is intended for users that have been using Access for some time, but have not yet mastered the process of putting all of the blocks together to build a complete application. A basic knowledge of tables, queries, forms, and reports is assumed.

How This Book Is Organized

Building Access 2 Applications is divided into three main sections, consisting of ten chapters. Instead of just being another Access reference manual, *Building Access 2 Applications* walks the reader through all of the steps necessary to create a Contact Manager, using the WinContact case study. After the first section, all of the steps to create WinContact are provided.

Part I, *Application Design*, consists of four chapters that give an overview of what an application is, and how to go about creating one. Chapter 1, *What Is an*

Application, defines what a database management system is, introduces Microsoft Access, and defines what an Access application is. Chapter 2, *Dranchak's Development Methodology*, introduces the reader to what a methodology is, and details a simple but effective methodology for building data-centric applications. The WinContact application, a case study that is used throughout the book, is also introduced. Chapter 3, *Windows Design Basics*, discusses what makes the Microsoft Windows interface a good choice for both the developer and user, as well as how to create a good interface for your application. Chapter 4, *Information Modeling*, introduces the art of information modeling and shows you how to create the logical data model for the WinContact application.

Part II, *Applications with No Code*, contains four chapters that discuss creating Access applications, using standard Access objects, but without macros or modules. Chapter 5, *Tables and Databases*, covers how to create the tables necessary for the WinContact application, as well as an overview of properties whose characteristics will be inherited by other objects created later. Chapter 6, *Queries*, discusses the relationship between tables and queries. Chapter 7, *Forms*, explains when forms should be used, and discusses how to create them. Chapter 8, *Reports*, discusses the use of reports to provide the end user with information.

Part III, *Enhancing Your Application with Macros*, the meat and potatoes of this book, details how to tie all of the objects in your database together to create an application. Chapter 9, *Macros*, provides an overview of what macros are, and how you create, edit, and save them. Chapter 10, *Using Macros to Modify the User Interface*, teaches you how to create a custom user interface that incorporates all of the other objects you have thus far created to finish the WinContact application.

Chapter 1

What Is an Application?

In This Chapter

Microsoft Access is a database management system that allows you to create custom database applications to meet your specific needs. This chapter discusses the fundamentals of database management systems, as well as what constitutes an Access application. You will learn:

- The difference between data and information.
- What a database is.
- What a database management system is.
- The chain of events that created the market for Access.
- Why there was a strong demand for a Windows database management system.
- How Access takes advantage of the Windows environment.
- What constitutes an Access application.

Information vs. Data

Data

Data is raw input with a wide range of possible interpretations, unless placed in a specific context. Take for example the following string of numbers:

201
203
212
516
718
914

Aside from the fact that these numbers appear to be sorted in ascending order and have three digits, what do they mean? Are they the output of a laboratory experiment? Or the street numbers for houses on a particular street in Algoma, Wisconsin? Perhaps they are last night's winning lottery numbers. The next list shows another set of data.

Connecticut
New Jersey
Manhattan
Long Island
Queens
Westchester

Perhaps this data set is a little less intriguing than the first. After all, Connecticut and New Jersey are states. But what about the others? Someone who lives in New York City would be able to tell you that Queens and Manhattan are boroughs of New York City, that Westchester is a county north of New York City, and that Long Island is a large island east of New York City and south of Connecticut. But if you weren't acquainted with the metro New York region, you wouldn't be able to make even these associations. Either way though, the question remains: What does the data represent? It is not a list of only states, and it is not a list of only boroughs of New York. In other words, you have no idea, because you don't know the context in which the data is meant to be viewed. Stated differently, there is no definitive relationship among the six words in this list. To define a relationship, you might combine these two lists as illustrated in Table 1.1, because, after all, they both have six elements. Now new possibilities arise from associating the location in the left column and the number in the right column. But the table still does not tell you what this relationship is. Is the number on the right the number of registered users (in thousands) of Microsoft Access in each location on the same line? Or is it the number of miles of interstate highways that are maintained by the federal government?

Table 1.1 Places and Numbers	
Connecticut	203
New Jersey	201
Manhattan	212
Long Island	516
Queens	718
Westchester	914

Information

In actuality, the numbers in the right column are area codes for the locations in the left column. But until you associate the sets, all you have are data. When the two are combined, as illustrated in Table 1.2, by labeling each column, a relationship can be inferred, and you finally have information. Information is data in context.

What Is a Database?

A database is an organized collection of data which, properly used, becomes information. Although this book focuses on using computers to manage your data, a database does not have to be computer-based. An address book that contains the names, addresses, and phone numbers of business contacts and friends is a database. So is the drawer in your file cabinet which contains all of your suppliers' catalogs. Although you might not realize it, there is even a relationship between your address book and the drawer in the file cabinet, because you have listed every supplier in your address book. Therefore, if you

Table 1.2 Metro New York Locations and Their Area Codes	
Location	**Area Code**
Connecticut	203
New Jersey	201
Manhattan	212
Long Island	516
Queens	718
Westchester	914

have a catalog for a supplier, you also have an entry in your address book for that supplier. Sometimes, you may be looking through a catalog and decide to call the supplier to place an order, so you turn to the back of the catalog to get the phone number. Other times, you will want to call the supplier, but instead of taking the catalog from the file cabinet to get the phone number, you open up your address book, which is sitting on your desk, and look it up. In other words, you are managing the database by deciding what information you need, and which source to get it from.

You have also probably structured the data in some manner that makes sense to you. When you add a supplier to your address book, you may make an entry under the name of the supplier and then write in the name of your contact. Or you may add an entry under the name of the contact and then, as an afterthought, include the company name. Hopefully, you also organized the catalogs in the file cabinet in some orderly manner. Perhaps they have been inserted in alphabetical order, based on the supplier's name. Perhaps you sorted them by product type, and then put them in alphabetical order. Maybe you just inserted the most recent catalog, without regard to supplier or product type, in the front of the drawer, creating a FIFO (first in, first out) hierarchy without really thinking about it. Again, by deciding on physical sorting and placement, you are the database manager.

What Is a Database Management System?

Although the human mind is capable of managing a great amount of data (and information), it has its limits. In the information age, more data must be constantly assimilated and evaluated. In addition, there may be other users for your data. Perhaps you are on vacation, and your co-worker Bob has to call a supplier. Although Bob knows which drawer of which file cabinet the catalogs are stored in, it might not be obvious to him that you sorted the catalogs alphabetically according to the last name of the supplier's representative. Although he will eventually find what he needs, it would have taken much less effort and time if he knew how the data was organized. It would have taken even less time if he could have just put in a request to the database manager, and never had to deal with the underlying data. Thus, it is important not only that the database manager handle the physical issues of the data and its storage, but also that he or she provides accessibility to other members of the organization who need to use the data, in a consistent manner. This allows them to use the data to help them with their jobs, not to make their jobs into that of the database manager.

This presents the problem of how to efficiently manage data and its relationships and provide common access for all who will use it. The solution is to use a tool designed specifically for this task, a database management system. A database management system (DBMS) is a software application used to manipulate the database. The sole purpose of a database management system is to convert data into information and to provide access to this information. Database management systems come in all shapes and sizes from hand-held personal information managers (such as Sharp's Wizard) to DB2 running on an IBM 3090 series mainframe with terabytes of data.

A Little History

Computerized database management systems originally ran only on mainframes. If you didn't have a mainframe, you weren't going to have a DBMS. Thus, DBMSs were usually owned and operated by large corporations, academic institutions, and the government because of the economies of scale. With the introduction of the minicomputer, many smaller business and institutions, which could not afford a mainframe, acquired the newer, less expensive hardware, and DBMSs appeared on this platform.

Traditionally, database management systems were implemented and maintained in the corporate world by the Information Systems Department (ISD). The end user had little or no interaction with the physical DBMS. Although users were often consulted during the design and implementation phases of a DBMS, they would be permitted to do little more than put in requests for reports or input data to a very restrictive input screen. Although DBMSs are designed to help the end user, because of the complexity of these early systems and their reliance on ISD, users often did not get the information that they wanted or needed. It also put them at the mercy of the ISD, which traditionally was backlogged because requests usually outnumbered the resources available to implement them. Good information is always timely, and when a user had to wait months or even years for a system to be developed, the value of that information was often devalued. This often frustrated users, and caused them to call ISD the "Ivory Tower," because they had no control over the situation. Although this was unfair to the end user, it was not really the fault of ISD. At least not originally.

Mainframes and minis are complex and esoteric, requiring a very specialized set of skills to operate. In addition to operating the hardware itself, analysts, designers, and programmers are necessary to write the programs to make the hardware perform the desired tasks. Although recently there are many more people available with the proper skill set, demand still outpaces supply for systems professionals. The typical end user usually does not have this set of skills. In addition, most end users are not really interested in databases or computer programming; they just want to get the information they need to get their jobs done. Although many were frustrated, this arrangement was (and sometimes still is) a necessity. Essentially, end users were powerless.

The First End-User Revolution

Then something happened. A new series of computer programming tools, known as 4GLs (fourth-generation languages) were introduced. Fourth-generation tools such as RAMIS and NOMAD allowed requests for data to be typed into the computer in English-like statements, unlike the cryptic syntax of traditional programming languages such as COBOL, FORTRAN, and APL. This enabled end users to create their own queries and to access data in the database. Instead of having to request a new report format from a programmer, end users could create the report themselves. Although many programmers were threatened by the idea of end-user data manipulation, it usually worked out for the best, because programmers were free to work on projects more important than just creating reports, and ISD's backlog was often reduced. It also worked out well because ISD could still control the database input and structure as well as other system programs, which meant secure data. The reduction in report formatting backlog provided time to create better-designed applications.

But by giving end users a little power and showing them how they could readily perform tasks that only ISD could accomplish before the advent of 4GLs, Pandora's box was opened. Users wanted even more control over the database, as well as individual applications. Unfortunately, they had no way to gain that control until 1982.

The Dawn of the Second Revolution

Although the personal computer had been kicking around for some time, it wasn't until IBM introduced its PC in 1982 that its use became widespread. Suddenly, all of the frustrated end users of the world had the means to have a piece of hardware that they could understand and control, as well as the capability to create, edit, and manipulate their own data, all without having to deal with ISD. Equally, if not more, important was the fact that the price of PCs and their software put them within the reach of small companies and individuals. Thus, everyone seemed like a winner: End users could gain more control over their data and cut down on the amount of time it took to get the information they needed; small businesses and individuals could now afford and utilize tools that their larger relatives had grown accustomed to.

But PCs were not without their problems. From the corporate point of view, PCs were just isolated islands of information. Although networks are commonplace now, for many years they were not. This meant that when a user wanted to utilize data generated from a mainframe, it was often printed out, and then manually reentered into a PC. And, if a user created a report with a PC, much of that data would eventually be reentered into a larger system (such as a large accounting system) on a mainframe or mini. Although there have always been creative solutions to these problems, the concept of managing and maintaining data on unconnected PCs is astronomically more difficult than managing a centralized data source, such as a mainframe. Thus, many ISD staff members were against using PCs.

Even today, with PCs connected via networks, the problems of isolated and redundant data are extreme. If two users each have a database that stores the figures for a company's gross margin, which one is correct? Hopefully, they both have the same data. More often than not, one will have the correct value sooner than the other, which leads to anomalies in the data and, ultimately to poor business decisions made on incorrect assumptions. Additionally, in the early days of PC use, there was little consistency between applications concerning command structure, syntax, and user interface. This made learning new applications tedious and time-consuming. Most of the knowledge gained from learning one application could not be transferred to successive applications. Consequently, most users used two, or perhaps three, applications at most. PC applications were abundant, but they were not always intuitive or easy to learn. To make matters even worse, users would often start by using a single package like Lotus 1-2-3. When they found that a package couldn't meet all of their needs, they could not upgrade or redevelop, but had to purchase a new software package to meet the new requirements. And most of what they had learned to operate the previous application was totally inapplicable for the next. Because the new package was usually designed by a different company, and because there were few if any design standards, a word processor like WordStar would look and behave radically different from a spreadsheet.

On the other hand, users were becoming much more productive because they had tools like spreadsheets to perform calculations that they had previously performed with a calculator or perhaps even a pencil and paper. Word processors had a dramatic impact on the creation of documents, and presentation graphics programs changed the way that presentations are done.

But most of these gains were in the area of personal productivity. Although users were often more productive, they still lacked the skills to create custom applications because PC programs still had to be developed using traditional programming languages. With the advent of Ashton-Tate's dBASE product line, a new set of tools became available to do custom development on the PC, without having to use traditional development languages. dBASE also provided a "data-centric" view for an application, which forced users and developers alike to think in terms of databases, input forms, and reports. Although the use of these languages was still out of the grasp of most end users, it opened the door for a new breed of developer who didn't have to develop using only traditional languages. This allowed many users, in large organizations and small businesses alike, to develop their own custom applications. These tools were also embraced by many forward-thinking ISD shops. Suddenly, both end users and systems professionals were doing PC development work.

The Third Revolution

Microsoft introduced its graphical user interface (GUI, pronounced goo-ey) for DOS, Windows in 1985, although it wasn't until 1990 with the introduction of the dramatically improved Windows 3.0 that the Windows phenomenon took off. Although Windows is an overlay to DOS, and still faces some of its restrictions (16-bit architecture, 640k base memory limitation, and so on), it provided a pretty new face, as well as workarounds to these and many other problems. Perhaps the greatest advantages of Windows over DOS are:

- A consistent, graphical user interface.
- The ability to share data between applications (via DDE and OLE).
- Task switching.
- Limited multitasking.
- Device independence.

- Use of memory beyond 640k.
- The operating system, not the application, handles peripherals (printers, etc.).
- The ability to run DOS applications (in a window or full screen).
- An object/action paradigm (it is truly an object-oriented interface, but was not developed using object-oriented programming techniques).
- Development environments that include both traditional tools and languages (such as C, Basic, and Pascal), as well as visual programming tools (such as Visual Basic, Visual C++, and ObjectVision).

Future versions of Windows will overcome the aforementioned limitations of DOS (especially as Windows matures and becomes a more robust 32-bit operating system), in addition to having the advantage of:

- A scalable, 32-bit architecture.
- Integrated network support.
- Symmetric multiprocessing.
- The ability to run software written for other operating systems (UNIX, OS/2, etc.).
- A common macro language standardized for all Windows programs, which will allow the easy development of tightly integrated, custom application suites (Visual Basic, Applications Edition).

Note

Because Windows is a family, no longer a single product, not all members of the family will have all of the above features.

Led by Microsoft's own Excel and Word for Windows, sales of Windows applications such as spreadsheets and word processors have been, to say the least, strong. Yet, as of the fall of 1992, when Access was first introduced, there were only a few Windows database management systems to choose from, and none of them had taken a strong position in the market. There was a growing demand from professional developers, who had previously used tools like Borland's dBASE and Paradox to create stand-alone applications, as well as from end users who had outgrown the nonrelational database capabilities that their spreadsheets offered. Enter Access!

What Is Access?

Microsoft Access is a Windows-based relational database manager that truly exploits the Windows environment. It is not a rewrite of a previously existing DOS database; it was designed purely for the Windows environment. It features:

- Drag and drop creation and editing of queries, reports, macros, and forms.
- Support of Window's Multiple Document Interface (MDI).
- The ability to include OLE objects (such as sound, video, or almost anything else you can store on your hard disk) both as records in a database, and as objects on a form or report.
- Wizards that walk you through complex operations.
- A powerful macro language that allows the automation of most routine tasks without programming.
- A programming language, Access Basic, which is modeled on the widely accepted Visual Basic, but with additional database extensions.
- The ability to create distributable, royalty-free, stand-alone applications using the Access Developers Toolkit (ADT).
- The ability to simultaneously attach to, and even join across, other database formats such as dBASE, Paradox, and Btrieve.
- The ability to import and export files in several standard formats including Excel, Lotus 1-2-3, Fox Pro, and ASCII.
- A scalable architecture that allows Access to be used as a stand-alone database, a multiuser file server database, and the client application of any client/server engine that supports ODBC.
- Support for referential integrity at the database engine level.
- Data validation that, if created at the table level, is automatically migrated to forms and reports.
- An extensible architecture that allows access to functions in any Windows dynamic link library (DLL).
- The ability to create and use libraries of reusable code.
- The ability to create and/or use third-party Wizards.

If you are used to using Windows products such as Excel and Word for Windows, Access will look very familiar to you. It sports toolbars, a floating toolbox, rulers (where appropriate), and the familiar Print Preview. It also features comprehensive on-line help.

What Is an Access Application?

An Access application is a collection of Access objects which work together to solve a problem. Both the problem and the solution can be simple or complex. For example, if you need to display the city that corresponds with a zip code, your corresponding application would probably be relatively simple. As a matter of fact, you might not even think of it as an application. On the other hand, if you run a small airline and need to automate the reservation process, as well as schedule flights and manage employees and aircraft maintenance, the underlying problem is very complex. It is actually several problems, which you seek to solve in an integrated manner. As a result, the corresponding application will most likely be very complex. Sometimes, but not often, problems and applications have an inverse relationship. In other words, a simple problem might result in a complex application (usually because of a poor application design) or a complex problem might result in a simple application (because of good application design).

Access Building Blocks

Access has seven classes of objects that are the basic building blocks of all applications:

- Databases are the containers in which all other objects are stored. Access database objects differ from the database that was described earlier in this chapter. Traditional databases store only raw data and information about the data's interrelationships. Access database objects also store the raw data and relationship information, but they store everything else associated with that data as well, including forms, reports, macros, and programs. Figure 1.1 illustrates this conceptual architecture. An Access application must contain at least one database, even if there are no tables in it.

- Tables are the objects in which the actual data is stored.

- Queries are the objects that are used to retrieve information (in a table-like format) from one or more tables. Queries are also used to perform various operations on tables that modify data. *Select queries* are parallel to *Views* in SQL Server.

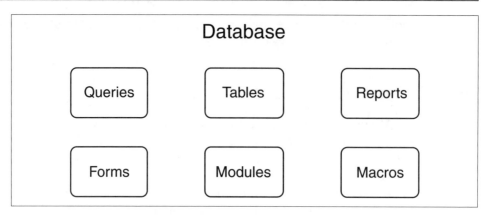

Figure 1.1 Access's conceptual architecture.

- Forms are used for inputting, editing, and viewing data. Forms are the interface through which the user interacts with the data.
- Reports are used for retrieving and printing data in special layouts, and have the capability to perform totals and other calculations for groupings of related data.
- Macros are chains of predefined actions which through the manipulation of other objects can be used to automate repetitive tasks and modify the user interface.
- Modules are custom procedures created using Access Basic Code (ABC) for advanced applications whose requirements cannot be satisfied using macros and the other objects.

This book assumes that you are familiar with at least the basics of all of these, except for macros and modules. If you are not, you might be able to get through this book, but you should really spend some time with the Access manuals and/or tutorial.

With these seven building blocks, *anyone* can create an application using Access. Actually, you don't even need all seven. A working, but somewhat limited, application can be built using just a database, tables, and forms. In addition, three more kinds of objects that interact with the preceding seven are:

- Dynasets are the resultant data sets that are returned from a query. They are fully editable (unless using right joins or unless the application has been developed to prevent editing) and updatable.

- Snapshots are static pictures of a dynaset, which cannot be updated or edited.
- Controls are the objects used on forms and reports that accept user input and display program output, both on the screen and in hard copy.

If you are interested in creating royalty-free, distributable applications, either for internal distribution within your own organization or for resale, you need the Access Developers Toolkit (ADT). The ADT gives you several additional tools to assist you in putting all of your building blocks together to build a freestanding structure, including:

- The Windows Help Compiler.
- Several utilities to help you build custom help files.
- A program that allows you to create a custom setup program for your application.
- All of the necessary runtime files needed to distribute your application.
- Several OLE custom controls.

It is the mission of this book to help guide you in putting all of these pieces together to create useful applications, which will make you and/or your users more productive.

Chapter 2

Dranchak's Development Methodology

In Chapter 1, you learned that an Access application is a set of Access objects that are combined to solve a problem. How do you go about creating an application that successfully solves your problem? In this chapter you will learn:

- What a methodology is.
- The six steps of Dranchak's Development Methodology.
- How to identify the problem you are trying to solve.

Case Study: Saugatuck Marketing Group

Throughout this book, we will build an application for a fictitious company, Saugatuck Marketing Group (SMG). SMG is in the business of providing promotional services to businesses in the information technology arena, specifically software development firms. Account executives are responsible for handling relationships with existing accounts, as well as prospecting new accounts. They use several methods to prospect new accounts, including print advertising, direct mailings, and trade shows. In practice though, they have found that most of their revenue comes from repeat business. As a result, more time is spent with current accounts than with finding new business.

SMG's Technology Profile

Although they are a fairly small company of 43 employees, SMG has a centralized Information Systems Department (ISD) with a staff of five. Most of their mission-critical applications run on an IBM AS400, although there is an Executive Information System (EIS) that was written using Microsoft Excel and Word for Windows. There is also a custom-written Windows application (called Expense Tracker) that is used for tracking client expenses. SMG has a Novell network in place with two file servers, and has standardized on a suite of applications for all users which includes Windows 3.1 (running on DOS 6.0), Excel for Windows, Word for Windows, Powerpoint for Windows, Project for Windows and Access, and Wall Data's Rumba (for AS400 connectivity under Windows). Windows for Workgroups is under evaluation, and it looks likely that it will be implemented in the near future.

There is also a prototype client-server application in place which was developed using Microsoft SQL Server for NT. Client development environments are currently under evaluation, but front ends have already been developed using Excel and Pioneer Software's Q+E, and Access. Every employee in the company has an IBM-compatible machine. Office-bound employees have a minimum configuration of a 486DX2 66 with 16MB of RAM, and 340MB of disk storage, and are of course connected to the network. Access to the AS400 is through a gateway on the network. Traveling employees (sales staff) have a minimum configuration of a 486SL-based notebook with 8MB of RAM, and 200MB of disk storage, and use pocket network connectors when in the office.

Although there are all levels of users in the company, the majority are very computer literate because of the focus of the company's clientele (information technology). Many routinely write macros in Word and Excel. As a matter of fact, both the EIS application and the client expense tracking system were started by end users, but then completed by ISD when they started to grow in complexity. Because of the pressures of maintaining the older applications, as well as moving forward with the evaluation and implementation of client-server and PC-based technologies, ISD has not been able to respond to all requests and demands as quickly as SMG's business needs require. Instead of hiring additional staff, they have chosen to outsource much of the new technology. They have been careful to select vendors that can complete development projects using new tools, as well as teach ISD staff the techniques and methods. Thus, after one or two projects, SMG not only has successful, functioning applications, but also the knowledge to develop and support similar projects. This technique is known as *technology transfer*.

The Methodology

Software development has traditionally been considered a science. Generally, if you wanted to become a computer programmer, you would probably go to school and study computer science, perhaps even earning a Ph.D. in the discipline. Why is it considered a science? Probably because computers, their operating systems, and development languages are all based on very strict rules of behavior. But calling software development a science would be like calling the routine of an Olympic figure skater a science, just because the skater had a confining set of rules within which to perform his or her routine.

Similarly, you could ask, is story writing a science? It too uses a language that has rules and syntax just like a computer language. Clearly, story writing is not a science, but you can apply scientific methods to aid in the process. A *method* is a systematic procedure or a technique; a *methodology* is a body of methods, assembled for the purpose of solving a problem or producing a result. If you were writing a story, you could look at a body of works by a particular author that you admire, and analyze the style. Perhaps you could find a common thread that consistently runs throughout all of the works. You could take this knowledge and try to apply it to your own work. Perhaps you could also find out what kind of methodology the author used when he or she was writing. Perhaps he or she went to a mountainside retreat to find inspiration. Or sought the chaos of a large metropolis to get the adrenaline pumping.

So, is it correct to think of software development as a science? No! It is an art, and a very creative one at that. It is always tougher to create a masterpiece when the artist is bound by rules (such as those imposed by a software development language). While some of you might celebrate being labeled an artist, others might feel frustrated, because it has been easier to just follow the rules and be considered a scientist. Truly, the software developer must be both artist and scientist. He or she must know which rules restrict him or her, as well as how to use creativity to circumvent traditional approaches when the occasion calls for it.

Since its inception, the computer community has been trying to take the art out of development, and make it pure science. It has been seeking a methodology that could help developers quickly write successful programs, with no bugs, by assigning rules to the process of writing a program. Most of the traditional methodologies start at point A, end at point B, and have clearly defined steps in between. These methodologies are often rigid, and are unforgiving if something that should have been included in a preceding step is omitted. On the other hand, the absence of rules or methodology will lead to chaos. Although some people can achieve incredible results following some seemingly random path to get from beginning to end, strictly intuitive developers are very rare. The trick is to find a methodology that fits the task at hand, and then apply it to a specific problem or scenario.

Dranchak's Development Methodology (DDM) provides a contextual framework to speed the development of a successful Access application. This methodology is not the be-all and end-all to all software development projects. Although formulated with Access as the development tool in mind, it could be applied to other data-centric development environments that use an event-driven graphical user interface. You might even be able to apply it to nondata-centric event-driven development environments such as a Visual Basic, but it would not be applicable to writing a traditional COBOL program, which is going to run in a batch environment.

Figure 2.1 graphically illustrates the process and, although it is somewhat linear in nature (it does after all have a starting and ending point, and it could be argued that these are the same two points because you wind up back at the problem definition when the problem is ultimately solved), it is highly iterative. An *iterative* process is one that repeats all or some of the steps until a condition is met. In this case, the software application that satisfied the original objectives (more on objectives and defining the problem in a moment) would be the condition to be met that would stop the repetition of the steps. Throughout this book it is emphasized that the more prepared you are at the early steps of iteration, the fewer iterations you will have to go through. This ultimately leads to a shorter development cycle and a more thorough solution.

Step 1: Identify the Problem

The first step in the process is to identify the problem. Although this sounds easy—and it sometimes is—this is where most development problems start. If the developer does not correctly analyze the problem and understand what the user wants, all of the following steps will be working toward an incorrect objective. This will ultimately lead to failure or a lot of work rewriting the application.

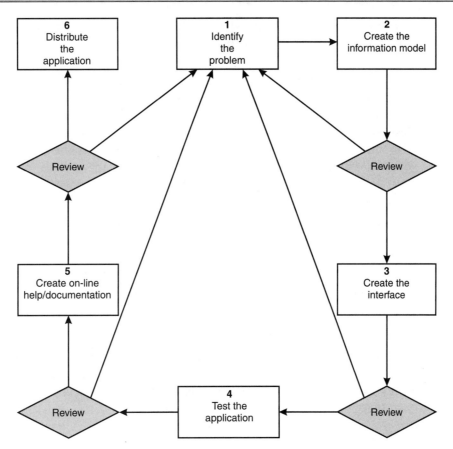

Figure 2.1 The six steps of Dranchak's Development Methodology.

Ask the Right Questions

To identify the problem, the developer must sit down with the user and determine what he or she really wants and really needs. This is done through a formal interview. Notice that after each step in DDM, the step is reviewed, and passed back to the beginning step. Identify the problem. This means that the first interview should be the longest and most formal, the one that yields the most information. Successive interviews and meetings, both formal and informal, will ensue until the project has been completed. For clarity's sake, it is assumed that there is only one user and one developer, but real-world situations will usually have more than one user, and often will have more than one developer.

How do you go about interviewing the user? How do you get the information that you need to implement the system? Read on.

Open-End Questioning   Although people have different personalities, there is a technique you can use to obtain useful information from almost any user. It is called open- and close-end questioning. As the developer, it is your responsibility to ask questions that will give you enough information to correctly assess the situation. Open-end questioning is the process of asking questions that will encourage users to tell you about their business, their functions, their needs, and their expectations. Your interviewing process should always start with open-end questions, some examples of which are:

- What can you tell me about your department?
- What is your particular role?
- Can you explain the relationship you have with ISD?
- What is the process by which you gather your information?

SAUGATUCK MARKETING GROUP

SMG chose DASL, a local firm that specializes in custom software development, to design and implement WinContact. Here is a transcript of the first part of the interview between Ian Joseph, SMG's liaison for the project, and Stephen Krandas, the DASL developer assigned to the project.

IJ: We need a contact manager.

SK: Why?

IJ: I spend at least 50 percent of my time at client meetings. I always have my notebook computer with me, as well as a daytimer and a portfolio. Why should I carry all three? I need the notebook because we have both Word and Excel files specific to the customer that we reference while at the meetings—you know, things like proposals, memos, year-to-date costs. We also have a custom Windows application called ET, which is used to help track customer expenses. I use my portfolio mostly for taking notes at the meetings, and my daytimer is used as my calendar and contains my list of names, numbers, and addresses.

SK: What about when you are not in the field?

IJ: Well, when I am in the office, there is the usual cycle of calling a customer, discussing new or existing contracts, setting up a follow-up date, and then doing some kind of work that is required before the follow-up date. Thus, I am perpetually moving between my notebook, my daytimer, and the phone. It seems like it would be more efficient to have an application on the notebook that would help me better manage the correspondence between myself and my customers.

Oh, I almost forgot! It's very rare that I ever utilize features such as mail merge, even though I know Word offers some powerful tools that could make me more productive. I've gone so far as creating a few Word templates, but essentially, every time I send someone a letter, I manually type his or her whole name and address. I keep putting off setting up a mail merge file mainly because I'm just too busy to take the time, but also because I know in the back of my mind that I will someday have an application that will help me work the way I want to, so I don't want to have to do the work of data entry twice.

SK: Have you considered any of the personal information managers (PIMs) that are currently on the market?

IJ: Well, actually I have. But, first of all, ISD doesn't support any of them, which means that the company won't buy me one. None of them is on an approved software list. I decided that the cost of these packages could be justified as a personal purchase, because of the potential increase in my sales bonus if the tool would help me close one new sale. I read some magazine reviews, and narrowed the field down to two. As it turns out, I didn't really have to decide, because my wife (who is very knowledgeable about computers) bought me one for my birthday, based on some discussions we had had at the dinner table.

At first I was very excited, but the deeper I got into understanding the product, the more frustrated I became. It ultimately came down to the fact that it didn't seem intuitive, and it was hindering my productivity, not enhancing it. Essentially, it didn't work in the way I like to work. It also didn't have some features that I thought were very important.

SK: Such as...?

IJ: I don't know. That's essentially why you are here. I was able to convince my boss that if we could have a contact management application developed that met our needs and fit the working patterns of our entire department, the project could pay for itself within a very short period of time. Even if it did not directly improve sales, quicker responses to customer requests would lead to improved relationships with our customers. Both my boss and I are sort of hacks, so we started playing around with Access, thinking maybe we could develop the application ourselves.

SK: Why Access?

IJ: Well, even though we're computer literate, we're not really programmers. I mean, I took COBOL in college, but I'm not a programmer. Access looked good because it seemed like we could create an application that used some forms and tables, and maybe even a few macros, but didn't really require any real "coding" in the traditional sense. We also decided that we had to stay in the Windows environment, and not move backwards to DOS, and what else is there in user-oriented database management systems? Actually it was ISD that really set us straight on that. Besides, Access is on their approved software list, so not only can we purchase it, we will also be able to get support for it. ISD also said that part of their strategy includes a new technology called client-server, and that Access can be the client side in the system. I wasn't quite sure exactly what that meant, so they explained to me that if our needs grow beyond what Access can offer, we have a migration path to a different back end, like Microsoft's SQL Server.

SK: I assume that you didn't finish the application yourself. Why not?

IJ: I eventually reached the conclusion that it wasn't the best use of my time to complete this application myself. As much fun as I had doing it, it's really outside the scope of my responsibilities. I should be spending my time with customers, not hacking code. That's why we decided to bring you in—to realize our vision of what a contact manager really should be.

Close-End Questioning After getting an understanding of the big picture, you should turn the questioning in a direction that will result in very specific answers. This is called close-end questioning, because it results in a very specific, closed answer. Some examples of closed questions are:

- Are you happy with the current system?
- Specifically, which features do you like?
- Which features do you dislike?
- What is the current response time from the host?
- What do you think an acceptable response time would be?

It is from the answers to the specific questions that you will be able to design your system.

SAUGATUCK MARKETING GROUP

Here is a transcript of the second part of the interview between Ian Joseph and Stephen Krandas, in which Stephen is trying to hone in on the specifics that will guide his design.

SK: What features did you dislike in the PIM that you purchased?

IJ: First of all, I absolutely hated the calendar and the way appointments were handled.

SK: What did you dislike about it?

IJ: It brought up a page—like in a daytimer—and every month had its own tiny calendar. When you double clicked on any month, the year's page went away, and you jumped to the first day of the month. Each day of the month had a separate page in the daytimer, and you had to page through each one to get to the day you wanted. Maybe there was some kind of shortcut, but I never came across it.

SK: If you don't like that kind of interface, what do you envision?

IJ: I'd like to see a graphical representation of a complete month, maybe like the Calendar applet that comes with Windows. I would like to see simultaneously the appointments for any given day. If I click on a different day, then I would expect to see that day's appointments.

SK: The calendar applet has two different views: month and day. It sounds like you would like to see both of those views combined into one form. Is that correct?

IJ: More or less. Conceptually it's correct, but I really don't like the look and feel of Calendar. It looks like it did under Windows 1.1, and I prefer more of a 3-D look.

SK: Do you think two buttons, maybe Next and Previous, would be appropriate for moving from month to month?

IJ: Yeah, that would be a good starting point. A series of buttons, or perhaps a list box would also be good, in addition to the Next and Previous buttons. A slider control would be really neat. Could you do that in Access?

SK: Access doesn't include a slider control, but the Access Developers Toolkit (ADT) does. Back to the idea of a series of buttons, do you mean 12 buttons, one for each month?

IJ: Yes, exactly.

SK: I think that the full name of a month would be impractical—it would use up too much space on the form. What do think of just a three-letter abbreviation like Jan., Feb., Mar.?

IJ: That sounds good, but I think that even the first letter of the month, arranged in the correct order, will be sufficient.

SK: What about the appointment list? Any thoughts?

IJ: Just a list with the time, who the appointment is with, and the ability to have a note. I'm not sure if I'd like to see a list of all times, at half-hour intervals, or if I'd prefer only to have the time show up when I add an actual appointment. The list would then resort the appointments, of course.

SK: We can try both, and see which you like better. What about who the appointment is with? Would you like to see a drop-down list with all of the contacts in the database? It would cut down on typing.

IJ: What if I have an appointment with someone who is not in the database, like my doctor?

SK: We could allow you to add entries that are not in the database, or would prompt you to create a new entry at that time. I think it's safer to allow entries that are not in the database.

IJ: That sounds good to me.

SK: What other features would you like to see?

IJ: A to-do list and a phone book, as well as the ability to print reports with different sortings.

SK: What do you mean when you say a phone book? Do you mean just a contact and his or her phone number? Or do you mean something more like an address book?

IJ: When I say phone book, I mean something that is all-encompassing. Something that will tell me everything I need to know about a contact, including name, address, multiple phone numbers, fax number, e-mail address, and notes.

SK: What about the date of last contact, and something that defines his or her relationship to you, you know, customer, vendor, personal, SMG, etc.

IJ: Yes, exactly. And his or her company, of course! He or she shouldn't be able to have an entry, unless there is an association with a company. Also, companies should appear in a list box, so that we don't have to keep retyping.

Hopefully, you get the idea. Instead of continuing on with the interview here, in the sections and chapters to follow, you will often just see what the analyst inferred from the conversation.

Define the Scope

The scope defines the overall context of the problem you are seeking to solve. A scope for the preceding contact manager application might be *the design and implementation of a Windows-based contact management application.*

Define the Goal(s)

The goals of a project provide a nonspecific overview of the issues at hand. Goals are nonquantifiable; they contain no references to resources or dates. Some examples of goals are:

- To provide better information to top executives.
- To decrease the response time for customer inquiries.
- To increase sales revenue.
- To provide host connectivity to all field personnel, at a reasonable cost.

SAUGATUCK MARKETING GROUP

After the conversations with SMG's vice president of sales, Louis Rich, it was determined that the two primary goals for SMG's sales department are:

- To improve account executive productivity.
- To increase customer satisfaction.

Define the Objective

An objective is a measurable goal you wish to accomplish. The objectives for WinContact are:

- Reduce the number of physical items an account executive must carry to customer meetings to just a notebook computer.
- Reduce the amount of time spent on customer contact by 50 percent.
- Decrease the response time to customer requests for proposals.
- Improve the quality of customer–account rep communications.
- Design and implement a contact management application for the sales department which will:

    Run in, and take advantage of, the Windows environment.

    Be developed in Microsoft Access.

    Be distributed without a runtime royalty.

    Provide phone/address book.

    Provide a to-do list.

    Provide an appointment calendar.

Step 2: Create the Information Model

Define the Output

In the development of traditional computer programs, before you begin to design your application, you must know both your input and your output. This is because most traditional applications process the input(s), to arrive at a calculated output. A simple example is a program that converts a Fahrenheit temperature to a Celsius temperature where the input is a number that represents a temperature measured in degrees Fahrenheit, for example, 32°F, the freezing point of water. The desired output is the corresponding centigrade temperature, measured in degrees Celsius. The corresponding centigrade freezing point of water is 0°C. To get from the input to the output, a calculation must be performed. That calculation, in English, is:

```
Temperature Celcius=1-(32/Temperature Fahrenheit)
```

Unlike traditional applications, DBMSs are usually more concerned with the manipulation and sorting of data than with calculated outputs, although there will be times when the sorted data has calculations performed on it.

Before you can design the internal workings of your application, you must define the output that is required. Output refers to both printed reports, and on-screen data. Especially in this day and age of the "paperless office" and graphical user interfaces, there is more and more emphasis being placed on electronic delivery of information. It is essential to the design of a good database to know what output the user expects. Once the output has been determined, you can then map it to the known inputs, or determine which inputs are needed.

SAUGATUCK MARKETING GROUP

There are ten reports that SMG considers critical to running its business, which need to be created by WinContact. These reports are:

- Contacts and phone numbers, sorted by contact last name.
- Contacts and phone numbers, sorted by contact postal code.
- Contacts and phone numbers, sorted by contact state.
- Contacts and phone numbers, sorted by lead source.
- Company names and contacts who have not been contacted in 30 days.
- Company names and contacts who have not been contacted in 60 days.
- Company names and contacts who have follow-up calls scheduled for the current business day.
- Company names and contacts who have follow-up calls scheduled for the next business day.
- All contacts sorted by type of relationship (current customer, past customer, prospect, vendor, personal, co-worker, etc.).
- List of all phone calls to a client, including date, length of call, follow-up date, and call notes.

Define the Logical Data Structure

After you have viewed the outputs and inputs, you should start thinking about your data structure. The logical data structure represents how the user will view the data, and is not concerned with the actual implementation issues. The actual logical data structure will be created in Chapter 4, based on the inputs and outputs defined above.

Define the Physical Schema

The physical schema is the actual design of your database for the specific software you are using. If you were using dBASE IV, your physical schema would consist of one or more DBF files at the DOS level, each with a name of no more than eight characters. If you were using an SQL server, your physical schema would consist of one or more database devices (an OS/2 or NT file), one or more databases (container used for storing objects, similar to Access), and then one or more tables, each with a file name of no more than 30 characters, no spaces allowed. On the other hand, an Access physical schema consists of one or more database objects, each with one or more tables, each with a file name of up to 64 characters, with embedded spaces allowed.

Implement the Physical Schema

This is simply a matter of taking the results of the physical schema definition and entering it into your application. Using Access, for example, you will create tables that consist of one or more fields. You will then set the properties of these fields. If you are using a CASE tool like Asymetrix InfoModeler, the tool will automatically implement the physical schema for your database.

Create Test Data

As early as possible in the development cycle, a set of test data must be created.

Why? There are really two reasons for this: First of all, the designer of the application (probably you) must verify that the application performs as expected as development proceeds; second, the user/customer should be able to test the application with valid data. There are two rules to follow when defining your sample population:

1. The sample data must be significant.
2. The sample data should not be any larger than is necessary to make it significant.

Step 3: Create the Interface

Define the Overall Flow of the Application

Before you can start to actually develop your user interface, you must think about, and decide on, the flow of your application. Flow means where the user starts, where the user ends, and what he or she sees at each of these points and in between. Do you want the user to see a toolbar when the application first starts? Do you want him or her to see a startup splash screen with information about the application? If the answer to this is yes, what should they see next? A blank workspace, with no windows open? This would mean that the user has to make a selection from a menu, which is a two-step process: first, opening the menu, then selecting a command.

Do you want users to start with a form in which they will browse through customers? Or would you rather that they start with a form (window or dialog box) that presents choices of where to go next? If they choose the latter, which options do you offer, and how do you offer them? Do you use radio buttons or push buttons? A list box? All of the above? And what happens when they make a choice? Do they come to another form that prompts them to enter information that pertains to their choice?

How will the forms look? Do you want to use colors? If yes, which ones and how many? Do you always want push buttons to appear in the same location on every form? Should all push buttons be the same size? Should you use text or images, or both, in push buttons? When you have a data entry form, which control should be in the upper left-hand corner (which is where most people start working)? Should you group related controls together? If so, how do you decide on those groups?

Reports should also be part of this scrutiny, because whether viewed on screen or printed on paper, they are allowing the user to interface with the data. Although Windows handles the direct interaction with the printer, the developer must give consideration to how reports are going to look and how long they will take to print. Although laser printers are common these days, there are still many people using dot-matrix printers. A report that includes graphic images such as bitmaps will look awful on most dot-matrix printers, if they even print any of it! What if the user has a color laser available? You would probably incorporate colored objects into reports that were to be printed on this printer. Thus, the developer must be able to plan ahead based on the environment in which the user will be operating.

The answers to all of these questions, and many more, define the overall flow of an application. If you are new to application development, you may have taken these things for granted when you used shrink-wrapped software. But vendors like Microsoft spend millions of dollars on usability studies to try and understand what users like and dislike, and what is easy and what is difficult. Even though you don't have the resources that Microsoft does, you do have a wealth of experience. Think about software that you like and dislike. Which packages felt natural to you? Which ones were frustrating because they didn't "work like you"? Now apply this experience to the problem you face creating a work flow that will help your application meet its objectives.

And don't forget about the users. It is during the design phase that most ideas should be gathered. Ask your customer what they expect to see when the application boots up. Also ask what they expect to happen when they click on a button labeled Print. Should a dialog box ask them how many copies and which pages? Or do they expect the whole document (or report or whatever) to print, without further interaction?

SAUGATUCK MARKETING GROUP

As the designer of the application, you've decided that you want an initial splash screen to appear when the application first boots up. You will use it to display your company logo, and feed your ego a little by adding some text that credits you as the developer of this application. Of greater importance is the inclusion of copyright notice and version information. You checked this decision with the users, and they had no problem with it, because they're used to seeing splash screens in most commercial applications that they use.

What happens after that? The idea of opening a blank document (as in Excel or Word for Windows) doesn't really seem ideal. Why? Because users are not using this application to start with a blank canvas and to develop a masterpiece. They are using it to put data in and get it out, in certain predefined formats that make it meaningful to them. There is some degree of flexibility, but only because you have given them choices.

You already know that users are going to input data, edit data, browse data, and print data. You also know that the users regard this application as having three focuses:

- Companies
- Contacts at companies
- Correspondence with contacts

Does it make sense to start with a certain form, such as the phone book, and then provide push buttons and/or menu commands to navigate around the rest of the application? This is, after all, a contact manager, and you could argue that this form is "the center of the universe." In other words, from your application's perspective, it is a contact-centric universe. After all, you can't send a letter unless you've chosen a contact to send it to, right? Wrong! What if you want to send a form letter to all prospects? Or print a report of all contacts sorted by area code? Perhaps the idea of starting from a form that offers some choices such as the following is the way to go:

- Add/edit/view contact
- View/print report
- Add/edit/view lead sources
- Add/edit/view relationships
- Help
- Exit

Perhaps creating a form with buttons for contact, report maintenance, help and exit, and then tying them into a list box that has the appropriate choices for the selected button would work. Figure 2.2 illustrates a flowchart for the application.

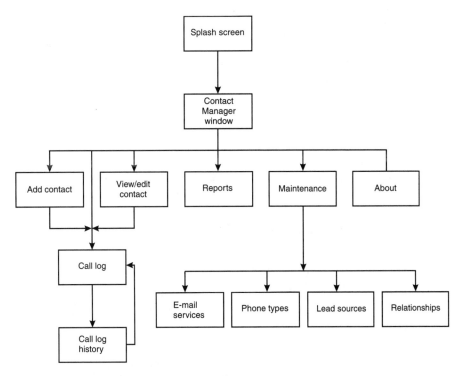

Figure 2.2 Program flow hierarchy.

Table 2.1 All Forms	
Form	Description
Splash Screen	First screen displayed when application starts.
Control Center	The control panel that provides access to all other functions/forms.
Add/Browse Contact	Form in which all information about a contact is added/edited/viewed.
View/Print Report	Form from which predesigned reports are selected.
Add/Edit Company	Form from which companies are added/edited.
Add/Edit Lead Sources	Form from which lead sources are added/edited.
Add/Edit Relationships	Form from which relationships between contact and user are added/edited.
Add/Edit E-Mail Service	Form from which e-mail services are added/edited.
Add/Edit Phone Type	Form from which phone types are added/edited.
Phone Log	Form used to add entries to the phone log.
Phone Log History	Form used to edit/view the phone log's history.
About Screen	Form that displays pertinent information about the application.

Now that you have developed and documented the overall flow of your application, you must come up with a list of all of the forms that are necessary. Remember that no matter how hard you try, you will probably leave out a few forms. This is okay, because as discussed earlier, this is an iterative process. As long as you have the majority of your design, you will probably be fine.

Based on the flowchart in Figure 2.2, a list of all forms and a brief description of each one's main function is illustrated in Table 2.1. At this point, the names are informal references, which may or may not be modified as the project proceeds.

Create Your Reports

Although electronic delivery of information is becoming more popular every day, paper is still the preferred medium of delivery. Hopefully, as more computers become interconnected and software allows easy transmission of complex electronic documents (not just short text files), paper use will be reduced, and thousands of tons of paper will be saved. Either way, Access has the bases covered through report objects. Although most users will still use Access to create paper reports, Access's excellent implementation of the now standard Windows Print Preview feature makes on-screen viewing both easy and convenient.

Note

During the early development of this book, almost all of the communication between the author and the publisher was performed using electronic mail. It was only when the editor's workstation began having network connection problems (which did not get resolved quickly), that communication reverted to the old hard copy/overnight mail combination.

Although forms allow a great deal of control over the way you add and browse data, they are somewhat limited, because they usually work with an updatable Dynaset. This prevents transactions from getting too complex. Reports, on the other hand, offer greater flexibility in the layout and presentation of your data. Perhaps the biggest advantage of reports over forms is the ability to combine groups of data, and then perform aggregate functions [such as sum( ), max( ), min( )] across the group. Although you can achieve some degree of grouping on forms through creative queries, especially if you write direct SQL code (more on this later), reports are truly the vehicle for performing these kinds of data gymnastics.

Reports really consist of two pieces: the report itself and the underlying data source. You cannot have a report without an underlying data source. Although a report can be bound to a table, it is highly recommended that you do not do this. All reports should be bound to queries.

In Step 2: (Create the Information Model), you created the layouts for all of your reports (at least those you've been able to anticipate). To create these reports, all you have to do is note any changes that may have occurred in the design of the physical schema (such as changing the name of a field), and use the drag and drop capabilities of the Query Builder to create the underlying query. When the query is complete, use the drag and drop features of Report Design mode to create your reports. Since you already created a test data set, it should be easy to test your reports and see if they perform as expected. (You will learn about queries and SQL in Chapter 6, Queries, and reports in Chapter 8, Reports.)

Design and Implement the User Interface

Create All Required Forms

Forms are the most common objects used for allowing the user to interact with the application. Although you can have an application with no custom forms (by defining a table, allowing the user to input data into the table from the table's Datasheet view, and then just printing and editing from this same context), this is definitely not very user-friendly Another severe limitation to this method is that you are limited to editing a single table at a time. Thus, if you have tables that should be joined, you have to manually edit each table, one at a time, and hope that you don't make any mistakes. Queries do allow you to edit more than one table at a time, when using a Datasheet view, but, again this is very clumsy, especially if you have more fields than will fit on a single screen.

Forms, on the other hand, allow you to edit/view more than one table at a time (using a query as an underlying data source), as well as allow you to lay out your data fields in almost any design you can think of, instead of the restrictive spreadsheet-like interface of Datasheets (although you can use a datasheet view in a form). Forms also allow for the inclusion and use of OLE objects, graphics, text, command buttons, and other Windows controls to make the presentation of data more user-friendly. Forms are used to:

- Browse data (browse meaning view and/or edit data).
- Enter new data.
- Prompt the user to make selections (such as choosing one of three predefined reports).
- Pass messages back to the user.

Coverage of form basics starts in Chapter 7, Forms, and continues throughout the book, as you learn more advanced features (such as triggering macros from buttons on forms) and how to apply them to forms.

Create Macros to Automate Tasks

After you have created your forms, you will have to create macros that tie them together in meaningful ways, with as little interaction from the user as possible.

By automating the opening and closing of forms, printing of reports, and so forth, you are helping the user to be more productive. Instead of having to learn all of the intricacies of Access and how its various objects interact, the user can focus on getting the results he or she needs quickly. You will use macros to make complex tasks seem easy (such as synchronizing two forms), and to reduce the possibility of errors. Macros are started when certain events occur. Some of the events that can trigger a macro are:

- The push of a command button.
- Entering a control.
- Opening a form.
- Exiting a form.
- The meeting of conditional criteria such as the name of a form or a certain value in a control.
- Selection of a custom menu command.

Thus, by assigning macros to events, you can automate what happens when a certain event occurs. For example, if you have a form for data entry, you can place a push button on it with the text OK, and assign a macro to it that will close the form, write the record to the underlying tables, then open another form. You can also use macros to print reports with little or no user interaction.

Remember, this is an iterative process. In the examples in this book, you will not finish creating all of your forms before you create all of your macros. You will start some forms and leave them in an unfinished state until you know how to create the appropriate macros. In the real world, you will probably create a form and its macros, and finish the two pieces together before moving on to the next form.

SAUGATUCK MARKETING GROUP

Before you can create macros to automate tasks, you must know the tasks you want to automate. Keeping the theme of iteration in mind, you will probably come up with more ideas as you go along, but the more you can plan in advance, the better off you will be. Based on his conversations with Ian Joseph and the results of the program flow, Stephen Krandas created the following list of actions:

Display custom help for each form.

Open the splash screen when the application is started.

Close the splash screen after some fixed time period.

Open and display the Control Center.

Update the list box in the Contact window to respond to the button selected.

Open and display the Add/Browse Contacts form.

Print the current contact.

Automatically return to the Contact window when finished with the Contact form.

Open a phone log for the current contact while in the Contact form.

Return to the Contact form without recording changes to the phone log.

Return to the Contact form after recording changes to the phone log.

Display the phone log history from the Phone Log form (which is tied to the current selection in the Contact form).

Display the phone log history from the Contact form, based on the current contact selected.

Return to the Contact form after displaying the phone log history.

Open the View/Print Reports form from the Contact window.

Select a predefined report from either a list box, various buttons, or a combination of both.

Exit from the Report form without selecting a report, and return to the Contact window.

Automatically return to the Contact window after a report has been viewed or printed.

Open and display the Maintenance form from the Contact window.

Exit from the Maintenance form without making a selection, and return to the Contact window.

Open and display the Lead Sources Maintenance form from the Maintenance form.

Return to the Maintenance form without recording changes to the Lead Sources Maintenance form.

Return to the Maintenance form after recording changes to the Lead Sources Maintenance form.

Open and display the Relationships Maintenance form from the Maintenance form.

Return to the Maintenance form without recording changes to the Relationships Maintenance form.

Return to the Maintenance form after recording changes to the Relationships Maintenance form.

Open and display the E-Mail Service Maintenance form from the Maintenance form.

Return to the Maintenance form without recording changes to the E-Mail Service Maintenance form.

Return to the Maintenance form after recording changes to the E-Mail Service Maintenance form.

Open and display the Phone Type Maintenance form from the Maintenance form.

Return to the Maintenance form without recording changes to the Phone Type Maintenance form.

Return to the Maintenance form after recording changes to the Phone Type Maintenance form.

Display the Add/Browse Contacts form from a custom menu.

Display the View/Print Reports form from a custom menu.

Display the Maintenance form from a custom menu.

Display the About Application form from a custom menu.

After creating a list of all of the tasks you want to automate, you should group them together, by form, if possible. Notice that, except for the last several entries (which deal with menus), this list of tasks is grouped by form. It is no coincidence. You will see that you can use macro groups, and it makes sense to organize all of the macros associated with a form into a single macro group. After creating the macros, you must decide which events will trigger them. Most of the tasks just listed will be triggered by pushing a command button on a form. Therefore, you will have to assign the correct macro to the correct control's On Push property. Coverage of macro basics starts in Chapter 9, Macros, and will lead you through the creation of most of the macros necessary to carry out the tasks listed.

Create Macros to Build Custom Menus

Once you have created custom forms, it makes sense to remove the standard Access menus and replace them with menus and commands that are specific to your application. For example, it doesn't make sense to have Access's default View menu available when a user is using a custom form in the contact manager application. The standard View menu for a form is illustrated in Figure 2.3.

Figure 2.3 Standard Access form View menu.

Do you want any of these options available to the users of your application? Since it is a custom application, you don't want them editing the design of the form, so that eliminates Form Design. As the application designer, you will have made a choice whether you want the user in Form or Datasheet views. That eliminates the Form and Datasheet commands. If the form has a subform, there will be a Subform command on the menu. Again, you will have made a decision how you would like to handle the subform, so allowing the user to make another choice does not make sense. Finally, there is the Options command which allows the user to edit Access's global settings. Once again, this is something the user should not be allowed to edit, because it can affect the way your custom application works.

Does it make sense to have this menu with the standard commands? No, but it does make sense to eliminate the whole View menu, or possibly to create a custom View menu with commands specific to the application. Creating a new View menu with several commands that apply filters to the form, and thus change the "view," seems like a smart alternative.

Assuming that contacts are categorized by their relationship to the application's user, a new View menu for a form that displays contact information might have the following commands:

- All contacts
- Customer contacts
- Vendor contacts
- Prospecting contacts

All of these commands affect the view of the data. Also note that custom menus have access to any and all of Access's standard menu commands. This means that you can create new menus that combine custom menu commands with standard Access menu commands. It also means that you can create a custom menu, and create new labels for Access's standard commands. Windows interface issues are covered in depth in Chapter 3, Windows Design Basics, while actually using macros to create menus will be covered in Chapter 10, Using Macros to Modify the User Interface.

Create Access Basic Code for Functions Not Addressable from Macros

Although macros are versatile and cover many tasks, they do have their limitations. Enter Access Basic. You can use Access Basic to create custom procedures that can be used to achieve results that are not possible with macros. You can create functions that return values (in the same way you would write a custom function in Excel) and you can write subprocedures to perform tasks that are not available to macros (such as creating a snapshot from a query). It is through Access Basic that you can make calls to dynamic link libraries to make functions available that are not possible to create in Access Basic, or that you may have created for some other application. It is possible to use functions directly in unbound controls (on both forms and reports), as well as to set default values in bound controls. It is also possible (and very common) to call functions from macros. Likewise, macros can be called from functions. Further, you can use Access Basic to create forms and other objects in their entirety. Unfortunately, although Access Basic provides a great deal of power, it is beyond the scope of this book. See Access's on-line help and printed documentation for more information on Access Basic.

Step 4: Test the Application

Test in the Standard Access Environment

Testing is the act of making sure that all features of your application perform as expected. When you designed and implemented your information model, you also created data that was designed to test your application. This is just the first step of the testing process; however, it is another iterative procedure, which is outlined in Figure 2.4. There are two kinds of testing:

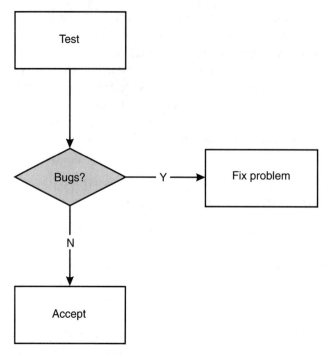

Figure 2.4 The testing process.

- Informal interactive testing (IIT)
- Formal noninteractive testing (FNIT)

Informal Interactive Testing (IIT) is the process you go through as you develop the application. For example, if you create a query against two tables, you run it, and then compare the results to what you expected the results to be. If the results are correct, you move on to the next item of business. If the results are incorrect, you analyze the situation and try to identify and correct the problem. Another example would be creating a form. You create the form in Design mode, and when you feel comfortable with it, you toggle to Form mode. You quickly realize that it is not quite what you expected it to look like, so you toggle back to Design mode to make some modifications. You also might try entering data in several forms, and then try running a report to see if the results come out as expected. If the results are not correct, then you know that you have a flaw somewhere in the processing chain. The two keys to Informal Interactive Testing are (as the name implies):

1. The testing process is informal.
2. The testing process is interactive.

Informal means there is no set pattern to the testing flow and no formal result set against which to check it. It also means that the developer does not log or track errors in any formal manner. Interactive means that when an error occurs (an error is any deviation from the expected result), the developer interactively responds to it, in whatever way he or she feels is appropriate. The two keys to formal noninteractive testing are:

1. The testing process is formal.
2. The testing process is noninteractive.

Formal means that there is a single expected outcome for every possible action, and this is the criterion to which the actual outcome will be compared. If there is a deviation, there is an error. The developer must know what all of the actions and the possible outcomes are. If there is a deviation, the error is logged, and will be addressed. The process is noninteractive because the developer (or the user) will not stop to fix the problem. He or she will continue with the rest of the tests, noting all errors (unless an error causes the application to come to a complete halt). Once all errors have been logged for a session, the developer will go back and address each issue using IIT until all problems have been eliminated. Once this condition has been met, the original set of tests will be run again. Testing in the runtime environment is 100 percent FNIT, because the user/developer cannot access macros, modules, or design mode for tables, queries, forms, and reports.

Because the Access development environment is interpretive, not compiled, testing in Access will be 80 to 90 percent IIT. When the application is at the point where you consider it bug-free, you will move it to the runtime environment as described next. Furthermore, there are two subclasses of testing for both of these methods:

1. Positive testing
2. Negative testing

Positive testing is the process of determining whether the desired outcome results from an action. Negative testing is the process of doing something other than what you are supposed to do at any given point in the application to see what happens. Negative testing is tightly coupled with error handling and data validation. For example, if you try to enter a person's name into a control that has a date datatype, Access will prevent you from doing this, and will present a message box that informs you that you have tried to enter a value that is inappropriate for the field you are editing. It would be more appropriate if an error message was returned that said, "You must enter a valid date in the format MM/DD/YY. Please change your entry." It is up to you as the developer to try to have the insight to trap errors that occur when users perform an invalid action. Negative testing is used to check these errors and how the system handles them.

IIT and FNIT should include both positive and negative testing. There will be times during your development that you accidentally enter an invalid value, and this will be part of the IIT negative process. After you design and implement an appropriate handler for this event, you should add it to the list of actions to be tested, and include what the correct outcome should be (that is, a message box that guides the user to correct the problem). Thus, it becomes part of the FNIT negative process.

Microsoft Test is a software tool that allows you to automate your testing and capture the results of the tests. Instead of manually going through every permutation of program flow, you create a test script that you play every time you make a major change to your application. You then compare the results of the test script with your expectations. Although initially it takes more time to set up a test script, if your application is complex, you will save time and energy in the long run. The testing process, because of its interactive nature, is not covered in any single chapter, but is referred to throughout the book as the application is built.

Prepare the Application for Distribution

If you plan to distribute your application using the ADT runtime, the time to debug it is after you feel comfortable that it is working as it should. As explained in the following section, you will have a much more difficult time debugging your application in the runtime environment. Thus, you should not move to this step until the application has been thoroughly tested in the development environment.

Test in the Access Distribution Environment

Although your application should work 100 percent correctly in the runtime environment if it worked 100 percent correctly in the development environment, this is not necessarily 100 percent true. Therefore, you must once again run your suite of tests against the stand-alone application. If errors do occur and you have not provided an error trap, you will get very little help from Access in finding your error. You are not allowed to access the modules or macros while in runtime. As a result, instead of the traditional message that takes you to the line where the problem occurred for a module error, you will get a message saying that an error has occurred and that you are not allowed to access the module. After this message, you will usually be thrown out of the application.

One area that can cause problems is code that uses the text in a Window title bar. If your application uses DDE to talk to Word and has a DDEExecute message to execute a WordBasic command that will return focus to Access, you might use a statement like:

```
DDEExecute chan, "[AppActivate ""Microsoft Access"",1]"
```

If, in runtime, your application has different text in the title bar (as it should), such as "My Contact Manager," the DDE call will fail, and your application will hang up without telling you why (other than perhaps in which module the error occurred).

It is also important to install the application on as many machines as possible, using your setup disks. Different environments can cause different problems to show up. Using the previous example of having a DDE conversation with Word, consider what would happen if the test machine has WINWORD.EXE not in a WINWORD directory, but in a directory called WORD. If the correct directory is in the path, the DDE conversation will work fine; if, however, the correct directory is not in the path, an error will occur. Testing on several machines can help uncover such potential bugs.

Although it is impractical to test every possible variance of user actions, user input, and the environment, the more you can test before releasing your application, the better off everyone is going to be. It is possible to do limited testing and just distribute the application and wait for bugs to come in, but this is not recommended. This method will upset the users (who might lose data), as well as give you a bad reputation for delivering unreliable applications.

An intermediary solution is to perform a reasonable amount of testing, and to then distribute the application to a small number of users for their feedback. This is called a *beta test*. When distributing the application in beta, make it clear that nothing is final, and that the user risks losing data. If this is clear from the outset, beta testing helps both the developer and the user. The developer gets feedback about likes and dislikes, as well as a larger population of potential situations in which bugs might arise. The users get an opportunity to start working with the software sooner than they would have otherwise, and the opportunity to communicate directly with the developer. Although feature sets should be frozen at the time of beta, small changes have a tendency to get worked in. Once again, this is part of the iterative process.

Step 5: Create Documentation

On-Line Help

Almost all commercially shipping Windows applications come with on-line help. Although you sometimes see an application with no on-line help, this is a rare bird in this day and age. The quality of the on-line help varies from poor to excellent, just as do the products themselves (although a poor product can have greater help and an excellent product can have terrible help). Some commercially available products don't come with any printed documentation, only on-line help. On the other hand, very few custom applications have on-line help. Many developers have neither the time nor the inclination to create a help system. Yet, because of the excellent help systems of many mainstream applications, users have come to expect good on-line help. As a result, it is imperative that you create an on-line help system for your application. Although some printed documentation is still required (at least to tell the user how to install the software), the trend is toward less printed documentation and more on-line help. Several years ago it was common to see help that would make references to the printed documentation for more detailed information. Now, as Access demonstrates, the trend is reversed. Access documentation often says, "See on-line help for more information."

The Windows Help Engine

Windows provides an application called WINHELP.EXE, which is an application that allows any Windows program to display help files in a consistent format. WinHelp is called the help engine because it is an engine that allows any file created, following certain formatting guidelines, to be compiled into a file which can be viewed using WINHELP.EXE. This engine provides the capabilities for an application to call both general and context-sensitive help. The developer of a Windows application does not have to worry about creating a mechanism to view help. He or she merely has to create a file that can be read by the help engine. As such, it allows developers to create custom help for their applications. There are only three requirements:

- A development environment that supports help-context IDs.
- A copy of the Windows help compiler (and its associated utility programs).
- A word processor that can create rich text format (RTF) files (such as Word for Windows).

Access provides the first, the Access Developers Toolkit provides the second, and you provide the third. If you choose not to purchase the ADT (because you have no interest in creating distributable applications), the Windows help compiler is available from several other sources such as the Windows SDK and Visual Basic Professional edition. The one thing that you need to provide is a little creativity.

Printed Documentation

There are really two kinds of printed documentation, user and system. User documentation is written with the end user in mind. It contains instructions and definitions to help the user use the application. System documentation is for the developer(s). It contains objectives, specifications, flowcharts, data diagrams, and source code (if applicable). It is designed to help the developer get from the concept to the final product. More important, it is for those who will have to maintain and modify the application in the future, so that they can understand what happens "under the hood," and why. Traditionally, system documentation has been a hodge-podge of various printed documents. They often exist independently, and are not put together in any organized fashion. In the heat of the moment, system documentation is often skipped or ignored, yet it is one of the most important components of an application.

It is especially easy using a tool like Access (or even Word for Windows), which supports OLE, to assemble a single systems documentation application. Although your first reaction might be to ask why use a database for documentation instead of a word processor, the answer is simple. Although a word processor is the conventional tool for creating traditional documentation, which is very text rich and linear, Access provides a great environment for multiple data types—OLE objects such as flowcharts, word processing documents, graphics, audio, and video, and even the data itself. Access provides systems documentation tools such as the Analyzer Wizard. Why export your data dictionary to a word processor when you can use it and your favorite word processor in a single application on-line? You will also probably use Access to track your testing (you could actually store your automated test scripts in your database) and help with the development of your help system (tracking subjects as well as storing the source text as OLE objects).

Although the trend is toward on-line help and away from printed documentation, most developers still want to provide some printed documentation. At a bare minimum, installation and startup instructions must be printed.

Step 6: Distribute the Application

This is perhaps the easiest step in the process. At this point you should have:

- An error-free application
- On-line help
- Printed documentation

You have two choices: Distribute the application's MBD file(s), or distribute the application with the ADT runtime. If you choose the former, all users you distribute the application to must have a copy of Microsoft Access. When they run your application (depending on the security you have implemented), they will be able to modify the application, and it will still have all of the standard Access tools. If you choose to create a runtime, you will distribute a special runtime version of Access which does not allow the user to modify the application. It makes your application look like a stand-alone, custom windows application. Which is right for your users? It really depends on the organization as well as the project.

If you use the ADT, you will use the Setup Wizard to create a set of installation diskettes, which you will distribute to your users. These setup disks will include your application's MDB file(s), as well as all of the files required by the Access runtime. After they are created, you simply distribute them to your users. When they get the disks, they run a file called SETUP from the first disk, and your application will install itself, using a standard Windows setup program.

If you have completed all of the previous steps, you will have an application that solves your problems. All you have to do is create the setup disk(s) using the Setup Wizard provided with the ADT, and then distribute your application.

Chapter 3

Windows Design Basics

An Overview of the Windows Interface

One of the key factors in the overwhelming success of Windows is its consistent look and feel. Although each Windows application has its own unique interface characteristics, there is a certain amount of common ground between applications. This makes life easier for users because they come to expect certain behavior from certain objects, which simplifies moving from one application to another. Once a user has gotten over the hurdle of learning Windows basics, and perhaps one application, all of this knowledge is transferable to each additional application that is acquired. Instead of having to relearn the standard interface (menus, syntax, and command structure), users can focus on how to use the unique features of that application to solve their problems. They don't have to worry about how to open, save, and close a file; they learn that if their applications follow Windows interface guidelines, these functions will always be found on the File menu, where applicable.

Notice the key operative: *if their applications follow Windows interface guidelines*. Unlike some other graphical user interfaces, which are fairly restrictive, Windows gives the developer a wide degree of latitude when it comes to interface issues. Although it is recognized that certain applications have specialized interface needs (such as a program for an ATM that responds to a touch screen), it is beneficial to the user for the aforementioned reasons to provide a consistent interface. Thus, Microsoft left the door fairly open for interpretation. But Microsoft found that many developers were designing applications that were not consistent, even if they were within the same organization. As a result, Microsoft published *The Windows Interface: An Application Design Guide*, to guide developers through interface design issues. Although this book does not cover all issues of interface design, it does cover the areas that are expected to be consistent.

From the developer's point of view, this standardization can be either a blessing or a curse. From the negative side a consistent standard means:

- Working within restrictive guidelines (less freedom of expression).
- Taking the time and energy to learn and embrace the standards.

On the positive side:

- Your application has the potential to be more widely accepted because it is already familiar to most users.
- You do not have to waste time reinventing the wheel.

In reality, the two positives far outweigh the negative factors. Although you are restricted, you are also free of the burden of developing the interface environment and features. Ultimately, the creative programmer can bypass or modify many features of the Windows environment. The only time the standards should be deviated from is when there is absolutely no way to achieve the desired objective while working within the standard. Also, learning the standards is just like learning Windows. Once you make the initial investment, every additional application will be easier to develop because of the effort you put in up front.

Although some developers will always shy away from the standard to create a unique interface, the ones who succeed are few and far between, and the industry press is often harsh to those who deviate from the standards. If a software developer decided to put the main menu of his or her application on the bottom of the screen instead of the top, this would probably not be well received by the press or end users. These standards might seem to slow innovation, but this is not at all the case. The windows API (Application Programming Interface) will continue to evolve and incorporate ideas from Microsoft, as well as other vendors.

The trick for developers is to be innovative and creative with the areas that they have control over, while not deviating from the standards. Access makes it easy for the developer to follow the standards established by Microsoft, yet leaves wide latitude for interpretation. The rest of this chapter discusses standards within the Windows environment, especially as applied within the Access environment. Technical implementation of these features is discussed throughout the rest of this book, as you develop the application.

Windows and Forms

Parents, Children, Windows, and Forms

The Windows environment supports three kinds of windows:

- Application windows
- Document windows
- Dialog boxes

An application window, also commonly referred to as the parent window, provides the main framework or workspace for a Windows application. By definition, a Windows application can have one—and only one—application window. Document windows, commonly referred to as child windows, appear within the application window. Figure 3.1 illustrates the Access workspace, and identifies the parent and child windows. In traditional, file-based applications such as word processors and spreadsheets, files are opened for editing within a document window. Although this paradigm makes sense for many applications, there are many applications that are not document- or file-based. As such, document windows are often referred to by the type of document they contain or by some other meaningful name. Excel, for example, calls document windows by the type of file that they contain: chart window, macro window, and so on. Dialog boxes are special instances of document windows, and are discussed later in this chapter.

Like Excel, Access document windows are referred to by the kind of object they contain:

- Database windows
- Table windows
- Query windows
- Form windows

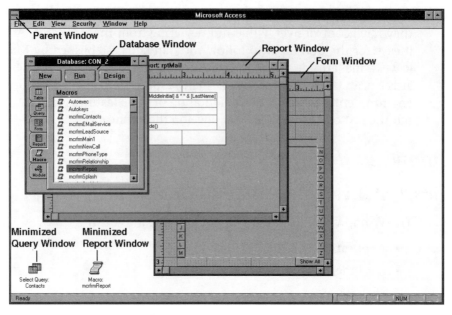

Figure 3.1 Access workspace.

- Macro windows
- Report windows
- Module windows

Although there are seven types of document windows in addition to the application window, Access only allows you to modify two of those:

- Application window
- Forms

It is with the application window and forms that you will develop your application's interface.

Document Interfaces: SDI vs. MDI

Windows applications that allow for the display/editing of one or more document windows use a Multiple Document Interface (MDI). Access supports MDI. Applications that only allow for a single document to be open at a time use a Single Document Interface (SDI). Although Access is not an SDI application, it can be made to look like and behave like one, if that is what you desire.

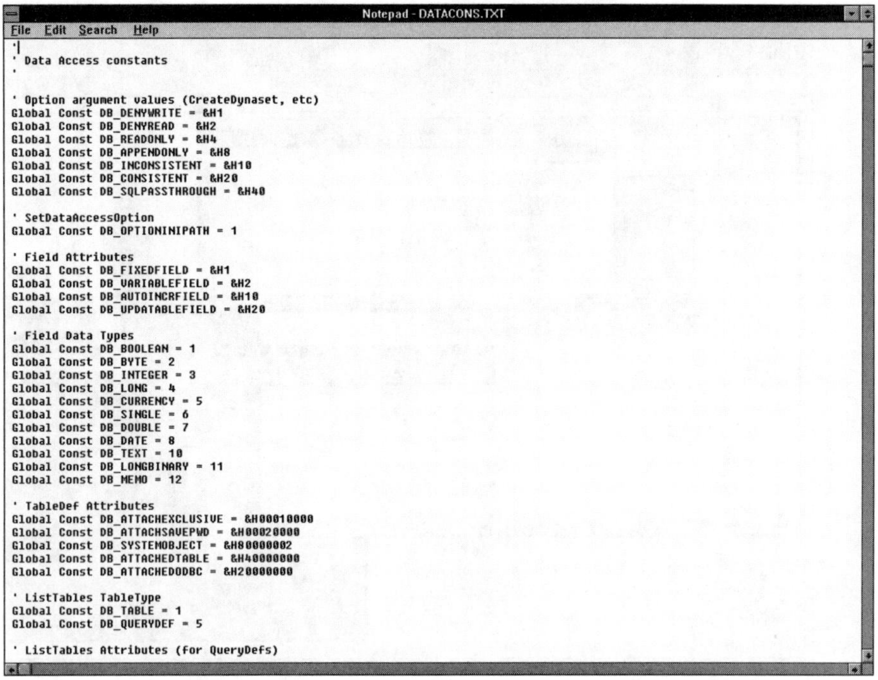

```
Notepad - DATACONS.TXT
File  Edit  Search  Help
'
' Data Access constants
'

' Option argument values (CreateDynaset, etc)
Global Const DB_DENYWRITE = &H1
Global Const DB_DENYREAD = &H2
Global Const DB_READONLY = &H4
Global Const DB_APPENDONLY = &H8
Global Const DB_INCONSISTENT = &H10
Global Const DB_CONSISTENT = &H20
Global Const DB_SQLPASSTHROUGH = &H40

' SetDataAccessOption
Global Const DB_OPTIONINIPATH = 1

' Field Attributes
Global Const DB_FIXEDFIELD = &H1
Global Const DB_VARIABLEFIELD = &H2
Global Const DB_AUTOINCRFIELD = &H10
Global Const DB_UPDATABLEFIELD = &H20

' Field Data Types
Global Const DB_BOOLEAN = 1
Global Const DB_BYTE = 2
Global Const DB_INTEGER = 3
Global Const DB_LONG = 4
Global Const DB_CURRENCY = 5
Global Const DB_SINGLE = 6
Global Const DB_DOUBLE = 7
Global Const DB_DATE = 8
Global Const DB_TEXT = 10
Global Const DB_LONGBINARY = 11
Global Const DB_MEMO = 12

' TableDef Attributes
Global Const DB_ATTACHEXCLUSIVE = &H00010000
Global Const DB_ATTACHSAVEPWD = &H00020000
Global Const DB_SYSTEMOBJECT = &H80000002
Global Const DB_ATTACHEDTABLE = &H40000000
Global Const DB_ATTACHEDODBC = &H20000000

' ListTables TableType
Global Const DB_TABLE = 1
Global Const DB_QUERYDEF = 5

' ListTables Attributes (for QueryDefs)
```

Figure 3.2 Notepad, an application that uses a Single Document Interface.

Notepad: An Application That Does Not Support MDI

Perhaps the best example of an SDI application is Notepad, which comes standard with Windows. It only allows you to edit one document at a time. If you try to open a second document for editing, it prompts you to save changes (assuming you have actually edited the document), closes the document, and then opens the next document. If you want to simultaneously edit two Notepad documents, you must start two separate instances of the Notepad application. Figure 3.2 illustrates Notepad.

Excel: An Application That Does Support MDI

Although Access is an MDI application, it is not the best example to start with for an illustration of MDI, because Access does not "think" in terms of files and documents, but rather in terms of objects, some of which are documents, some of which are not. Microsoft Excel, on the other hand, is a great example of an

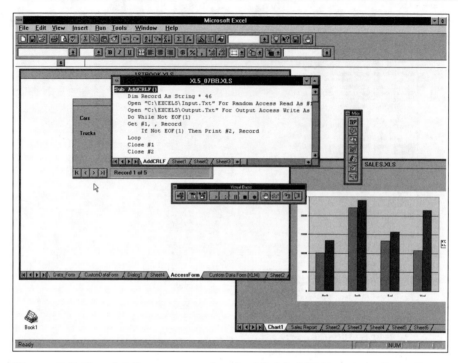

Figure 3.3 Excel 5.0, an example of a Multiple Document Interface.

application which has a Multiple Document Interface because it allows for many documents/files to be opened simultaneously. If you have one spreadsheet open in Excel and wish to open a second, you simply select File → Open, and choose the file you wish to edit. The first document remains open, and the second one is opened in another child window. Figure 3.3 illustrates an Excel workspace with several files open.

Window Components

It is easiest to analyze the environment of a Windows application by breaking it into two discreet areas: the actual window (object) and the objects placed within the context of a window. The first half of this chapter details window objects, while the second half details controls, the objects placed within a window. Figure 3.4 illustrates the Access application window and identifies its key components.

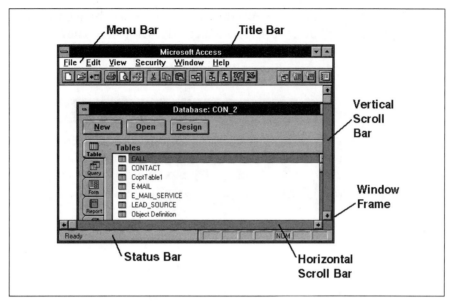

Figure 3.4 Access application window.

All Windows application windows should have the following components:

- Window frame
- Title bar
- Status bar
- Menu bar

And, although not required, an application can also have a vertical scroll bar and a horizontal scroll bar.

Window Frame

The window frame is the border that appears around the perimeter of a window and visually separates it from other windows. The width of the frame is determined by the developer, and the color is determined by the colors set in the Control Panel. In addition to visually distinguishing one window from another, the frame is also used to resize the window. When the mouse cursor passes over the frame, it changes into a double-headed arrow, which shows in which directions the frame can be resized. When the user clicks on the frame and drags, a gray outline appears that shows what the window's new size will be if the mouse button is released. Access does not allow the developer to change the width of a window frame, although a secondary interior frame may be created using Access's line or box controls.

Note

You will rarely see an application without a window frame. Technically, you won't see this at all, because the window frame is the overall framework of the application, although it is possible to write an application that works within Windows but has no graphical interface.

Title Bar

The title bar appears at the top of the window and has three primary functions:

- To display title text for the window (possibly the application).
- To provide a means for changing the size of a window.
- To provide a means for changing the location of a window.

These means are accomplished through three subobjects of the title bar:

- Control menu
- Maximize/minimize buttons
- Title

The Control menu provides a vehicle for the user to size and move the window. Figure 3.5 illustrates a Control menu for an Access form, and Figure 3.6 illustrates the Control window for Access 2.0.

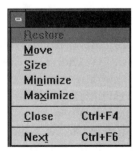

Figure 3.5 Control menu for an Access form.

Figure 3.6 Control menu for Access.

Commands on the control menu are used to:

- Restore the current window to the previous size when it was neither maximized or minimized.
- Move the current window to a new location.
- Minimize the current window.
- Maximize the current window.
- Close the current window.
- Switch to either another form (if the window is a child form) or to another application (if the window is an application window or parent).

Unless you open a form in Dialog mode (modes are covered later in this chapter), Access automatically provides a Control menu for forms.

The Maximize, Minimize, and Restore buttons, which are illustrated in Table 3.1, are used to change the sizing of the current window. These buttons always appear as a pair, as illustrated in Table 3.2. The Minimize button is always to the left, and the right button changes based on the state of the current window (maximized or not maximized).

Table 3.1 The Maximize, Minimize, and Restore Buttons	
Appearance	**Button Name**
▼	Minimize
▲	Maximize
▲▼	Restore

Table 3.2 Maximize, Minimize, and Restore Button Pairs

Appearance	State of Current Window
	Active and maximized
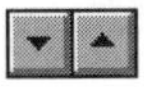	Active, but not maximized

Access automatically displays sizing buttons on all forms. You can prevent them from being displayed by using a form's pop-up and modal properties, as well as by using a macro to open a form in dialog mode.

The title of a window is centered between the Control menu and the sizing buttons. It is a text string that uniquely identifies the window. If it is an application window, it contains the name of the application, with the first letter capitalized. If the application contains a child window (form or document window) which is maximized, the title should contain the name of the application, followed by a single space, a hyphen, another space, and then the name of the document, as illustrated in Figure 3.7. If it is a form (or a dialog), it should contain either the name of the current document (which is not necessarily applicable in Access, since Access doesn't use "documents") or the name of the command (menu item text) which opened the form (the dialog box that results when you select File → Run Macro... has the title Run Macro).

Access handles titles on child forms by providing a form property that sets the title. If you have the ADT, you can change the application window's title; if you do not have the ADT, you cannot.

Note

As is the case with many examples in this book, saying you cannot change the title of the Access application window without the ADT really means that Access does not provide a tool to do it with. You could actually hack the code with a C program that makes calls to the Windows API and dynamically modify the window's handle. This is not recommended, however, even for the most advanced users!

Microsoft Word - BAA_CH03.DOC

Figure 3.7 Title bar example for Word for Windows.

Scroll Bars

Scroll bars are designed to help a user quickly navigate through an application's windows, in the event that the virtual window is larger than the physical window. Access, like most other Windows applications, is implemented with this feature both in the application window and all child forms. Although you cannot turn the application window's scroll bars on and off, you can control vertical and horizontal scroll bars on custom forms through the forms Scroll Bars property. Figure 3.8 illustrates an Access window with both vertical and horizontal scroll bars.

Although scroll bars are commonly referred to as a single unit, they actually consist of three distinct components:

- Scroll arrows
- Scroll box
- Scroll bar shaft

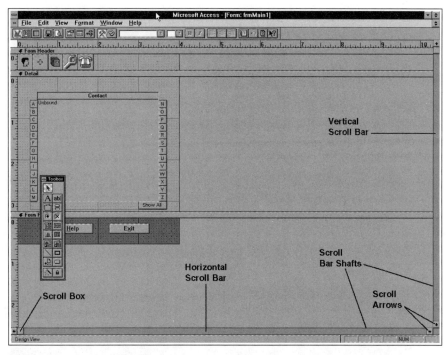

Figure 3.8 Vertical and horizontal scroll bars in Access's Form Design window.

When a user clicks on one of a scroll bar's two scroll arrows, the window scrolls one line at a time in the direction of the arrow. Scroll arrows offer the smallest unit of navigation of the choice scroll bar components. The scroll box, on the other hand, provides the largest unit of navigation of the scroll bar components. When you click and drag on a scroll box, you navigate in the direction you drag. In most applications, the velocity at which you scroll through a window is logarithmic, not linear. Access is no exception to this rule. Some applications, such as Microsoft Excel, actually tell you what line you will be at when you release the mouse button. But because Access does not always "think" in terms of lines (like Excel "thinks" in terms of rows), this feature doesn't make any sense, and is therefore not implemented. The scroll shaft actually serves two functions. First, it is a visual indicator of where you are in a window, based on the position of the scroll box. Second, it provides the middle-of-the-road unit of navigation. If you click in the scroll bar above the scroll box, you will move up one screen. It is the equivalent of pressing the Page Up key. If you click in the scroll bar below the scroll box, you will down one screen, the equivalent of pressing the Page Down key.

Status and Message Bars

A message bar, illustrated in Figure 3.9, is a horizontal bar at the bottom of the screen that displays status information about a selection, an object, or a running process. It also is a special message bar that displays additional information. The Access default status bar displays the current state of several options, which can be toggled either on or off, such as information and status messages from the application. Table 3.3 lists the abbreviations that appear in the right side of the status bar.

Access does not allow you to put a status bar in a form, nor does it allow you to change its style. Access does allow you to create text and messages to be displayed in the status bar, using several different properties (depending on the object) or commands, or allows you to hide it altogether.

Menu Bar

The menu bar is used to display the titles of the menus available to an application at any given point in time. This last qualifier is mentioned because

Turn control wizards on or off

Figure 3.9 Access message bar.

Table 3.3 Access Status Bar Text	
Status Bar Text	**Meaning**
FLTR	A filter is applied.
MOV	Move mode is on.
EXT	Extend mode is on.
CAPS	Caps lock is on.
NUM	Num lock is on.
SCRL	Scroll lock is on.
OVR	Overtype is on.

Access, like many other applications, has dynamic menus that change depending on where you are working in the application. Access allows you, the developer, to take advantage of this by calling different menu bars to be associated with different forms. By selecting an item on the menu bar, the user opens the menu associated with the item that was selected. The menu bar is always directly below the application's title bar.

Menus

Menus are lists of commands that are available to an application. The commands can be either implicit (if you select a file name from the most recently used file list, the program actually opens the file) or explicit (the Open command on the File menu). There are three kinds of menus available in the windows interface:

- Drop-down
- Cascading
- Pop-up

Drop-Down Menus

A drop-down menu is one that drops down from the menu bar when the corresponding menu bar text is selected. Drop-down menus are the most common menus used in Windows applications. Figure 3.10 gives an illustration.

Figure 3.10 Access's File menu, an example of a drop-down menu.

Cascading Menus

A cascading menu is a submenu that appears to the right of a menu item when the item is selected. Cascading menus are also known as child menus. The menu item from which the child appears is known as the parent item. An example of a cascading menu is Access's New command, which is illustrated in Figure 3.11.

Pop-Up Menus

A pop-up menu appears at a location in the application's workspace, and is not attached to the menu bar. Figure 3.12 illustrates a standard Access pop-up menu, which is invoked using the right mouse button. Figure 3.13 illustrates an Access form that has been coerced to look (well, somewhat) and behave like a pop-up menu.

Figure 3.11 A Cascading menu (Access's New menu).

Figure 3.12 An Access pop-up menu.

Menu Components

All menus (except for pop-ups) consist of two items: a title and an item. A menu's title appears in the menu bar of the application if it is a drop-down menu, and to the left of the menu if it a cascading type. Pop-up menus do not have titles. The title is a single word that describes or groups all of the items in the menu it represents. Although it is technically possible to create a title with spaces (more than one word), this should be avoided at all costs, because it will be confusing to the user. When a title is selected, the menu will be displayed.

A title is selected either by the user clicking on it or by use of a mnemonic Access key. An Access key is an underlined letter in the title, which, when pressed in combination with the Alt key, will invoke the menu. Access keys are often referred to as combination keys or hot keys.

Items are the individual elements on a menu that invoke an action when selected. Like titles, they can be accessed either by clicking or by an Access key. Unlike titles, they can be, and often are, more than one word. Also, pop-up menus should not allow Access keys, although they are technically possible to implement. This is because the pop-up is invoked using the mouse. As such, using access keys does not really make sense.

Related actions are grouped on a menu, and it is common to further divide items into subgroups, and to insert a solid line between the groups. Figure 3.14

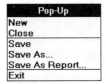

Figure 3.13 An Access form disguised as a pop-up menu.

Figure 3.14 File menu showing like commands grouped together and separated by lines.

illustrates the Access File menu (when form object is selected). Notice that there are four groupings of actions:

- Open/Close actions
- Save actions
- Print actions
- Miscellaneous actions

A line is placed between each group to make it easier for users to find the action they are seeking. When a menu title is selected, text that describes the contents of the menu should appear in the status bar. Likewise, when a menu item is selected, descriptive text should appear in the status bar.

Window Modes

Focus is a state that determines whether an object can receive input at any given point in time. Only one object can have focus at a time. In Excel, for example, when you open a new spreadsheet, and cell A1 is highlighted, the input you type will be entered into the cell. Cell A1 has the focus. If you subsequently move to cell B10, it has focus. Objects such as command buttons also can receive focus, and although an OK button might not take input in the traditional sense, when you push it, you are actually inputting an action to the program.

A window's mode determines whether users may continue to work with other windows in an application, or if they must stay within the active window and close it before continuing. There are four different modes under which windows can be opened:

- Modal
- Modeless
- Pop-up
- Dialog

Modal

A modal form is one that must retain focus until it is closed. When a modal window is opened, all other windows are disabled, although menus and toolbars are still enabled.

Modeless

A modeless form is a one that does not have to retain focus while it is open. In other words, it can be open, and then you can leave it to work in other windows. The Access Database window is an example of a modeless form. You can reduce it to an icon, hide it, or just select another form to work on. Until you close it, it will always be there for you to continue doing whatever it was that you were doing before you switched focus to another object. Generally speaking, all Access objects (Database window, Form, Report, Macro, and Module design windows) are modeless, and all user-created forms are by default modeless.

Pop-Up

A pop-up form remains on top of other windows (forms) within the application. They are often used to create "floating" toolboxes (such as the Access toolbox) and palettes. Examples of pop-up forms are the Access Toolbox, Property Sheet, Field List, and Palette, which are illustrated in Figure 3.15.

Dialog Boxes

A dialog box is a special occurrence of a modal window; they also disable menus and the toolbar. Although Access does not have a dialog box form type, it allows the user to create them using two methods:

- Setting a form's modal and pop-up properties to Yes.
- Opening a form from a macro (or module) and setting its Window Type property to Dialog.

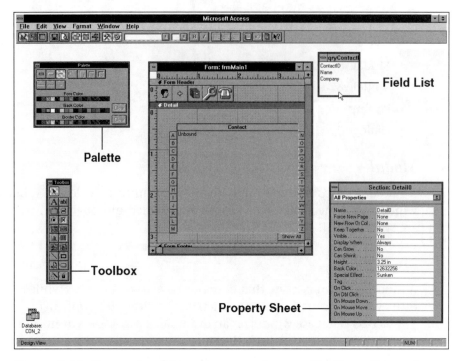

Figure 3.15 Example of Access pop-up forms—Toolbox, Property Sheet, Field List, and Palette.

The first method creates a form that will always behave as a dialog box whenever it is opened. The latter method allows you to selectively open a form in Dialog mode. Therefore, you can use the same form in more than one scenario, and have it behave differently, when appropriate.

Windows Controls Overview

When a user is presented with a window to make a choice (that will influence the resultant action of the program which displayed the dialog), the program is temporarily passing control over to the user. Thus, the objects a user can select in the window are known as controls, because they allow the user to control the flow of a program. Every object in a window is a Windows control.

The purpose of a control is to pass information to the user and/or to receive input from the user. The Windows environment has a set of standard controls, in addition to customizable controls, for those applications whose needs cannot be met by the standard controls. Access supports the following standard controls.

- Static text
- Text boxes
- Command buttons
- Option buttons
- Check boxes
- Toggle buttons
- Group boxes
- Single selection list boxes
- Combo boxes
- Bound OLE object frames
- Unbound OLE object frames
- Lines
- Rectangles

The standard Windows controls that Access does not directly support are:

- Extended selection list boxes
- Spin boxes
- Sliders
- Read-only pop-up text fields

Controls Supported by Access

Static Text

Label controls are used to display static text that is not editable by the user. Labels are often bound to other controls, and are used to identify and provide direct keyboard access (via access keys) to controls, although they do not have to be bound to a control. As you will see in Chapter 7, you have the option of having bound labels automatically created every time you create a control. Table 3.4 lists controls and where their respective labels should be placed. In addition to the suggestions in this table, the following rules should be followed:

Table 3.4 Controls and Suggested Label Locations

Control	Location
Command Button	Inside the button.
Option Group	Above the frame and centered, below the frame and centered, or on top of the top frame line, starting in the upper left-hand corner.
Check Box	To the right of the box.
Option Button	To the right of the button.
Text Box	To the left of or above the control, followed by a colon, and left-aligned with the section in which it appears.
Toggle Button	Inside the button.
Combo Box	To the left of or above the control, followed by a colon, and left-aligned with the section in which it appears.
List Box	To the left of or above the control, followed by a colon, and left-aligned with the section in which it appears.
Unbound Object	No label.
Bound Object	Below the object, centered. Using a text box control to display a related field is an even better option.
Subforms/Reports	Above the control, left-aligned.
List Box	To the left of or above the control, followed by a colon, and left-aligned with the section in which it appears.

- Capitalize the first letter of every word in a label, except articles, conjunctions, prepositions, and the *to* in infinitives.
- Provide a unique Access key (this will be covered in Chapter 5).
- Use a bold font.
- Dim unused labels/controls.

Although these rules can be broken, they, like most other rules listed in this book, will help you achieve a consistent look and feel for your application.

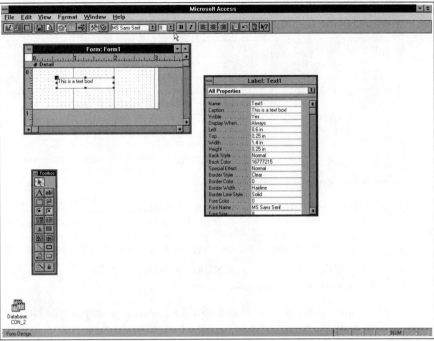

Figure 3.16 An Access form in Design mode with a text box

Text Boxes

Text box controls allow the user to type information or to display calculated values. Figure 3.16 illustrates a form with a text box. In Access, text box controls are usually bound to a field in a table or query, and are the primary vehicle for data entry.

Command Buttons

A command button is a rectangular control that initiates an action when it is pushed. A command button usually contains a label to specify the action that will take place when the button is selected. The developer can provide a keyboard shortcut (known as an access key) simply by placing an ampersand (&) in the label string directly in front of the character in the label, which should be pressed in combination with the Alt key. Access also allows the developer to place a bitmap image (BMP) on the face of a button. If a bitmap is placed on the face of a button, the label text is not displayed. The text of all command buttons should be System 10 Bold, to be consistent with other Windows

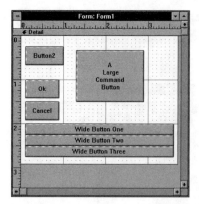

Figure 3.17 Examples of command buttons.

applications. They should also have access keys, and you should deviate from this standard only in very special situations. Figure 3.17 illustrates several command buttons on a form.

There are three buttons that should appear on every form: Help, Cancel, and OK. Each form should have one and only one of each of these buttons. The Help button should display a window's help topic about the current form. The Cancel button should close the form, and undo any changes that may have been made via the form. All forms have a Cancel property which may be used to identify one and only one button on a form as a Cancel button. The OK button should close the form, and commit any changes which may have been made via the form. It is recommended that you use these labels, although you will periodically encounter situations where a different label will be more

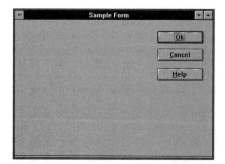

Figure 3.18 Help, Cancel, and OK buttons in the upper right-hand corner of a form.

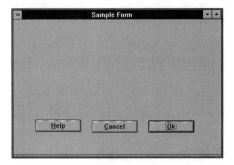

Figure 3.19 Help, Cancel, and OK buttons at the bottom of a form.

appropriate (such as a button labeled Next, which closes the active form and navigates the user to a second, related form).

These three buttons should be placed in the upper right-hand corner of a form or across the bottom. Figure 3.18 illustrates the former, and Figure 3.19 illustrates the latter. It is becoming more common to place them at the bottom, and have the region graphically separated by using a different color for the form footer. Figure 3.20 illustrates this concept.

Option Groups

Option group controls are used to create a graphical or functional grouping for a set of related controls. When used in conjunction with check boxes, radio buttons, and/or toggle buttons, they are often called group boxes. Related controls are placed inside the frame, and are bound to the same field as the

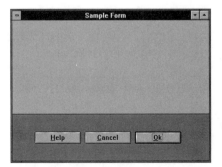

Figure 3.20 Help, Cancel, and OK buttons at the bottom of a form, in a form footer.

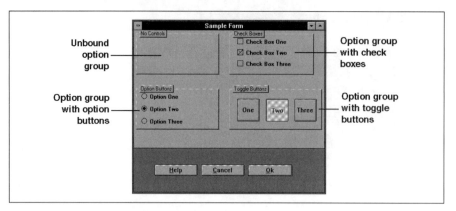

Figure 3.21 Form with option groups.

frame. Figure 3.21 illustrates four separate option groups, one without controls, one with check boxes, one with option buttons, and one with toggle buttons.

Option Buttons

Option buttons are small hollow circles that, when selected, have a large dot in the center, as illustrated in Figure 3.22. Option buttons are used to:

- Indicate/select the state of a yes/no or true/false condition when used stand-alone.
- Represent a single selection from a list of mutually exclusive options when used in an option group.

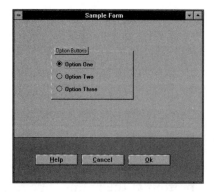

Figure 3.22 Option Buttons: selected and unselected.

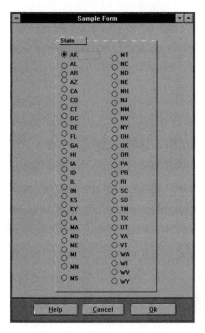

Figure 3.23 States option group: incorrect use of option buttons.

You should never use more than three option buttons to represent a mutually exclusive option. If there are more than three items, a list box/combo box should be used instead. Figure 3.23 illustrates a form that incorrectly uses option buttons (in an option group) instead of a list box; Figure 3.24 illustrates the correct use of option buttons, both stand-alone and in an option group.

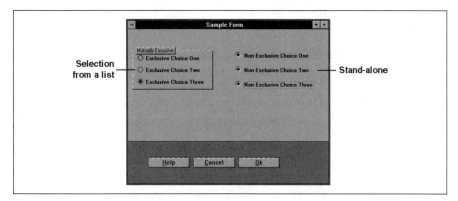

Figure 3.24 Option buttons: stand-alone and selection from a list.

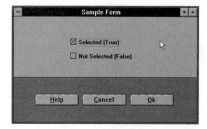

Figure 3.25 Check boxes: selected and unselected.

Although check boxes are preferred for displaying data of a yes/no datatype, there are certain cases where it is more appropriate to use option buttons. It is visually much easier to decipher the state of a check box than to read the contents of a text box such as true/false or -1/0 (the actual stored values). But option buttons have traditionally been associated with mutual selection; thus, users might become confused if they were to see a single option button used to represent a yes/no datatype.

Check Boxes

Check boxes are small squares that, when selected, have an X appear inside, as illustrated in Figure 3.25.

Check boxes are used to:

- Indicate/select the state of a yes/no or true/false condition when used stand-alone.
- Represent a single selection from a list of mutually exclusive options when used in an option group.

Figure 3.26 illustrates both of these scenarios. You should never use more than three check boxes to represent a mutually exclusive option. If there are more that three items, a list box/combo box should be used instead.

Check boxes are the preferred control for displaying data of a yes/no datatype because it is visually much easier to decipher the state of a check box than to read the contents of a text box such as true/false or -1/0 (the actual stored values).

Toggle Buttons

Toggle buttons are rectangular, 3-D buttons, which, when selected, have a large dot in the middle, as illustrated in Figure 3.27. Toggle buttons can contain text

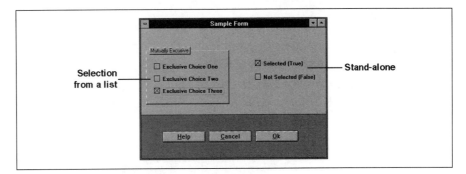

Figure 3.26 Check boxes: stand-alone and selection from a list.

or graphics, but not both (unless the text is encapsulated in the graphic). Toggle buttons are used to:

- Indicate/select the state of a yes/no or true/false condition when used stand-alone.
- Represent a single selection from a list of mutually exclusive options when used in an option group.

Figure 3.28 illustrates both of these scenarios. You should never use more than three toggle buttons to represent a mutually exclusive option. If there are more than three items, a list box/combo box should be used instead.

Check boxes are preferred for displaying data of a yes/no datatype, but there are certain cases where it is more appropriate to use toggle buttons. Although it is visually much easier to decipher the state of a check box than to read the contents of a text box such as true/false or -1/0 (the actual stored values), most

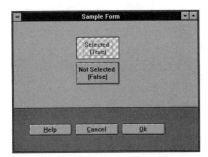

Figure 3.27 Toggle buttons: selected and unselected.

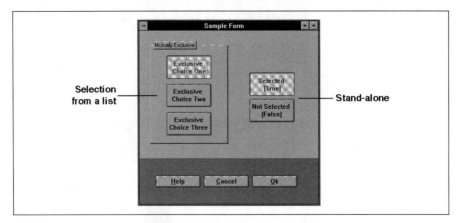

Figure 3.28 Toggle buttons: stand-alone and selection from a list.

Windows users get confused when a toggle button is used to represent yes/no data.

Single Selection List Boxes

Single selection list box controls are used to present the user with a list of choices from which they can select only one choice. List boxes are useful for making a selection from a long list. If there are more entries in a list than the control has room to display, a vertical scroll bar will be displayed on the right side of the control. Figure 3.29 illustrates two simple list boxes, one with a vertical scroll bar and one without.

Figure 3.29 Two simple list boxes, one with vertical scroll bar.

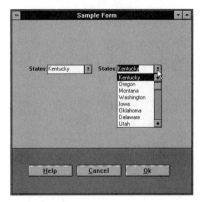

Figure 3.30 Combo box: contracted and expanded.

Combo Boxes

Combo box controls are, as the name implies, a combination of two types of controls: the edit box and single selection list box. Initially, the control looks like a text box with an arrow on the right, but when you select the arrow, the control expands, and a list box appears. Figure 3.30 illustrates a combo box, both expanded and contracted. Combo boxes are used when you want to present the user with a list of common choices, but not necessarily limit them to that list. For example, let's assume you have a created a form for order entry, and have a list of products. It makes sense to display a list of standard products, but perhaps allow the user to input additional products for custom orders. A custom item would not be added to the list of standard products, but the system would have the flexibility to handle it properly. Access also allows the developer to limit the input to this list. This can help users quickly navigate through a long list of choices, because when the user types into the box, Access tries to match the input with an item on the list. Thus, if you had a combo box with a list of states, and typed C, California would be selected, because it is the first item in the list that starts with C.

Additional Features of List and Combo Boxes

List and combo boxes behave identically—it is just a question of whether the list is always displayed or whether you can type an entry. Access goes far beyond the list boxes that most Windows users are familiar with by providing the ability to:

- Display multiple columns.
- Determine the width of columns.
- Hide columns that you want bound, but not displayed.
- Display column headings.
- Display a horizontal scroll bar if more than one column is displayed and the list box is not wide enough to display all of the columns.
- Fill the list using a hard-coded list, a table/query, an SQL clause, or a field list.
- Bind the control to a field in a table/query.

Bound Object Frame Control

Bound object frame controls are used to display/edit OLE (Object Linking and Embedding) objects that are saved as part of an Access table. An OLE object is any object (photo, chart, video clip, Excel worksheet, and so on) that was created in an application and that can be linked/embedded in another OLE-compliant application. Bound object frames are always *bound* to an OLE object datatype in the underlying Access table. A good way to visualize a bound object frame is to think of it as a looking glass with a special filter, which allows you to see a document (or other object) that is stored in a data table. Depending on the application and its OLE implementation, you will see either the document itself (such as a Paintbrush document), or an icon that represents the server application (such as with Winword 1.1). It is also possible to display just an icon, even if the server application can display the complete document. Figure 3.31 illustrates an object frame.

A bound object frame does not display anything when in Form Design view, but displays the corresponding object in Form view (Or Report view). From Form view, the object can be edited directly by double-clicking on it or by selecting the appropriate command from the Edit menu. Figure 3.32 illustrates how the Word object in Figure 3.31 can be selected, and how the default Edit menu changes to reflect that an OLE object has been selected.

Unbound OLE Objects

Unbound object frame controls are used to place OLE objects that are not stored in an Access table on forms (and reports). Unbound OLE objects are usually

Figure 3.31   Bound object frame: a Word 6.0 object.

visual enhancements, such as a logo, a chart, or possibly a video clip with instructions how to use an application or an OLE custom control.

Like bound object frames, depending on the server application's OLE implementation, either the document itself or an icon representing the application may be displayed. Unbound OLE objects are usually visual enhancements, such as a logo, a chart, or possibly a video clip with instructions how to use an application. Unlike bound object frames, unbound object frames cannot be used to edit the object in Form view, although the object can be edited in Form

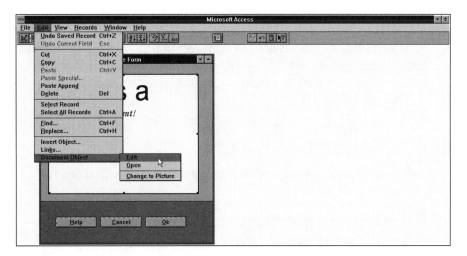

Figure 3.32   Edit menu for bound Word object.

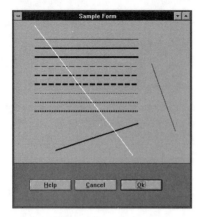

Figure 3.33 Lines, lines, and more lines.

Design view. Essentially, this gives you, the developer, control to edit the object, but limits the user to viewing it.

Lines

The line control is used to draw lines. Lines are used to visually enhance forms and reports. A form with several lines of varying thicknesses and angles is illustrated in Figure 3.33.

Rectangles

The Rectangle control is used to draw rectangles. Rectangles are most often used to visually group related controls. Rectangles can achieve various looks by altering borders and fill. Figure 3.34 illustrates several rectangles, each with a different look and feel.

Controls Not Supported by Access

There are five kinds of standard Windows controls that are not supported by Access:

- Multiple selection list boxes
- Extended selection list boxes
- Spin boxes

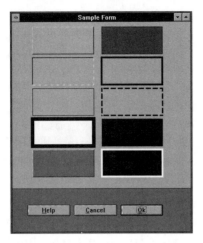

Figure 3.34   Rectangles, rectangles, and more rectangles.

- Sliders
- Read-only pop-up text fields

These are mentioned not to be critical of the product, but to point out that there are some areas of the Windows interface that are not directly supported. It is better to be aware of these limitations than to beat your head against a wall trying to figure out why it isn't in the documentation. In addition to the controls described, Access supports third-party OLE custom controls. Three OLE custom controls are provided with the ADT.

What Makes a Good Interface?

As discussed in Chapter 2, application development is an art. Interface design in particular is the most visible and, thus, visual part of an application. Although there is great debate about many of the characteristics that make an interface "good," it is generally agreed that a well-designed interface will be:

- Consistent
- Simple
- Subtle

Consistent means two things: First, it means that your application conforms to Windows standards for interface design, as discussed throughout this chapter; second, it means that your application follows the same pattern for all similar objects or components. Earlier, it was suggested that you put command buttons either at the bottom or in the upper right-hand corner of a form. Don't, for instance, create half of your forms with buttons on the bottom and half with buttons on the top. Put them all in the same place. If you must deviate, do so for a good reason (for example, on a long form that looks bad with buttons on the bottom). As far as the buttons themselves, wherever possible, make them the same height and width. Make sure they are the same distance from the bottom, and that they are the same distance from the control above them. Finally, make sure that on every form they have the same amount of spacing between them.

Simplicity means that the application interfaces with the user in a clear and uncomplicated manner. Information overload occurs when too much information is presented, and the user gets confused or, even worse, just shuts down and gives up. Too much information can be a menu with too many items, a form with too many controls, or a chart with too many labels. It is a common mistake for developers to present the user with too much information at once, resulting in information overload.

Always try to make the user's choice as clear as possible. Force users to focus on the correct item. Don't overwhelm them. Figure 3.23 demonstrates this concept very well. It overwhelms and makes it difficult for the user to focus on the important issue—which state is selected. If this option group was the only item to select on a form, it might not be that bad, but imagine it on a form with more address information. First of all, it would waste a large amount of screen space; second, it is not quick and easy to decipher. Figure 3.35 illustrates a customer address form that includes this option group. It should be obvious how confusing this looks. Figure 3.36 illustrates the same form, but uses a combo box instead of the option group. In about one-fiftieth of the space, you get a control that you can interpret much more quickly. Although your eye eventually figures which state is selected in the option group, it takes much longer for you to scan all 50 buttons, and determine their state, than to look at a combo box with only the state that is selected.

Subtle means that you coerce users into making a choice or focus their attention in a manner that seems natural to them. In other words, you direct their actions, but on a subconscious level. The example of using the combo box for states instead of the group box demonstrates this concept very well. If a user is viewing an existing record, both the option group and the combo box tell

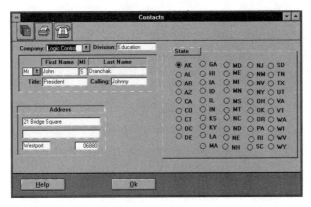

Figure 3.35 A poorly designed form: address form with state option group.

him or her which state is selected. But as the developer, you have decided that it would take too long to focus on the selected state using the option box method. You have also decided that it is superfluous to display the list of 50 states, when all the user is concerned with is the current selection. Therefore, without the user being consciously aware of it, you have made him or her focus only on the currently selected state and ignore the other 49.

Likewise, when a user is inputting new state names, you have decided that it is more efficient for him or her to either type in the state or select it from the drop-down list than to scan and select one of the 50 option buttons. Having this option group would also cause the user to lose focus on the whole form. If

Figure 3.36 A well-designed form: address form with state combo box.

you have 50 percent of your form dedicated to one underlying field, the user might infer that this field is more important than all the others, which might not be the case. Again, you have quietly guided him or her to the proper choice in a natural manner. In interface design, often what you don't put on a form is as important as what you do put on it.

Another example of subtlety is the use of expanding forms or subforms. Perhaps you know that you would like to keep a group of related controls together on a form. You also know that the form would be too busy with all of the controls. Finally, you know that some of the information, although related, is viewed very infrequently. With this knowledge, you could provide a button, labeled Details, that displays a subform or pop-up window with the detail information. This way you keep your interface clean, while allowing users to access important information, which they don't necessarily always need to see. This method is subtle, because you're not forcing the viewer to look at the details, but you are offering him or her a quiet option that makes it possible with a minimum of fanfare.

Zen Computing

Ultimately, you want users to just "feel" the interface, without thinking about it. They should not have to search the interface for data or commands, because it is well-presented and intuitive. They should be able to ignore the interface and just assimilate the actual information presented. Zen computing! As the designer, it is your role to be the Zen master who allows the user to transcend thinking about the interface. You want the user to "feel at one" with your application.

Chapter 4

Information Modeling

What Is Information Modeling?

In Chapter 1, you learned that information was data in context. Information modeling is the process of taking the data and its context, and molding it into a meaningful model that can be used by your DBMS. There are four ways that your data is represented at various points in your system's life cycle:

- External view
- Conceptual view
- Logical view
- Physical view

In the development of your system, you are concerned with getting from the external view to the physical view. Your ultimate goal is to get from the external view to the physical view and then back to the external view. Users will interact with your application through the external view. The external view is the data itself and the context it is in. Table 4.1 illustrates an external view. It includes printed reports, tables, and so on. Using the example of the Saugatuck Marketing Group, the largest single piece of the external view is probably the salesman's phone book or Rolodex.

The conceptual view is an English-like representation of the external view. Creating the conceptual view from the external view is the process of verbalizing the facts that are represented by the data of the external view. Figure 4.1 is a portion of the conceptual view of the data illustrated in Table 4.1.

Table 4.1 External View

| EMPLOYEE | | | | | |
EmployeeID	FirstName	MiddleInitial	LastName	SocialSecurity#	EntryDate
1002	John	M	Smith	000-24-9891	1/1/93
1003	Tom	I	Turk	781-35-7829	1/1/93

The logical view represents your information as entities, attributes, and relationships, following the rules of relational theory. Figure 4.2 illustrates this view of the data represented in Table 4.1, as well as some additional information. Although it is easy to explain to an end user what this figure means, it would not necessarily be evident to someone who wasn't familiar with relational theory and database management systems.

The physical view is the physical implementation of the logical view. In Access, it is an MDB file with tables, fields, indexes, keys, and so on.

This chapter focuses on getting from the external model to the logical model. It is the goal of information modeling to accurately translate your data from the external view to the logical view.

Relational Databases

Relational Theory

Many computer users' first exposure to databases is through spreadsheet applications such as Excel. Microsoft user studies have determined that nine out of

---

Employee is identified by EmployeeID.
Employee has a FirstName.
Employee has a MiddleInitial (MI).
Employee has a LastName.
Employee has a Social Security # (SS#).
Employee was added to the system on EntryDate.

Figure 4.1 Conceptual view.

EMPLOYEE

EmployeeID
FirstName
MiddleInitial
LastName
SocialSecurityNumber
EntryDate

Figure 4.2 ER diagram for the Employee table.

ten Excel users use their spreadsheets for list management. It is typical for a user to just start typing a list of related information, and suddenly, a database is born. One of the benefits of this is that it requires no preparation. Figure 4.3 illustrates a simple contact list as it might start life in Excel, and although this format is fine for four contacts, as illustrated, and might even work for ten contacts, it would not be very useful for 100 or 1,000 contacts.

What is wrong with this picture? First of all, there is no order, beyond that by which entries were added to the list. This certainly is acceptable for some applications, but it is not for a contact list. If you have 100 entries in your list, and there is no order to the list, you would waste a lot of time browsing through the list. You could sort this array by the name column, which would yield somewhat undesirable results because it contains first and last names. Figure 4.4 illustrates an expanded version of this list, sorted by the name column. Not very useful, is it?

Ideally, you want to be able to separate items in the list such as first name, last name, company name, and so on, and then sort by these. If you have a working knowledge of Excel's database features, you know that with a very

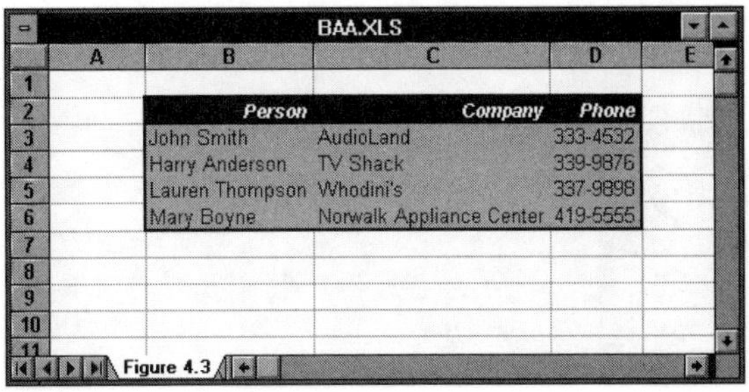

Figure 4.3 The beginning of an Excel contact list.

Person	Company	Phone
Bruce Allen	Stereos R Us	718-0009
George Ross	hdTV	718-1112
Harriet Fletcher	American Television	333-2321
Harry Anderson	TV Shack	339-9876
John Smith	AudioLand	333-4532
Justin Thames	Media Concepts. Ltd.	333-4321
Kary Wisten	Media Concepts. Ltd.	333-8989
Lauren Thompson	Whodini's	337-9898
Lisa Doyle	hdTV	333-1234
Mary Boyne	Norwalk Appliance Center	419-5555

Figure 4.4 Expanded version of an Excel contact list, sorted by

small amount of work, you can do this. Figure 4.5 shows the example data, defined as an Excel database and sorted by the contact's last name. This makes it much easier to look for a contact in the database, because you know that there is an alphabetical sort (by name) on the data. A problem arises, however, as soon as you add new contacts, because you have to constantly redefine and resort your database to keep it current. What if you don't want to manually scroll through the database to find a contact? Excel can handle this by using search criteria. Further, what if you want to see only the contacts at Microsoft? This can be accomplished using search criteria and extract range.

Excel stores data in a flat file format. This is because data is stored, as represented in the preceding example, as a series of rows and columns. Although this is useful and efficient for small lists, it becomes inefficient for large lists, especially if you have many columns of data (fields in Excel terms), with lots of replicated data. A simple example will help to clarify this.

Assume that your database has entries for contacts at Microsoft, Lotus, and Borland. Assume also that your contact list contains 300 entries for each of these companies. Then suppose that Borland and Lotus merge to become Borlus. In Excel, you would have to find every occurrence of Borland and change the text to Borlus, and every instance of Lotus, and change it to Borlus. If you are an

LastName	FirstName	Company	Phone
Allen	Bruce	Stereos R Us	718-0009
Anderson	Harry	TV Shack	339-9876
Boyne	Mary	Norwalk Appliance Center	419-5555
Doyle	Lisa	hdTV	333-1234
Fletcher	Harriet	American Television	333-2321
Ross	George	hdTV	718-1112
Smith	John	AudioLand	333-4532
Thames	Justin	Media Concepts. Ltd.	333-4321
Thompson	Lauren	Whodini's	337-9898
Wisten	Kary	Media Concepts. Ltd.	333-8989

Figure 4.5 Excel Database, with separate columns for first and last name, sorted by last name.

Table 4.2 Contact Table

CONTACT			
First Name	**Middle Initial**	**Last Name**	**Company**
Bill		Gates	Microsoft
Steve		Ballmer	Microsoft
Jim		Manzi	Lotus

Excel power user, you could accomplish this quickly using search and replace. But what if a temp (or a string of temps) maintains your list for you and they don't know about this feature? They would spend hours manually changing every occurrence of Borland and Lotus to Borlus. In addition to the names changing, all of the address information would have to be changed to represent the new company's address (assuming, of course, that all employees of both companies now share the same address).

An alternative to the flat file model is the relational model. In the relational model, instead of all information being stored in a single, large table, information is stored in several smaller tables, which can be viewed together to create the net effect of the one large table. Tables 4.2 and 4.3 illustrate the single table you have been working with, broken into new two tables—one that stores information about the contact and one that stores information about the company the contact works at.

Notice that both tables have a column for company name. This is because the two tables are related to each other by company name. In English, you might make the following statements:

- Each contact works for a company.
- Each company is located at an address.

Table 4.3 Company Table

ADDRESS					
Company	**Street1**	**Street2**	**City**	**State**	**Zip**
Microsoft	One Microsoft Way		Redmond	WA	99999
Lotus	55 Cambridge Parkway		Cambridge	MA	99999

The first statement articulates a fact about a contact, then about a company. Notice that both statements, like their respective tables, contain a reference to a company. This indicates that there is a relationship between the two tables.

In the original example (the Excel contact database), if a company changed its address, you would have to find every occurrence of the company's address and change it. If you had 50 contacts at one particular company, you would have to find each occurrence and change it. Again, if you use search and replace, the job becomes much easier, but there is still a chance for error. What if you had incorrectly input the address in several instances? Search and replace would not find these instances, and your data would be inaccurate.

On the other hand, in the preceding example (two separate tables), if a company changes its address, you only have to change it once. You don't even have to do a search and replace. After the change is made, every time you look at the combination of both tables (more on this in a moment), the new address magically appears with each instance of the company. In the following section, you will be introduced to the basic building blocks of a relational model.

Entities, Attributes, and Relationships

The relational model has three basic building blocks:

- Entities
- Attributes
- Relationships

Entities: Person, Place, Thing, or Idea

An entity is a person, place, thing, or idea. Examples of entities are:

- A man
- A car
- Seagulls
- A book you are reading
- Love

In the English language, all of the above are nouns. Notice that in the above examples, if you were trying to tell another person about the entity (the noun), you would have to identify the noun (for instance, "Look at a car"), and you could not identify which one without an adjective ("Look at the red car"). In Access, entities are mapped to objects called tables. You will typically create a table for every entity you wish to model, and you will give the table the same name as your entity. From this point on, the words entity and table will be used interchangeably, but remember that the entity is a noun, and the table is a logical and/or physical representation of the entity.

Attributes: Characteristics That Identify an Entity

To identify a particular instance of an entity, you must use the characteristics of that entity that identify it or its attributes. Examples of the entities just given with one more attributes to identify them are:

- John Smith (man)
- Red 1969 Corvette (car)
- Flock of seagulls (seagulls)
- *Building Access Applications* (book)
- Puppy love (love)

The name of the attribute is called the attribute name, and it is a noun, although the attribute itself is an adjective that describes the entity. From this point on, the terms attribute and attribute name will both be referred to simply by the term attribute, but it is important to distinguish between attributes and attribute names. The man John Smith is identified by two attributes: first name and last name. The car, red 1969 Corvette, is identified by three attributes: color, year, and model. The seagulls are identified by the attribute group. The book is identified by its title. Love is identified by its type.

Note

If both entities and attributes are nouns, how can you tell by reading an English sentence which is which? By the context of the sentence.

In Access, attributes are mapped to fields. Fields are properties of the table object. When you create a table, you assign names (and other various properties) to the fields that correspond to the entity's table. To facilitate creating a logical model, you must identify all of the entities that you wish to represent in your system, and then identify the attributes that will be used to describe them. Consider the following example:

A color has three components: hue, luminosity, and saturation, and is referred to by ColorName.

This is actually a statement of fact. Facts are the basis for creating your information model. As such, it is important that facts are not complex; rather they should be elementary. An elementary fact states a single fact, and consists of three components:

- A subject
- A predicate
- An object

The sample sentence does not meet the criteria to define a simple fact because it contains four facts about a color. Therefore, this complex fact must be broken into four simple facts. These are:

- A color has hue.
- A color has luminosity.
- A color has saturation.
- A color is referred to by its ColorName.

Now consider the following sentence:

The car is a red 1969 Corvette.

This complex fact should be broken down into the following three elementary facts:

- Car is painted color.
- Car was built in year.
- Car is identified by model.

Notice that in all three of these elementary facts, car is the subject, and the attribute (really the attribute name) is the object, and they are connected via a predicate.

In the first sample sentence, color is the subject, and would thus be the entity. Hue, luminosity, and saturation are objects, and would thus be attributes of an instance of a color. In other words, the values for the attributes hue, luminosity, and saturation are the adjectives that describe and identify a color.

In the second sample sentence, car is the subject, and color is the object. Thus, car is the entity and color is an attribute of an instance of car, along with year and model. Based on the context, one is an entity and one is an attribute. Is one of these assumptions wrong? No, it varies with the context. Either of them can exist independently, but they can also exist together.

From the examples you know that you have two entities, car and color. Car has three attributes: color, year, and model. Color has four attributes: hue, luminosity, saturation, and ColorName. You also know that ColorName in the color entity is the same as color in the car entity.

A common way to represent entities and attributes is to list the entity, followed by all of the attributes, enclosed in parentheses, and separated by commas. Thus, the information from the example is represented as:

CAR (Color, Model, Year)
COLOR (ColorName, Hue, Luminosity, Saturation)

Another common way to display entities and attributes is to use a diagram in which each entity is a graphical object, with the name of the entity (or table) at the top of an entity's object, and the attributes (or fields) listed in a single column below the name. The Access Table window and Query window both represent entities and attributes (more or less) in this manner. Figure 4.6 illustrates the example in the Access Query window.

To define your entities and their attributes:

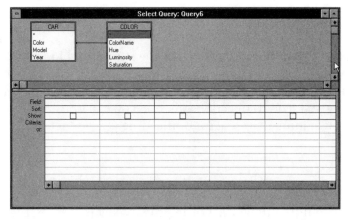

Figure 4.6 CAR and COLOR entities in the Access Query window.

1. Examine the external model.
2. Convert the external model into a conceptual view by writing down all of the facts you derive from the physical model that relate to the system.
3. Convert complex facts to elementary facts.
4. Convert the subjects of your elementary facts to entities and the objects to attributes to create the logical view.
5. Create primary and foreign keys to maintain referential integrity (covered shortly).
6. Normalize your tables (covered shortly).
7. Move your information model to Access.

Relationships: A Link Between One or More Entities

Entities are linked to one other via relationships. In Figure 4.6, the CAR table has a relationship with the COLOR table. The relationship could be stated in English as:

"CAR is painted a COLOR"

where is painted is the relationship, and CAR and COLOR are the entities. It is usually through relationships that one or more tables are joined, based on common attributes. After being defined in English as facts, relationships are defined in relational database terms using foreign keys. These are covered later in this chapter.

Keys

Referring back to the example of the car, do the attributes color, year, and model provide enough information to uniquely identify a car? Probably not, but it really depends on the context (or Universe of Discourse). Say, for example, you ran a company that rented collectible cars, and you had a business rule that said "you cannot own more than one car of the same year/model."

What Is a Primary Key?

The attribute or attributes that uniquely identify an instance of an entity constitute the entity's primary key. The primary key is used by the DBMS (as well as the users) to identify each instance of an entity. A composite key is a

Table 4.4 Sample Employee Data					
EMPLOYEE					
FirstName	MiddleInitial	LastName	SocialSecurity#	EmployeeID	EntryDate
John	M	Smith	000-24-9891	1002	1/1/93
Tom	I	Turk	781-35-7829	1003	1/1/93
Kary	K	Fetini	912-44-1094	1004	1/31/93
Melinda	S	Smith	781-11-1964	1005	3/1/93
Natasha	Y	Smirtya	451-30-1534	1006	3/3/93
Tom	L	Qapmoc	631-59-9891	1007	3/28/93
John	M	Smith	010-68-2224	1008	7/4/93
Harriet	K	Vanderbuilt	798-14-7898	1009	9/1/93

primary key that requires more than one attribute to uniquely identify the instance of an entity.

It follows then, if the primary key is used to identify each unique instance of an entity, that each and every instance of an entity must contain data in the attribute or attributes that constitute its primary key. A null value is an instance in which the attribute has no value. It means that there is a space (or other place holder) or a zero for an attribute. Although it is acceptable for some keys to have null values (for example, you may desire to track a person's birth date, but it is not critical to the overall performance of your system), it is not acceptable to have a null value in an attribute that is used as a primary key. If null values were allowed, you (and the DBMS) would have no way to identify an instance as being unique.

A candidate key is an attribute (or group of attributes) that is under consideration for use as the primary key. Consider the data illustrated in Table 4.4. Which attributes are candidate keys, and which attribute (or attributes) will constitute the primary key? As defined in Chapter 1, information is data in context. Table 4.4 tells you little or nothing about the context. In real world situations, you will know much more about the actual data. Some of it may be written. Other times it will just be an informal understanding. Before identifying the candidate and primary keys, some assumptions must be presented:

- An employee has one and only one FirstName.
- An employee has one and only one MiddleInitial.

- An employee has one and only one LastName.
- An employee has one and only one SocialSecurity#.
- An employee has one and only one EmployeeID.
- An employee was entered into the system on an EntryDate.

Additionally, since the data is assumed to be significant, the following conclusions can be drawn, based on the data presented:

- More than one employee can have the same FirstName.
- More than one employee can have the same MiddleInitial.
- More than one employee can have the same LastName.
- More than one employee can be added to the system on the same Entry-Date.
- More than one employee can have the same combination of two or more of the following attributes: FirstName, MiddleInitial, LastName.

From this information and the sample data, you can determine the primary key by looking at each of the candidate keys, and then deciding whether one of them identifies an instance as unique.

FirstName is not acceptable as a primary key because more than one employee can have the same first name. Likewise, MiddleInitial and LastName are not viable selections for the primary key because more than one employee can have the same MiddleInitial or LastName. Because FirstName, MiddleInitial, and LastName are not unique, it follows that the combinations (FirstName, Middle-Initial), (MiddleInitial, LastName), and (FirstName, MiddleInitial, LastName) are also not unique. This is also stated explicitly in the constraints listed. Therefore, the combination of any of these three attributes cannot be used as a composite primary key. SocialSecurity# is acceptable because only one individual can have a specific Social Security number. EmployeeID is also acceptable because there is a one-to-one correspondence between employees and EmployeeIDs. EntryDate is not acceptable because more than one employee can be added to the system on the same date.

An alternate primary key is a key that can be used as the primary key, but is not, except in special circumstances. It is common practice to identify and document alternate primary keys so that, if the system has to be modified in the future, others will be able to quickly see which other keys can be used. The question now is, which attribute should be used as the primary key, Social-Security# or EmployeeID? Although the assumptions and constraints don't mention it, there is some small chance that an employee may not have a Social Security number. What if the company decides to hire several employees who are not U.S. citizens? If you had chosen SocialSecurity# as the primary key, you would have to either assign the new employees "fake" social security numbers or change the primary key of the table. The latter could be especially problematic because of joins and foreign keys, which are covered in the next section. Thus, in consideration of future events, EmployeeID will be selected as the primary key. SocialSecurity# could be used as an alternate primary key based on the current constraints, but it would be best to change the constraints to allow null values for Social Security number, which would, as discussed, prohibit it from being used as a primary key.

As discussed earlier, a common way to represent entities, attributes, and primary keys is to list the entity, followed by all of the attributes enclosed in parentheses and separated by commas. The attribute or attributes that constitute the primary key are moved to the beginning of the list of attributes and then underlined. Thus, the example would be:

EMPLOYEE (<u>EmployeeID</u>, FirstName, MiddleInitial, LastName, SocialSecurity#, EntryDate)

In reality, the table would probably be restructured (at least for display purposes, as illustrated in Table 4.5) so that the primary key would be the first column. This makes the primary key easily recognizable even to individuals

Table 4.5 EMPLOYEE Table with Primary Key as the First Column

EMPLOYEE					
<u>EmployeeID</u>	FirstName	MiddleInitial	LastName	SocialSecurity#	EntryDate
1002	John	M	Smith	000-24-9891	1/1/93
1003	Tom	I	Turk	781-35-7829	1/1/93
1004	Kary	K	Fetini	912-44-1094	1/31/93
1005	Melinda	S	Smith	781-11-1964	3/1/93
1006	Natasha	Y	Smirtya	451-30-1534	3/3/93
1007	Tom	L	Qapmoc	631-59-9891	3/28/93
1008	John	M	Smith	010-68-2224	7/4/93
1009	Harriet	K	Vanderbuilt	798-14-7898	9/1/93

Table 4.6 Contact Table

CONTACT			
First Name	Middle Initial	Last Name	Company
Bill		Gates	Microsoft
Steve		Ballmer	Microsoft
Jim		Manzi	Lotus

who are not familiar with the design of the table. Note that when represented in table form the primary key is underlined for quick identification.

What Is a Foreign Key?

A foreign key is an attribute or group of attributes that references the primary key of another table. Examine the example from earlier in the chapter as illustrated in Tables 4.6 and 4.7 (note in Table 4.6 that three underlined heads together constitute the primary key). The Company attribute in the CONTACT table is a foreign key, because it is dependent on the existence of Company in ADDRESS table, where it is the primary key. In other words, you cannot add a contact to the CONTACT table unless the company he or she works for exists in the ADDRESS table. Foreign keys are used by DBMSs to connect or join two tables with related information.

Note that although the preceding example uses two attributes with the same name, there is no rule that states that this must be the case. Thus, the CONTACT table could have used the attribute name Employer, while the COMPANY_AD-DRESS table could still use the attribute name Company. Although not all DBMSs enforce it, it is highly recommended that both attributes be of the same datatype (more about datatypes in Chapter 5). Although some datatypes will

Table 4.7 Company Table

ADDRESS					
Company	Street1	Street2	City	State	Zip
Microsoft	One Microsoft Way		Redmond	WA	99999
Lotus	55 Cambridge Parkway		Cambridge	MA	99999

Table 4.8 Table with a Recursive Foreign Key

EMPLOYEE		
EmployeeID	Name	Supervisor
11203	Mary Smith	11233
11233	Madeline Jones	NULL
11222	Harry Mark	11233
11254	Elizabeth Ranqew	11203

be correctly translated and mapped together (that is, an integer datatype with a value of "22," and a text datatype with the string "22"), most will not. Imagine the DBMS trying to convert the a text datatype that contains the string "Database" into an integer. Although the foreign key is not the only attribute through which two tables can be joined, the foreign key always provides a solution that you know will work the way the database designer intended it to.

What Is a Recursive Foreign Key?

A recursive foreign key is one whose primary key reference is in the same table. Table 4.8 illustrates an example of a table from a personnel database, in which each employee has a unique EmployeeID (the table's primary key), Name, and SupervisorID. SupervisorID is a foreign key that references the primary key of the table EmployeeID. In other words, supervisors are represented in this system by their EmployeeID, and before an employee can be assigned a supervisor, that supervisor must exist in the table as an employee. Recursive foreign keys are often called "fish-hook" or "j-hook," as is illustrated in Figure 4.7, because of the way they are often graphically represented.

Figure 4.7 A recursive foreign key.

Indexes

An index is a list that helps speed data access. Like an index in a book, an index in a DBMS contains references to records, which help users find certain records or sort the records in a specific order. Like the primary key, an index consists of one or more attributes. The same attribute(s) that define the primary key can also define an index. There are two ways in which an index differs from a primary key:

- A primary key must uniquely identify an instance of an entity, whereas an index does not have to uniquely identify an instance, although it often does. As such, it can contain null values. When an index is used, you will often be looking for a group of similar records, not just one.

- You can have only one primary key, but you can have more than one index (or none, for that matter).

Consider the data illustrated in Table 4.9. Although the primary key is EmployeeID, more often than not, you will probably want to see the list sorted by LastName. Thus, if this was to be your main viewing order, you would create an index on the LastName attribute. Although indexes speed up data retrieval, they add overhead to updating and inserting, because every time a new record (row) is added or an existing row is modified or deleted, all associated indexes must also be modified. Although there are no hard rules, it is best to use as few indexes as possible. Ultimately though, it comes down to your decision of which is more important, read response or insert/update response.

Table 4.9 EMPLOYEE Table with Primary Key as the First Column

EMPLOYEE					
EmployeeID	FirstName	MiddleInitial	LastName	SocialSecurity#	EntryDate
1002	John	M	Smith	000-24-9891	1/1/93
1003	Tom	I	Turk	781-35-7829	1/1/93
1004	Kary	K	Fetini	912-44-1094	1/31/93
1005	Melinda	S	Smith	781-11-1964	3/1/93
1006	Natasha	Y	Smirtya	451-30-1534	3/3/93
1007	Tom	L	Qapmoc	631-59-9891	3/28/93
1008	John	M	Smith	010-68-2224	7/4/93
1009	Harriet	K	Vanderbuilt	798-14-7898	9/1/93

Cardinality/Constraints

What Is Cardinality?

Cardinality is the number of instances expected on each side of a relationship. For example, each U.S. citizen has one and only one Social Security number. Therefore, if there is an entity Person and an entity SocialSecurity#, for every instance of Person there would be an instance of Social Security#. This is called a one-to-one relationship. In most cases, if a one-to-one relationship exists, the second entity should probably be an attribute of the first entity, not a separate entity. Consider the example just discussed. To have a second entity Social Security number, you would be required to store some reference to Person in the Social Security number table. Does it make sense to do this? No, because it wastes storage space and creates the possibility of anomalies. Sometimes, there will be some other reason that will force you to make this decision.

On the other hand, consider two entities, Person and PhoneNumber. Many people have at least two phone numbers: a home phone and a business phone. It is not uncommon today to also have a fax number and a cellular number. Thus, instead of a one-to-one correspondence between Person and PhoneNumber, there is a one-to-many relationship because each person can have more than one phone number. This does not mean that they will have more than one (or even have one for that matter). It simply means that the information model (and thus the DBMS system/application you are creating) can accommodate more than one PhoneNumber per person. One-to-many relationships are the most common type you will encounter.

If a relationship has a maximum cardinality of one in at least one direction, it is known as functional in that direction. Assume for a moment that although one person can have many phone numbers, each phone number can only be assigned to one person. Therefore, the relationship is functional from the PhoneNumber assigned to Person direction. This is because, in mathematics, a function sets up a one-to-one, or many-to-one, correspondence between two sets. Functional dependencies are covered later in this chapter.

If there can be more than one instance in each of two entities, there is a many-to-many relationship. Though the phone example was just represented as a one-to-many relationship, it is truly a many-to-many relationship, because each person may use more than one phone number, and each phone number may be used by more than one person. An example of this would be several contacts who work at the technical support hotline for a large software vendor.

You might have instances for three different support technicians in your Person table, and three corresponding instances for these technicians in the Phone-Number table. Yet, you reach all three of these individuals through the same centralized number, which means that three instances in the PhoneNumber table have the same phone number for their BusinessPhone.

Constraints

A constraint is a rule that is used to verify and/or maintain the validity of data in the DBMS. There are basically two kinds of constraints:

- Relational constraints
- Business constraints

Relational constraints maintain the accuracy/validity of the data in the DBMS from the view of the relational model, and prevent anomalies from occurring. There are two relational constraints that are important:

- Entity integrity
- Referential integrity

As discussed, in the primary key section of this chapter, a primary key is used to uniquely identify an instance of an entity. It follows that no instance of the primary key can have a null value. This is known as the Entity Integrity Rule. It also follows that if the primary key is a composite key, none of the attributes can have a null value. If the Entity Integrity Rule is not enforced, the attribute(s) that uniquely identify an instance of an entity would not be identifiable, because the primary key would have no value(s).

As discussed earlier in this chapter, a foreign key is defined as an attribute or group of attributes that references the primary key of another table. Thus, it follows that to meet this criterion, the value of a foreign key must be either null or the value of a primary key in another table. This is known as the Referential Integrity Rule.

Business constraints are business rules that are applied against data entered into the system, which maintain the accuracy of the data from a business point of view. One example would be a mail-order software company that does business only in the metro New York area. If the company ships orders only to Connecticut, New York, and New Jersey, it might have a business rule such as:

The states to which the order will be shipped must be Connecticut, New York, or New Jersey.

This business rule should be mapped to the DBMS and become a validation rule in Access or a rule in SQL Server. To expand the example, suppose analysis of past orders indicates that 80 percent of the orders are shipped to Connecticut. This information should also be incorporated into the DBMS to cut down on data entry. The most common value would become the default value in Access, or the default in SQL Server.

The domain of an attribute is the universe of all possible values from which a value can be drawn for that attribute. Domains are driven by rules and facts which are applied to them. For example, the attribute month would have a domain of one of the 12 months listed in Table 4.10. The value 1993 is not part of the domain because it is not a month. The domain could be further narrowed by including a constraint such as, "Month must be the first month of the quarter." In this case, the new domain for month would be:

```
{January, April, July, October}
```

If this were the domain, and the user tried to enter February into the system, the system would reject the entry. Also note that you probably assumed that the full names of months are used. But are three-character abbreviations also permissible?

Translating business constraints into Access will be discussed in Chapter 5, Tables and Databases, but it is introduced at this point so that you can start thinking about them. It is important to state even those rules that seem self-evident, because even the best DBMS in the world is "stupid" when it comes to understanding your business, until you "teach it." In other words, if you don't tell the DBMS, it won't know.

Normalization

Data redundancy is when data is repeated within a table. Data integrity is the consistency of data within the database. Data redundancy can lead to a loss of data integrity, and there are three major causes for this:

Table 4.10 Months of the Year			
January	April	July	October
February	May	August	November
March	June	September	December

- Update anomalies
- Deletion anomalies
- Insertion anomalies

An update anomaly is when one or more (but not all) instances of redundant data are modified, but all (or some) of the others are not. Thus, the data is only partially updated and becomes inconsistent. A deletion anomaly is when a piece of data is unexpectedly lost because of the deletion of another piece of data. An insertion anomaly is when a piece of data cannot be added to the database because another piece of data is missing.

The process of making sure that there is no redundant data, so that referential integrity can be enforced, is known as normalization. Normal forms are rules for structuring relations. C. J. Date introduced the first, second, and third normal forms to move data from a state in which referential integrity could not be enforced to a state in which it can always be enforced. The higher the number of the normal form, the more the data is correctly normalized. Decomposition is the process of moving from n normal form to $n + 1$ normal form, by splitting a relation into multiple relations. In other words, it is the process of making sure that there are no redundant data, so that anomalies are eliminated. Brief examples of normal forms are provided here, but if you are interested in a more formal and thorough discussion of normalization (and relational theory), you should read *An Introduction to Database Systems*, by C. J. Date, the definitive source on the subject.

First Normal Form

A table is in first normal form (1NF) when all values are atomic. In other words, for a table to be considered 1NF, all values in the table must be atomic. Expressed in plain English, this means that no attribute value can be a set of values. Table 4.11 is an example of a table that is *not* 1NF. This table is not 1NF because Phone can have multiple values. Assuming that an employee can have up to three phone numbers, and that one is a home number, one is an office number, and one is a cellular number, what is the problem with this table? You never know which phone number you are accessing. Table 4.12 illustrates the same data, in first normal form.

Although this resolves the problem of the first normal form, it creates a new problem—a lot of redundant data. This is addressed with the second normal form (2NF).

Table 4.11 EMPLOYEE Table Not in First Normal Form

EMPLOYEE

EmployeeID	FirstName	MI	LastName	Phone	PhoneType
1002	John	M	Smith	{203-111-1234, 203-111-7864}	{H,W}
1003	Tom	I	Turk	{203-111-9912, 203-111-6543}	{H,W}
1004	Kary	K	Fetini	203-111-0088	H
1005	Melinda	S	Smith	{203-111-3214, 203-111-3215, 203-111-8989}	{W,C,H}
1006	Natasha	Y	Smirtya	203-111-7788	H
1007	Tom	L	Qapmoc	914-111-9891	H
1008	John	M	Smith	{203-111-7856, 914-111-8919}	{H,C}
1009	Harriet	K	Vanderbuilt	203-111-8888	H

Table 4.12 EMPLOYEE Table in First Normal Form

EMPLOYEE

EmployeeID	Phone	PhoneType	FirstName	MI	LastName
1002	203-111-1234	Home	John	M	Smith
1002	203-111-7864	Work	John	M	Smith
1003	203-111-9912	Home	Tom	I	Turk
1003	203-111-6543	Work	Tom	I	Turk
1004	203-111-0088	Home	Kary	K	Fetini
1005	203-111-3214	Work	Melinda	S	Smith
1005	203-111-3215	Cellular	Melinda	S	Smith
1005	203-111-8989	Home	Melinda	S	Smith
1006	203-111-7788	Home	Natasha	Y	Smirtya
1007	914-111-9891	Home	Tom	L	Qapmoc
1008	203-111-7856	Home	John	M	Smith
1008	914-111-8919	Cellular	John	M	Smith
1009	203-111-8888	Home	Harriet	K	Vanderbuilt

Second Normal Form

As just stated, the problem with the data in Table 4.12 is that there is a large amount of redundancy; multiple occurrences of the same fact exist. A functional dependency is when the value in one attribute determines the value of another attribute (or group of attributes) in the same instance. In other words, if a table has two attributes, A and B, attribute A is functionally dependent on attribute B, if and only if each value for B has precisely one value for A. This is notated as:

$$A \rightarrow B$$

which is read as attribute A functionally determines attribute B.

Two attributes in the same table, A and B, are functionally dependent. They must have the same value for the A attribute that they have for the B attribute. Thus, if there is more than one occurrence of a functional dependency in a table, redundant data will exist, allowing for the possibility of an anomaly.

The determinant is the attribute on the left-hand side of the dependency, because it "determines" the value of the attribute on the right side. A primary key is always a determinant because it uniquely determines the value of every attribute in an instance of an entity.

A table is in second normal form when it is in first normal form, *and* every nonkey attribute is dependent on only a part of the primary key. To eliminate this redundancy, a table must be decomposed to the second normal form. An entity violates 2NF if a fact can be determined knowing only part of the key of the entity. Consider the data presented in Table 4.13. The primary key of this entity is a composite consisting of EmployeeID and Phone.

This table violates 2NF because an employee's name (a composite consisting of the three nonkey attributes FirstName, MI, and LastName) can be determined with just part of the primary key, EmployeeID. An employee's name is determined by EmployeeID. Thus, it is not necessary to have a Phone to identify an employee's name. That is, employee name is functionally dependent on EmployeeID, and thus violates 2NF.

Several problems arise with this structure:

1. The employee's name is repeated in every row that refers to a Phone number for that employee. This wastes physical storage space.
2. If the name of the worker changes (assume for a moment that the person doing data entry in personnel typed in the wrong last name, and it is later

Table 4.13 EMPLOYEE Table in 1NF Violating 2NF					
EMPLOYEE					
EmployeeID	Phone	PhoneType	FirstName	MI	LastName
1002	203-111-1234	Home	John	M	Smith
1002	203-111-7864	Work	John	M	Smith
1003	203-111-9912	Home	Tom	I	Turk
1003	203-111-6543	Work	Tom	I	Turk
1004	203-111-0088	Home	Kary	K	Fetini
1005	203-111-3214	Work	Melinda	S	Smith
1005	203-111-3215	Cellular	Melinda	S	Smith
1005	203-111-8989	Home	Melinda	S	Smith
1006	203-111-7788	Home	Natasha	Y	Smirtya
1007	914-111-9891	Home	Tom	L	Qapmoc
1008	203-111-7856	Home	John	M	Smith
1008	914-111-8919	Cellular	John	M	Smith
1009	203-111-8888	Home	Harriet	K	Vanderbuilt

discovered), every row that refers to a phone for that employee must be updated. This is an *update anomaly*.

3. Because of this anomaly, the data might become inconsistent, with different rows showing different names for the same worker (assuming some of the instances were corrected and some weren't).

4. If an employee had no Phone (perhaps for a few days while they are moving), there would be no instances for that employee. This is called an *insertion anomaly*.

To decompose a non-2NF into 2NF:

1. Create a new table. All of the attributes of the offending functional dependency become attributes in the new table.

2. The primary key of the new table is determined by identifying the determinant of the functional dependency.

3. Eliminate the attribute(s) on the right side of the functional dependency from the original table.

4. If there is more than one offending functional dependency, repeat steps 2 and 3 until they are all removed and the original table is in 2NF.

Table 4.14 EMPLOYEE Table Decomposed to 2NF			
EMPLOYEE			
<u>EmployeeID</u>	FirstName	MI	LastName
1002	John	M	Smith
1003	Tom	I	Turk
1004	Kary	K	Fetini
1005	Melinda	S	Smith
1006	Natasha	Y	Smirtya
1007	Tom	L	Qapmoc
1008	John	M	Smith
1009	Harriet	K	Vanderbuilt

If the same determinant appears in more than one functional dependency, place all of the attributes functionally dependent on this determinant as nonkey attributes in a table having the determinant as a key. To avoid these problems, this table should be decomposed into the two entities, as represented by Tables 4.14 and 4.15.

Table 4.15 EMPLOYEE_PHONE Table Decomposed to 2NF		
EMPLOYEE_PHONE		
<u>EmployeeID</u>	<u>Phone</u>	PhoneType
1002	203-111-1234	Home
1002	203-111-7864	Work
1003	203-111-9912	Home
1003	203-111-6543	Work
1004	203-111-0088	Home
1005	203-111-3214	Work
1005	203-111-3215	Cellular
1005	203-111-8989	Home
1006	203-111-7788	Home
1007	914-111-9891	Home
1008	203-111-7856	Home
1008	914-111-8919	Cellular
1009	203-111-8888	Home

As a result of this decomposition, both of these entities are in 2NF.

Note

Because the second normal form is concerned only with functional dependencies that are dependent on only *part of a primary key*, it is safe to assume that if a table does not have a composite key, it is in second normal form (providing, of course, that it is in first normal form). To be considered part of a primary key, an attribute must be part of a composite key.

Third Normal Form

While the second normal form eliminates functional dependencies in which the determinant is part of the primary key, it does not eliminate functional dependencies in which the determinant is in a nonkey attribute. This allows for values to be repeated, which as you already know leads to anomalies A table is in third normal form when every determinant is the complete primary key. In other words, if a fact can be determined knowing some nonkey attribute, the entity violates third normal form. Consider the data in the variation of the EMPLOYEE table illustrated in Table 4.16.

It should be obvious that an employee's Salary is dependent on his or her LaborLevel. Thus, it is safe to day that Salary is functionally dependent on

Table 4.16 EMPLOYEE Table Violating Third Normal Form

			EMPLOYEE		
EmployeeID	FirstName	MI	LastName	LaborLevel	Salary
1002	John	M	Smith	55	$75,000
1003	Tom	I	Turk	35	$42,000
1004	Kary	K	Fetini	35	$42,000
1005	Melinda	S	Smith	45	$67,000
1006	Natasha	Y	Smirtya	55	$75,000
1007	Tom	L	Qapmoc	45	$67,000
1008	John	M	Smith	35	$42,000
1009	Harriet	K	Vanderbuilt	25	$35,000

LaborLevel. Since LaborLevel is not in the primary key, and you know that every employee of LaborLevel 55 earns $75,000, this table violates the third normal form. Notice that this table is the second normal form, because the primary key is not a composite key.

This functional dependence with a nonkey determinant means the following:

- The employee's Salary is repeated in the instance (row) of every employee having the same LaborLevel. This redundancy wastes physical storage space.

- If the Salary for a given LaborLevel changes, every row for employees with the same LaborLevel must be updated. Also, if a row is deleted, and it is the only one for a given LaborLevel, the Salary value for that LaborLevel will be lost. Thus, there is potential for update and deletion anomalies.

- If there are no employees with a certain LaborLevel, it is impossible to store a Salary value for that LaborLevel. This is an insertion anomaly.

To decompose a table to third normal form:

1. Create a new table that duplicates the old one.
2. Remove all attributes on the right side of any functional dependency that fail the third normal form criterion from the new table.
3. Create another new table that contains both sides of the functional dependencies that fail the third normal form criterion.
4. Repeat steps 1 through 3 for the new tables until all tables are in third normal form.

To avoid these problems, this table should be decomposed into the two entities as represented by Tables 4.17 and 4.18.

SAUGATUCK MARKETING GROUP

From examining Ian Joseph's phone book, Stephen Krandas determined the following facts:

- A contact has a name, title, phone number, fax number, and address.
- A contact works for or represents a company.

Furthermore, after discussions with Ian, they decided that, in addition to the above items, they wanted to track:

Table 4.17 EMPLOYEE Table Decomposed to Third Normal Form

EMPLOYEE

EmployeeID	FirstName	MI	LastName	LaborLevel
1002	John	M	Smith	55
1003	Tom	I	Turk	35
1004	Kary	K	Fetini	35
1005	Melinda	S	Smith	45
1006	Natasha	Y	Smirtya	55
1007	Tom	L	Qapmoc	45
1008	John	M	Smith	35
1009	Harriet	K	Vanderbuilt	25

- The first time the contact was contacted.
- The last time the contact was contacted.
- What the follow-up contact date should be.
- The kind of relationship SMG has with the contact (prospect, client, other?).
- The contact's birthdate.
- The source of the lead for the contact.
- The division of the company the contact works for/represents.
- The contact's e-mail address, if there is one.
- The contact's calling name.
- The contact's surname.

Table 4.18 LABOR_LEVEL Table Decomposed to Third Normal Form

LABOR_LEVEL

LaborLevel	Salary
25	$35,000
35	$42,000
45	$67,000
55	$75,000

In addition, (customer) would like to be able to:

- Keep free-form notes on a contact, with no limitation on the length of text.
- Track call history, including notes on each call.

By applying a little common sense to these facts, consultant derived that:

- A contact's name is made up of three components: FirstName, MiddleInitial, and LastName.
- A contact's address consists of five components: StreetAddress, MailStop/Box; City; State, and ZipCode.
- Although both Phone and Fax are phone numbers, they have different purposes—voice and fax. Additionally, since many contacts have more than one voice number (cellular and/or several field sites), it would be best not to limit either the amount of numbers or the type of number.
- A contact's e-mail address alone is not sufficient information. After all, is it a Compuserve address, an Internet address, or a private mail system? Therefore, it is important not to track just the e-mail address, but also the e-mail system. Additionally, it is not uncommon for contacts to have more than one e-mail address using different services. Therefore, the system should allow for the entry of more than one e-mail address and service.

From all of this information, the following simple facts were derived:

- Contact has FirstName.
- Contact has MiddleInitial.
- Contact has LastName.
- Contact is associated with Company.
- Contact has Title.
- Contact has E-Mail Address.
- Contact has E-Mail Service.
- Contact is called by Calling name.
- Contact has mail sent to StreetAddress.
- Contact has mail sent to MailStop/Box.
- Contact has mail sent to City.
- Contact has mail sent to State.
- Contact has mail sent to ZipCode.

- Contact is called at PhoneNumber.
- Contact is called at PhoneNumberType.
- Contact is associated with Division.
- Contact was first contacted on FirstDateContacted.
- Contact was last contacted on LastDateContacted.
- Contact should be contacted on FollowUpDate.
- Contact has Relationship (personal, customer/client, prospect).
- Contact was born on BirthDate.
- Contact has Surname.
- Contact learned of SMG from LeadSource.
- Contact has Notes.
- Call is made/comes in on Date.
- Call starts at StartTime.
- Call ends at EndTime.
- Call is made to/comes from Contact.
- Call has Notes.

It should be obvious from the way that these facts are grouped that there will be at least two entities:

- Contact
- Call

It is at this point that the facts should be reviewed for violations of the first normal form. There are four objects that immediately stand out as being multivalued:

- PhoneNumber
- PhoneNumberType
- E-Mail Address
- E-Mail Service

As discussed, most contacts have at least two phone numbers (voice and fax), and many have more. There is a one-to-many relationship between Contact and PhoneNumber, although there is only a one-to-one relationship between PhoneNumber and PhoneNumberType.

Although not as likely, many contacts also have more than one e-mail address. Like the PhoneNumber objects, there is a one-to-many relationship between Contact and E-Mail Address, although there is only a one-to-one relationship between E-Mail Address and E-Mail Service. Thus, these four objects should be removed from the list of facts, and replaced with the following facts:

- Phone is used by Contact.
- Phone is identified by Number.
- Phone transmits/receives Type.
- E-Mail is used by Contact.
- E-Mail is sent to Address.
- E-Mail is routed via Service.

As a result, there are now four entities in the model:

- Contact
- Call
- Phone
- E-Mail

Before proceeding with the normalization process, the primary and foreign keys must be determined. To do that, all of the facts must be converted into entities and attributes. This is simply a matter of making all of the objects of the simple facts into attributes of the entity (Subject) they correspond to. The resultant entities and attributes are:

- Contact (FirstName, MiddleInitial, LastName, Company, Title, Calling, Name, Street, Address, MailStop/Box, City, State, ZipCode, Division, FirstDateContacted, LastDateContacted, FollowUpDate, Relationship, BirthDate, Surname, LeadSource, Notes)
- Call (Contact, Date, StartTime, EndTime, Notes)
- Phone (Contact, Number, Type)
- E-Mail (Contact, Address, Service)

The next step is to identify the primary key for each entity:

Contact: There is no primary key available from this list of attributes, either singly or as a composite. It is necessary to create a new attribute, which will be used as the primary key. ContactID will be the name of the attribute, and it will be a number that uniquely identifies each instance in the table. Since there is an attribute named Contact in each of the other entities, these should be changed to ContactID.

Call: The combination of StartTime and EndTime uniquely identify an instance of Call. This works because it is assumed that the user can only make or receive one call at a time. A natural inclination would be to include Contact as part of the key, but this would be incorrect because the primary key is the minimum group of attributes needed to uniquely identify an instance. Instead of using this as the key, a new field, CallID will be created.

Phone: None of the attributes can be used individually, but a composite key consisting of Contact and Number does the job.

E-Mail: Like Phone, none of the attributes can be used individually, but a composite key consisting of Contact and Address provide a unique identifier.

The entities and their relationships with their primary keys are now defined as:

- Contact (ContactID, FirstName, MiddleInitial, LastName, Company, Title, Calling, Name, StreetAddress, MailStop/Box, City, State, ZipCode, Division, FirstDateContacted, LastDateContacted, FollowUpDate, Relationship, BirthDate, Surname, LeadSource, Notes)
- Call (CallID, StartTime, EndTime, ContactID, Notes)
- Phone (ContactID, Number, Type)
- E-Mail (ContactID, Address, Service)

Figure 4.8 represents these entities as Access tables. Note that the attributes that constitute the primary key are in bold.

Now that the entities are in first normal form, what about second and third normal forms? Because second normal form is only applicable to entities with composite keys, Contact is already second normal form. E-Mail and Phone are also second normal form, because all of these attributes are part of the key. Thus, there are no functional dependencies involving nonkey attributes, because there are no nonkey attributes. That leaves the Call entity. A quick examination reveals that there is no functional dependency between any part of the key and the nonkey attributes. Therefore, Call is also second normal form.

Third normal form is a little more tricky. Since the third normal form criterion is met if there are no functional dependencies based on a nonkey attribute, E-Mail and Phone are clearly in compliance, since they have no nonkey attributes. It is also clear that in Call there are no functional dependencies based

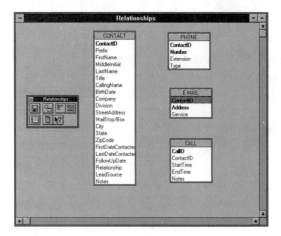

Figure 4.8 Access tables.

on the nonkey attributes. Can the value of Notes be identified only by ContactID, or vice versa? No. Therefore, Call is also third normal form. That leaves Contact up for review.

Contact will require a little more scrutiny, because of the large number of nonkey attributes. The most obvious potential functional dependency is:

ZipCode → City

In other words, once you know the ZipCode, you always know the City. Does it make sense to keep a separate table just for zip codes and their cities? Whether it makes sense or not, to achieve fourth normal form, it is necessary! Chapter 5 will address the issue of denormalization, which is the process of moving backward in the normalization process.

Another functional dependency that follows from the ZipCode City FD is:

ZipCode → State

Earlier in this chapter, the idea of decomposing a contact and the address of his or her company into two entities was presented. Does this make sense for SMG's application? Yes and no. Consider the functional dependency between a company and the attributes that constitute its address: If you know the company name, do you not know its street address, city, state, and zip? This is clearly a functional dependency that violates the third normal form. Perhaps. Now consider this scenario: There are two contacts; each works for Company X. Contact A works in the New York office, and Contact B works in the Los Angeles

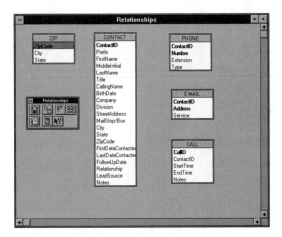

**Figure 4.9 Entities and their attributes in the Access query
window: fourth normal form.**

office. They are obviously in two different locations. Thus, in this case, just because you know the name of the company, you don't necessarily know the address. There clearly is not a functional dependency.

It could be argued that because address is considered the mailing address (from the fact that the statement *receives mail at* was used), there should only be one address per company (address being StreetAddress, City, State, and ZipCode), which would be a separate entity. A contact's personal address would be stored by using a MailStop/Box attribute in the contact entity. This is because many organizations with multiple locations have all mail come in through a centralized location, and then handle its distribution themselves. But although this is common, it is not universal. There are, and will continue to be, exceptions. Therefore, the model of one address per company cannot be built into SMG's information model because it is not always true. As a result, all of the company and address information will stay with the contact attribute, except for City and State, which will be moved to a new entity, Zip. The result of this change is illustrated in Figure 4.9.

Now that the entities are in fourth normal form, the only thing that remains to be done before implementing the physical model is to identify the foreign keys. The Contact entity has one foreign key, ZipCode, which is a primary key in the Zip entity. Appointment, Call, E-Mail, and Phone each also have one foreign key, ContactID, which is the primary key in the Contact entity. In other

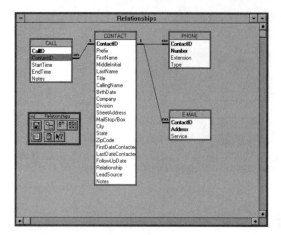

Figure 4.10 Relationships.

words, there cannot be an instance of a ContactID value in Appointment, Call, E-Mail, or Phone, unless there is a corresponding ContactID value in Contact. Likewise, a value cannot exist for the ZipCode attribute of Contact, unless it exits in Zip. Figure 4.10 illustrates the completed logical model, with lines drawn in to show relationships.

CASE Tools

For many years, information technology professionals have been using Computer Aided Software Engineering (CASE) tools to help them develop large systems. Historically, CASE tools have been expensive, as have been the environments in which they work. Although CASE tools for the PC platform have been in existence for some time, they have remained fairly pricey, and have often required more of an investment in time than the results were worth. After all, a developer can just sit down and bang out some code without even writing a specification, right? Wrong. Although some developers can get away with this kind of behavior some of the time, it is a pattern that will lead to failure.

Although you might not even realize it, Microsoft Access already has some CASE features built in. Consider the Report Wizards and Form Wizards. Although this book explores the depth of the product offerings, many people could satisfy most of their needs without ever manually creating a form or a report. But, as you will see later in this book, you can use the Wizards to either educate yourself about the process, or to take some of the tedious grunt work out of the process, so that you can focus on the details that will make your application a success.

One area in which Access does not provide very much help is database design. Although it is extremely easy to create tables and their relationships, Access does not really give you any guidance on how to do it. This chapter essentially was dedicated to overcoming this shortcoming, but you can go even further by choosing a CASE tool from a third party to assist you.

If used correctly, all developers can benefit from CASE tools. As mentioned earlier, CASE tools have traditionally been problematic because of the large amount of work involved in learning them, as well as the amount of time involved to follow whatever the respective methodology is. As a result, there has been a large backlash against CASE because developers thought that the time was better spent coding. The truth is, a systematic methodology should be used, no matter how small or large the project. The trick is to allow the methodology to facilitate your development, not inhibit it. Thus, a CASE tool that is not restrictive (in terms of forcing the developer to spend more time writing summaries of the work completed than the actual work itself took) and makes the developer more productive is better than no CASE tool.

The proper CASE tool can benefit every developer. The trick is finding the right tool to fit your requirements. Luckily, Access is not the only tool in the database tools world to take advantage of the Windows interface. If you are going to be creating simple, but critical, applications for your own mail-order business, your needs and expectations are going to be considerably different from those of a developer who is downsizing a minicomputer application which has more than 100 tables!

Asymetrix actually offers two information modeling tools that guide you through the process of designing your system's databases, and then creates them for you. Access Assistant, which is oriented toward the power user turned developer, will create tables, forms, queries, and reports, by stepping you through a series of questions, much like the Access Wizards. Although it does not offer a lot of depth, it is adequate for a large percentage of the applications that users will develop, mainly because it is so simple to learn and use. InfoModeler, on the other hand, is a much fuller-featured CASE tool. It requires more time and effort to learn initially, but offers much more depth. Serious developers will find the time spent learning FORML (Formal Object Role Modeling, the methodology that the product is based on) an excellent use of their time, once they see how helpful the tool is.

Chapter 5

Tables and Databases: Turning Your Logical Design into a Physical Schema

Databases

The first step in turning your logical design into a physical schema is to create the database object. In Chapter 1, you learned that an Access database object is a container that is used to hold all of the other Access objects that are required for your application. In addition to the standard Access objects (tables, queries, forms, reports, macros, and modules), it also contains data that it uses internally to manage your objects such as system tables and indices, and references to external objects (such as tables you want to attach). An Access database object is actually a single file that is stored on the file system of the operating system that your system or network server uses. As such, it can be stored on the DOS partition of your local hard drive, or on the NTFS partition of a Windows NT server to which you have access. Note that you can improve the performance of your application by using a high-performance file system like NTFS. Unlike many client-server DBMSs, the Access database is not fixed in size, but grows dynamically as you add objects. When you remove objects, however, it does not shrink dynamically; instead, you can compact your database after you remove objects to decrease its size. The maximum size for an Access database is one gigabyte (1GB), although this limitation can be worked around by spread-

Figure 5.1   New Database dialog box.

ing your tables and other objects across several database files. If you plan on using many gigabytes of data, you should consider using Microsoft SQL Server for Windows NT as your database engine, and Access as your front-end tool.

By default, Access database objects have the DOS extension MDB. Although you can use other extensions with Access databases, they will not be identified in any of the dialog boxes that allow you to select a database (such as the Open Database or Import/Attach dialog boxes), because Access always uses the *.mdb pattern to fill list boxes, although you can manually change this every time you open the dialog.

To create a database object:

1. Start Access, if it is not already running.
2. Select File → New Database. The dialog illustrated in Figure 5.1 will be displayed.
3. Select the File Name text box.
4. Type {Contact}.
5. Select OK. The database window illustrated in Figure 5.2 will be displayed.

Figure 5.2   The Contact database window.

Tables

Datatypes

Before Access can store a piece of data, it has to know what kind of data it is. Access offers support for eight different datatypes:

- Text
- Memo
- Number
- Date/Time
- Currency
- Counter
- Yes/No
- OLE Object

It is important that you select the proper datatype for the data that you plan on storing. Luckily, Access is fairly forgiving in case you make an incorrect choice. If, for example, you mistakenly define the Phone field as text, and later decide change it to Number, all you have to do is change the FieldType property.

A text field is used to store text or combinations of text and numbers such as addresses. A text field can be up to 255 characters long, and can include any character, including a blank space. You can impose a maximum limit other than (but not greater than) 255 characters by changing the field's FieldSize property to the size you want. Don't be deceived by the fact that you are setting a fixed length for the field. In reality, Access stores the data as a variable length field. The number that you specify in the FieldSize property is merely specifying a maximum allowable value.

FieldSize is also useful for enforcing primitive constraints. If you have a field for STATE, and want to restrict the user to using two-character abbreviations for states (such as CT, NY, CA), you could set the FieldSize property to 2. If the user trys to type in the full name of a state, Access would prohibit this and report an error when the attempt is made to add the third character. If you need to store text information that is more than 255 characters long, you should use a Memo field. Memo fields can contain up to 32,000 characters, but note that Memo fields cannot be indexed.

A Number field is used to store numeric values, especially those on which you wish to perform mathematical calculations, except for money (see below). There are five types of numbers that can be stored in a number field:

- Byte
- Integer
- Long Integer
- Single
- Double

A Date/Time field is used to store dates and times.

A Currency field should be used to store values for money or fixed-point values on which arithmetic operations will be performed. The currency datatype can be used to store numbers with up to 15 digits to the left of the decimal point and four digits to the right. The currency datatype uses fixed-point calculation, which is faster and more precise than the floating-point calculation used by single and double fields.

A Counter field is a special field in which Access automatically inserts sequential numbers, starting with the number 1, every time a new record is added to a table. In other words, Counter fields contain system generated numbers, which cannot be modified by a user (or developer). Counter fields are useful for creating "artificial" primary keys and indices. Counter fields are actually long integers.

A Yes/No field is one that can contain one of the binary data pairs illustrated in Table 5.1. Access actually stores the value -1 for the affirmative case, and 0 for the negative case.

An OLE Object field is a container used to store an OLE object that was created in another application. An OLE object is a binary object that conforms to Microsoft's OLE specification.

Table 5.1 Yes/No Field Data Pairs	
Format	**Value**
Yes/No	-1/0
True/False	-1/0
On/Off	-1/0

Table-Level Properties

Although you store your data in tables, Access provides several different avenues from which to input data into your tables. These are via:

- A table's datasheet view
- A query's datasheet view
- A form's form view
- A form's datasheet view

This book focuses primarily on using forms for data input (which allow more flexibility), but each of these four options is appropriate for different situations. For instance, what if you weren't sure which method a user would need for data entry (your application allows users to make the selection themselves), but wanted to make sure that certain criteria were met every time a user input data into a particular field, such as:

- Only certain values can be input.
- The same default value must be filled in.
- The same formatting must be applied for data entry.
- The same format must be applied for viewing data (even if in data entry mode).

Access allows you to define certain properties at the table level, and have them used by all other elements (elements are detailed in the "Expression Builder" section, later in this chapter) and/or objects that reference the table, such as queries, controls, or forms. The following field properties, once created at the table level, will be inherited by all objects that link to them:

- Input mask
- Default value
- Validation rule
- Validation text

In addition to being inherited, these properties are also dynamically linked. Thus, if you have three different forms that allow you to input data to the State field, changing the default value for the field at the table level will automatically be reflected the next time you use each of these three forms to input data.

There are also several properties that are inherited only at the creation time of the new control. In other words, when a new control is created, these properties are inherited, but it is only a temporary link. If you modify the value of the property in the table's definition, the change will not be reflected in any corresponding controls that refer to that property. These properties are:

- Format
- Input mask
- Caption
- Description (status bar text)

Although not as flexible as the properties that are dynamically inherited, with a little bit of planning, they could save you a lot of extra work.

Validation Rule

By default, whenever you enter data into a field, Access checks that data against the datatype of the field to make sure it is a valid entry. If, for example, you tried to type John in a Date/Time field, Access would display the message box illustrated in Figure 5.3. Although this will prevent many errors, it is often necessary to introduce data validation against additional rules, such as a business rule. The validation rule property allows you to create a custom rule against which all data entered for a field can be compared. A validation rule is applied after you have entered new data (or modified existing data), and left the field or control: in Windows terms, when the control you are working with *loses focus*. In a validation rule for a field, you can enter any valid expression, as long as it does not contain any of the items listed in Table 5.2.

For an example of a business rule, let's return to Saugatuck Marketing Group, whose physical location is in Connecticut. They have decided not to take on any customers outside of their immediate geographical location. They define their immediate geographical location to include Connecticut, New York, New Jersey, and Massachusetts. As such, since the contact database is designed to

Figure 5.3 Field error message box.

Table 5.2 Items Not Allowed in a Field-Level Validation Rule

User-defined functions
Domain functions
Aggregate functions
Current user function
Eval function
References to forms, queries, or table
References to other fields

help the company track its customers, this can be translated into a business rule that states:

All contacts must be located in Connecticut, New York, New Jersey, or Massachusetts.

This can be changed to fit the database by stating:

All entries in the CONTACT table must have State equal to CT, NY, NJ, or MA.

How can this be mapped into language that Access understands? Very simply. It was stated earlier that a validation rule can contain any valid expression that does not include the items listed in Table 5.2. Two of the most common Access operators that are used in validation rules are LIKE and IN. The IN operator, which checks the contents of a list for a match, has the syntax:

```
expression [NOT] IN(Value1,Value2,etc)
```

where:

- *expression* identifies the field for evaluation. When used in a validation rule, this is left out, and in reality refers to the field for which you are creating the validation rule.
- *[NOT]* is an optional argument that reverses the IN operator (only allows values not in the list).
- *Value1, Value2, etc* are the list of values against which the match is done.

As such, to translate this business rule into an Access validation rule, the text you enter would be:

```
IN ("CT","NY","MA","NJ")
```

The easiest way to create a validation rule is to use the Expression Builder, which is covered later in this chapter, where you will be walked through creating this rule.

Note

This section is referring to field-level validation rules. There is also a record-level validation rule, which is applied when a record is saved, not as each individual field is edited. Record-level validation rules allow the use of references to other fields. They can be used to cross-check the values between fields. Record-level validation rules are set from a Table's Property Window.

Validation Text

By default, when a validation rule is violated, Access displays a standard message box which informs users that the data they have tried to enter is prohibited, and also displays which validation rule was violated. Although this message might have some meaning to you as the developer, most end users are not going to understand the validation rule that you have created (nor should they). Therefore, Access provides you with an easy way to present a custom message to the user, every time a validation error occurs via a field's Validation Text property. Whatever text you type in as the value for this property will be displayed when the validation rule is violated instead of the default message. To define a simple validation error message, type the text into the Validation Text property. Building on the example of a validation rule that only allows NY, NJ, CT, and MA to be entered in the State field of the CONTACTS table, the validation text you would enter would be, "The State Must Be CT, NY, MA, or NJ."

Default Value

In order to save time and increase accuracy while performing data entry, Access allows you set default values for all fields at the table level using the Default Value property. Thus, if you had a State field, and 90 percent of your business was with customers in New York, you would probably want to set the default value to NY. In addition to table-level default values, Access also allows you to set default values at the form level, with the Default Value property of a control.

At this level, you can override the default value specified at the table level. Forms and their properties are covered in Chapter 7, Forms.

If you create a default value at the table level, when you add a control to a form or report that refers to it, the value will be inherited. If you later change the default value, the new value will also be inherited. If you assign a new default value to the control (via the control's properties), the form-level default value will override the table-level value. Thus, if you assign a value of "Jones" at the table level, and a value of "Smith" at the form level, even if you change the value of "Jones" to "Rose" at the table level, "Smith" will still be the default value for the form. If you would like to use the table default again, all you have to do is delete the form-level default through the control's Default Value property. Another advantage of this methodology is that no matter where you are adding/editing data (table datasheet view, form view, or even appending from an action query) the rules are always enforced.

Note

It is highly recommended that you use the "inherited" nature of table-based defaults and rules, and only use form-based solutions when absolutely necessary.

When you set a field's default value, you can use:

- Constants
- Variables
- Functions
- Expressions

To set a field's default value, simply type the default into the corresponding edit box. If you would like to build an expression, you can use the Expression Builder, which is detailed later in this chapter.

What are some examples of default values? If you wanted to have the State field in the CONTACT table default set to NY, all you would have to do is type "NY" in the Default Value property. Note that if you do not add the quotes, Access will automatically add them for you. If you wanted to set the FirstDate-Contacted field (also in the CONTACT table) to the current date, you would type =NOW( ) in the Default Value property.

Format

A field's Format property determines how a field will be displayed. Most of the time, you will display a field differently than you store it. For example, you might use a Date/Time datatype to store both the time and the date, but then only display the time portion of it, so that the user thinks it is a time field. Depending on the field's datatype, various formatting options are available, although all have both standard and custom formats. The Format property works in tandem with the Decimal Places property. If you want the number of Decimal Places to be determined by the format, the decimal places property must be set to Auto, which is the default setting. You can override the format's setting by selecting a new value for the Decimal Places property. For example, if you want a percent format with six decimal places (instead of the default of two), you would change the Decimal Places property from Auto to 6. Each datatype has different standard formats available, as well as the ability to create custom formats, except for Text and Memo datatypes, which have no standard formats.

> **Note**
>
> The OLE Object datatype does not have a Format property.

Table 5.3 lists the standard formats that are available for Date/Time fields.

Table 5.3 Date/Time Standard Formats

Format	Example	Note
General Date	4/10/94 05:34:00 PM, 4/10/94, and 05:34:00 PM	If the value is date only, no time is displayed; if the value is time only, no date is displayed.
Long Date	Sunday, April 10, 1994.	Same as the Long Date setting in the International section of the Microsoft Windows Control Panel.
Medium Date	04-Apr-94	
Short Date	4/10/94	Same as the Short Date setting in the International section of the Windows Control Panel.

(continues)

Table 5.3 (*Continued*)		
Format	Example	Note
Long Time	5:34:23 PM	Same as the Time setting in the International section of the Windows Control Panel.
Medium Time	05:34 PM	
Short Time	17:34	

Table 5.4 lists the valid format characters for creating custom formats for Date/Time fields.

Table 5.4 Date/Time Formatting Characters	
Character	Description
: (colon)	Time separator. Separators are set in the International section of the Windows Control Panel.
/	Date separator.
c	Same as the standard General Date format.
d	Day of the month in one or two numeric digits, as needed (1–31).
dd	Day of the month in two numeric digits (01–31).
ddd	First three letters of the weekday (Sun–Sat).
dddd	Full name of the weekday (Sunday–Saturday).
ddddd	Same as the standard Short Date format.
dddddd	Same as the standard Long Date format.
w	Day of the week (1–7).
ww	Week of the year (1–54).
m	Month of the year in one or two numeric digits, as needed (1–12).
mm	Month of the year in two numeric digits (01–12).
mmm	First three letters of the month (Jan–Dec).
mmmm	Full name of the month (January–December).

(continues)

Table 5.4 (Continued)	
Character	**Description**
q	Date displayed as the quarter of the year (1–4).
y	Number of the day of the year (1366).
yy	Last two digits of the year (01–99).
yyyy	Full year (0100–9999).
h	Hour in one or two digits, as needed (0–23).
hh	Hour in two digits (00–23).
n	Minute in one or two digits, as needed (0–59).
nn	Minute in two digits (00–59).
s	Second in one or two digits, as needed (0–59).
ss	Second in two digits (00–59).
ttttt	Same as the standard Long Time format.
AM/PM	Twelve-hour clock with the uppercase letters AM or PM, as appropriate.
am/pm	Twelve-hour clock with the lowercase letters am or pm, as appropriate.
A/P	Twelve-hour clock with the uppercase letter A or P, as appropriate.
a/p	Twelve-hour clock with the lowercase letter a or p, as appropriate.
AM/PM	Twelve-hour clock with the appropriate morning/afternoon designator as defined in the International section of the Windows Control Panel.

Table 5.5 lists the standard formats that are available for the Number and Currency fields. Custom Number and Currency formats have four sections, each separated by a semicolon. These four sections are:

- Format for positive numbers
- Format for negative numbers
- Format for zero values
- Format for null or empty values

Table 5.5 Number and Currency Standard Formats		
Format	Example	Description
General Number	1234.5	Displays number as entered. This is the default.
Currency	$1,234.50	Uses thousands separator; displays negative numbers enclosed in parentheses; DecimalPlaces property setting is 2.
Fixed	12345	Displays at least one digit; DecimalPlaces property setting is 2.
Standard	1,234.50	Uses thousands separator; DecimalPlaces property setting is 2.
Percent	123450.00%	Multiplies value by 100; appends a percent sign; DecimalPlaces property setting is 2.
Scientific	1.23E+03	Uses standard scientific notation.

Table 5.6 lists format characters that are available for Number and Currency fields.

Table 5.6 Number and Currency Formatting Characters	
Character	Description
. (period)	Decimal separator. Separators are set in the International section of the Microsoft Windows Control Panel.
, (comma)	Thousands separator.
0	Digit placeholder. Displays digit or 0.
#	Digit placeholder. Displays a digit or nothing.
$	Display the literal character $.
%	Percentage. Value is multiplied by 100 and the percent sign is appended.
E- or e-	Scientific notation with a minus sign next to negative exponents and nothing next to positive exponents. It must be used with other symbols, as in 0.00E-00.
E+ or e+	Scientific notation with a minus sign next to negative exponents and a plus sign next to positive exponents. It must be used with other symbols, as in 0.00E+00.

Table 5.7 Standard Formats for Yes/No Fields	
Format	Description
Yes/No	Yes = -1, No = 0 (Default)
True/False	True = -1, False = 0
On/Off	On = -1, Off = 0

Table 5.7 lists the standard formats that are available for Yes/No fields.

User-defined formats for datatypes can have up to four sections, depending on the datatype. Custom Yes/No formats have three sections, each separated by a semicolon. These are:

- This first section is not used for this datatype, but does require a semicolon placeholder.
- Format for values equal to -1 (Yes).
- Format for values equal to 0 (No).

You may use any text for these sections. If your database is storing values for a field that tracked whether, on a given date, a lake was frozen (solid or liquid), you could use the format:

```
;"Solid";"Liquid"
```

This assumes that Solid is always -1, and Liquid is always 0. Text and memo datatypes do not have standard formats, although you can create custom formats. Custom text and memo formats have three sections, each separated by a semicolon. These are:

- Format if field contains text.
- Format if field contains no text (zero-length strings).
- Format if field contains null values.

Table 5.8 lists format characters that are available for Text and Memo fields.

Input Mask

An input mask determines how a field looks and behaves during data entry and whether character formatting will be saved in the table. When you select a field for data entry, if it has an input mask, it will be displayed. Take a field that contains a telephone number and area code, for example. Do you want users

Table 5.8 Text Formatting Characters	
Character	**Description**
@	Text character (either a character or a space) required.
&	Text character not required.
<	Force all characters to lowercase.
>	Force all characters to uppercase.

to type the value with no formatting (such as 2125551212); with hyphens in between (212-555-1212), or with parentheses around the area code [(212)555-1212]? Is the area code optional or mandatory? If you want formatting characters, should the user be required to type them? Should they be stored in each record, or should they just be a display mask? If you decide to use parentheses around the area code, instead of just letting users type into the field (and assuming they know the format you want the data in), you could present them with a template such as:

`(###)###-####`

Input masks consist of three parts:

- The format.
- A value that determines whether the formatting characters will be stored in the table with the actual data.
- The character that will be used as a placeholder in the format template.

Each of these arguments is separated by a semicolon. The format template is the only required argument; the other two are optional, but recommended. The valid values for the second argument are:

- 0—Store the formatting characters in the record.
- 1—Store only the actual data.

You can use any character as the placeholder. If you do not supply one, Access uses an underscore (_). The input mask for the telephone template just illustrated would be:

`!\(999)000\-0000;0;#`

Table 5.9 lists all of the characters that have special uses in masks, along with a description of what they do.

Table 5.9 Special Input Mask Characters

Character	Description
0	Digit [0–9, entry required, plus (+) and minus (-) signs not allowed].
9	Digit or space (entry not required, plus and minus signs not allowed).
#	Digit or space (entry not required, blank positions converted to spaces, plus and minus signs allowed).
L	Letter (A–Z, entry required).
?	Letter (A–Z, entry optional).
A	Letter or digit (entry required).
a	Letter or digit (entry optional).
&	Any character or a space (entry required).
C	Any character or a space (entry optional).
. , : ; - /	Decimal placeholder and thousands, date, and time separators. (The actual character used depends on the settings in the International section of the Microsoft Windows Control Panel).
<	Causes all characters that follow to be converted to lowercase.
>	Causes all characters that follow to be converted to uppercase.
!	Causes input mask to fill from right to left, rather than from left to right, when characters on the left side of the input mask are optional. You can include the exclamation point anywhere in the input mask.
\	Causes the character that follows to be displayed as the literal character (for example, \A is displayed as just A).

Although input masks are not difficult to master, the easiest way to create them for Text and Date/Time fields is with the Input Mask Wizard. The Input Mask Wizard is covered in greater detail later in this chapter.

Caption Property

When you add a bound control to a form or report via drag and drop, the default behavior (which can be changed) is for a label control to be automatically created and bound to it. Where does the text for this label come from? It is created from the corresponding field's Caption property. If there is no caption entered, it defaults to the field's FieldName property. Thus, as long as you have a FieldName (and all fields must), there is always a default value. Since you must have a FieldName, and it will always be used if there is no value for the Caption property, you may ask: Is there any real reason to type in a value for a caption? Read on.

Although Access offers support for long field names that can contain embedded spaces, there are often compelling reasons to avoid them. One might be that you wish to retain compatibility with a data source that has more restrictive field names. Take Microsoft SQL Server, for example. Although it supports field names that are fairly long (30 characters), embedded spaces are not allowed. Thus, if you are creating an application that must interface to SQL Server, it is advisable to follow its naming conventions. If you had a field called FirstName, this would clearly fit both the Access and SQL Server's naming conventions. But, is this the label that you would want to appear on the form or report next to the corresponding control? Although it is not *that* cryptic, it would be easier to understand if the label said First Name. By using a field's Caption property, you can separate the conventions for field names and the corresponding labels that will appear on forms and reports (they will appear on data sheets too). Remember that by using the Caption property (or even just letting it default to FieldName), you will get the same text for all forms, reports, and queries. In other words, the caption that the user sees will be consistent throughout your application.

Although you can override the default captions at the form level, once you do so, there is no turning back, short of manually reentering text in the label control. This is because captions are only inherited by label controls when the object is created. In other words, if you create a caption at the table level, create a text control that has a label bound to it (default behavior), and then go back and change the field's Caption property (at the table level), the change will not be inherited, as it would be with a field's validation rule. This is because the label control, while bound to the text control, is not directly bound to the corresponding field in the table. As such, it pays to take a little time in the beginning to define your captions, and enter them when you create your table.

Description Property

Although it would seem obvious that the purpose of the Description property is to provide a more detailed description of the fields, it is only half of this property's story. In properly written Windows applications, whenever you select an on-screen object (a button, a menu selection, a field), the status bar at the bottom of the screen gives you information specific to the object. How can you do this in your custom Access application? By using the Description property of the field. Whatever text you type in the Description property will be displayed in the status bar when you select the corresponding field in datasheet mode (Query, Table, or Form), or a control that is bound to the field in a form. Thus, to create status bar text for a field, simply type the text that you want to use in the field's Description property. For example, to give the FirstName field in the CONTACT table a more verbose description in the status bar, type Contact's first name in the field's Description property.

> **Note**
>
> If you would like to override this text at the form level, the corresponding property is called Status Bar Text.

Building the Tables

Recall from Chapter 4, Information Modeling, that five tables were identified to build this application:

- CALL
- CONTACT
- E-MAIL
- PHONE
- ZIP

Lookup Tables

SMG: DENORMALIZATION AND LOOKUP TABLES

After completing the logical data model, Stephen Krandas realized that SMG does not have a database available that contains a listing of all zip codes in the United States, and their corresponding cities and states, nor does the company wish to purchase one. Instead, he decided to denormalize the database design, and "decouple" this information. In other words, even though there is the chance of storing duplicate information for contacts that have the same city, state, and zip code, they will all be stored in the CONTACT table, with one slight twist: There will be a table that contains the abbreviations and names of all 50 states, and Puerto Rico. Instead of typing a value into the State field (or any control that is bound to it), the users will be presented with a list that is from this new STATE table. They will then select a valid state abbreviation. Because the STATE table is used to look up valid values, it is called a lookup table.

The sole purpose of a lookup table is to provide one or more primary tables with a predefined set of values. In other words, if a value does not exist in the lookup table, it cannot be used in the corresponding field into which data is being added (or updated). As such, instead of allowing users to type in the name or an abbreviation for a state, they will simply select a valid value from the STATE lookup table, which has two-character abbreviations for every state in the United States, as well as Puerto Rico.

Lookup tables are particularly useful when you need a consistent set of values across a field in one or more tables, for example, a field that you want to sort on. Using the state example, if one user entered Connecticut, and one entered CT in the state field, when you build a query which groups by the value in the state field (as will be done later in this book), you will incorrectly get two groups for the contacts in Connecticut, not one! One will contain the CT entries, and one will contain the Connecticut entries.

After talking with management, Stephen Krandas decided that there were several other fields in the CONTACT table, and one field each in the PHONE and E_MAIL tables that were suitable for lookup tables:

- CONTACT.Relationship
- CONTACT.Lead_Source
- PHONE.Type
- E_MAIL.Service

Note

From this point on, when it is necessary to refer to both a field name and the table it is part of, the convention TABLENAME.FieldName will be used. This is consistent with Access, provided you have no embedded spaces in names. If you do use embedded spaces, Access requires that the items be enclosed in square brackets, such as [TABLE NAME].[Field Name].

Relationship and Lead_Source are both fields in the CONTACT table that were identified as sort keys from the report definitions in the design phase. As such, it is important to make sure that the entries they contain are *accurate* and *consistent*. Likewise, there are only a limited number of E-MAIL services and PHONE types (although the number of both is growing every day). Therefore, it makes sense to have them also stored in a lookup table. Consequently, four additional tables are necessary:

- E-MAIL_SERVICE
- PHONE_TYPE
- RELATIONSHIP
- LEAD_SOURCE

Krandis decided to use another variation on lookup tables for these four. Instead of actually storing the text value in the primary table (as opposed to the secondary or child table, which is the lookup table), a value that represents the corresponding instance in the lookup table is stored in the primary table.

Examine the data in Table 5.10, which shows a few entries in the PHONE table. Imagine that this table actually contained 1,000 rows, 500 of which contained the word Facsimile. What if you decided that instead of Facsimile, you wanted your database to say Fax? You would have to go into the PHONE table, and perform an update that found every occurrence of the word Facsimile in the PhoneType field, and replace it with Fax. This assumes that every instance of Facsimile is spelled correctly. If you weren't using a lookup table, the chances of Facsimile being spelled correctly in every instance would be very low.

Now examine the data in Tables 5.11 and 5.12. Instead of containing text, the PHONE table contains numbers that refer to the corresponding PhoneType

Table 5.10 PHONE Table

ContactID	Number	Extension	PhoneType
1	212-555-1212	4545	Home
1	212-333-1212		Facsimile
2	203-555-1212		Home
2	914-555-1234	341	Business
3	914-555-4321		Facsimile

Table 5.11 PHONE_TYPE Table	
PhoneID	PhoneType
1	Home
2	Facsimile
3	Business

Table 5.12 PHONE Table			
ContactID	Number	Extension	PhoneType
1	212-555-1212	4545	1
1	212-333-1212		2
2	203-555-1212		1
2	914-555-1234	33	3
3	914-555-4321		1

in the PHONE_TYPE table. These values are often called pointers, because they point to a specific value in another table. Don't worry about the fact that a user won't know that a PhoneType value of 1 in the PHONE table is really a Home phone. As you will see later in this book, you store the number, but always display the corresponding text to the user. Using the previous example of changing Facsimile to Fax, you would only have to make the change once in the PHONE_TYPE table, and not have to write a query to perform the update operation.

Because the PHONE_TYPE table will use a counter (PhoneID's datatype = counter), you must be sure that the corresponding field in the primary table is a number datatype, with its Field Size set to long integer. A Long Integer will take up less storage space, and will improve the efficiency of lookups and joins. Figure 5.4 illustrates the modified information model, with the new tables.

Your Turn: Building the Call Table

Building a table is really a five-step process:

1. Create and save the table object.
2. Add fields and define properties.

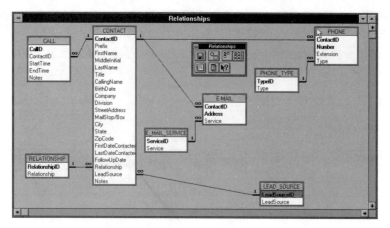

Figure 5.4 The new information model, which includes the new lookup tables.

3. Create the primary key.

4. Create indexes.

5. Define relationships between tables.

Creating primary keys, indexes, and relationships are covered in separate sections later in this chapter. To build the CALL table, follow the procedures outlined below.

To create and save the CALL table object:

1. Select the Table tab in the Database window.

2. Select New.

3. Select New Table. A Table Design window will open. Note that your cursor is in the first row of the Field Name column.

4. Select File → Save, or press the Save button on the toolbar. The dialog box illustrated in Figure 5.5 will be displayed.

5. Type CALL in the Table Name text box.

6. Select OK.

To add the CallID field to the CALL table:

1. Type CallID in the first row of the Field Name column.

2. Move to the Data Type column.

Figure 5.5 Save As dialog box.

3. Select Counter from the drop-down list. Notice that as soon as you select Counter, the properties pane changes, and displays the three properties associated with the Counter datatype: Format, Caption, and Indexed. Note that the default value for Indexed is No.

4. Move to the Description column.

5. Type Call ID. Remember that the description is used for status bar messages.

To add the StartTime field to the CALL table:

1. Move your cursor to the Field Name column in a new row.

2. Type StartTime.

3. Move your cursor to the Data Type column, and select Date/Time from the drop-down list. Notice the properties listed in the properties pane.

4. Add the text Call Start Time to the Description column.

5. Click on the Format property's text box.

6. Select General Date from the drop-down list.

7. Select the Input Mask property. Notice that the Build button appears on the right-hand side of the edit box.

8. Select the Build button. The dialog box illustrated in Figure 5.6 will be displayed.

9. Select Yes. The first screen of the Input Mask Wizard, which is illustrated in Figure 5.7, will be displayed.

Figure 5.6 Must save table first dialog box.

Figure 5.7 Step 1 of the Input Mask Wizard.

Note

Depending on datatype of the field that you are working with, the Input Mask Wizard will have different options available. For example, the Text datatype has a password mask available, whereas the Date/Time datatype does not.

10. Select Medium Time from the list box.

Hint

If you would like to see the way that the mask looks, try typing data in the Try It edit box.

11. Select Next >. The Input Mask Wizard changes, as illustrated in Figure 5.8. This step allows you to customize the mask.

Figure 5.8 Step 2 of the Input Mask Wizard.

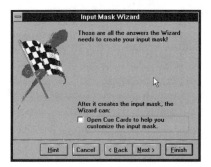

Figure 5.9 Step 3 of the Input Mask Wizard.

12. Since the defaults are acceptable, Select Next >. The Input Mask Wizard changes, as illustrated in Figure 5.9. This is the final step.

13. Select Finish. The new mask will be placed in the Input Mask property's edit box. Remember, you can now modify this mask.

14. Select the Caption property.

15. Type Start.

To add the ContactID field to the CALL table:

1. Move your cursor to the Field Name column in a new row.

2. Type Contact.

3. Move your cursor to the Data Type column, and select Number from the drop-down list.

4. Add the text Contact ID to the Description column.

5. Click on the Field Size property's text box.

6. Select Long Integer from the drop-down list.

> ### Note
>
> Long Integer is selected because this field is a foreign key that will relate to the CONTACT table's ContactID field. Since you will define ContactID as a Counter datatype in the CONTACT table, all fields to which it is related must be of the same base datatype (a Counter datatype is really a special long integer number), and because there can only be one Counter field per table (which CallID already is).

7. Change the Required property to Yes.

To add the EndTime field to the CALL table:

1. Move your cursor to the Field Name column in a new row.
2. Type EndTime.
3. Move your cursor to the Data Type column, and select Date/Time from the drop-down list. Notice the properties listed in the properties pane.
4. Add the text Call End Time to the Description column.
5. Click on the Format property's text box.
6. Select General Date from the drop-down list.
7. Select the Input Mask property.
8. Type 09:00\ >LL;0;_.
9. Select the Caption property.
10. Type End.

To add the Notes field to the CALL table using the field builder:

1. Move your cursor to the Field Name column in a new row.
2. Select the Build button on the toolbar or Select Build from the shortcut menu. The Field Builder, illustrated in Figure 5.10, will be displayed.
3. Select the Business option button, if it is not already selected (it is selected by default).
4. Select Contacts from the Sample Tables list box. Notice how the contents of the Sample Fields list box changes, as illustrated in Figure 5.11.
5. Select Note from the Sample Fields list box. (It is the last item in the list.)
6. Select OK. Note that the field is added to the table.
7. Change the FieldName to Notes.
8. Add the text Call Notes to the Description column.

Note

This method was used to illustrate that, once you know what you are doing, using builders or wizards can often slow you down. To add the Notes field without using the Builder would have only taken three steps!

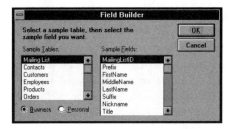

Figure 5.10 The Field Builder.

To add the Notes field to the CALL table without using the field builder:

1. Move your cursor to the Field Name column in a new row.
2. Type Notes.
3. Move your cursor to the Data Type column, and select Memo from the drop-down list.
4. Add the text Call NotesD to the Description column.
5. Click on the Required property's text box.
6. Select No from the drop-down list.
7. Change the Allow Zero Length property to No.

> ### Note:
>
> One of the strengths of Access is the ability to utilize a memo field in certain applications. The memo field allows a user to enter up to 32,000 characters of text. This provides the developer and the user with flexibility when designing an application. Memo fields can be used to store notes and detailed descriptions within numerous applications including inventory control, customer visit tracking, and follow up and medical history tracking.

Figure 5.11 Field Builder with Contacts table selected.

To create the primary key for the CALL table:

1. Select any column in the CallID row.

2. Select the Key button on the toolbar. Notice that a key icon appears next to the record indicator in the CallID row. Also note that the Indexed property has automatically been changed to Yes (No Duplicates).

Table-Building Tools

Access provides users with several tools to help them build tables and set the values of their properties:

- Field Builder
- Input Mask Wizard
- Expression Builder
- Table Wizard

The Field Builder and Table Wizard are exclusive to the process of creating and modifying tables, but the Input Mask Wizard and Expression Builder are found in other design modes of Access (the Expression Builder is also available in Report, Query, and Form design modes).

Field Builder

The Field Builder, which is illustrated in Figure 5.11, is a tool designed to help you quickly add new fields to a table, without having to manually set all of the properties that might be associated with particular field. Think of the Field Builder as a database of common tables and fields from which you can copy default values. These tables are broken down into two categories, Business and Personal. These categories contain a number of typical tables, each with various corresponding fields. There are 26 business tables and 19 personal tables. When you select either Business or Personal, the list of tables in the Sample Tables list box changes. As you select various tables in the list box, the list of fields in the Sample Fields list box changes. All three of these controls are linked. Before you can use the Field Builder, you must first create a new table, then place your cursor in the New Field column. Once these criteria are met, there are two ways you can invoke the Field Builder:

- The Build button on the toolbar.
- The Build command from the Table Design Shortcut menu.

Hint

The tables and fields that the Field Builder allows you to work with are an Access database, stored in WZTABLE.MDA. You can use the Add-In Manager to modify the defaults, or even directly manipulate the wizard, although this is not recommended.

Hint

The Table Design Shortcut menu is displayed by clicking on the right mouse button when the cursor is anywhere over the field pane of the Table Design window.

To use the Field Builder:

1. Invoke the Field Builder.
2. Select the option button for the kind of table you would like to choose a field from (Business or Personal).
3. Select the table from which you would like to select a field from the Sample Tables list box.
4. Select the field that you would like to add from the Sample Fields list box.
5. Select OK. The field will be added to your table.
6. Repeat steps 1 through 5 until you are finished adding fields.

At this point, you can manually edit any of the new fields' properties if you do not like the default values/settings. Note that the Field Builder is actually a subset of the Table Wizard.

Input Mask Wizard

The Input Mask Wizard is a tool that allows you to create an input mask without having to worry about the syntax issues of building the mask. Like most wizards, there is a trade-off between ease of use, and flexibility, although you can modify any mask that has been created by the Input Wizard. As a matter of fact, the wizard will prompt you to see if you would like to open Cue Cards to help you do this. As defined earlier, an input mask is a predefined template that must be

Figure 5.12 First screen of the Input Mask Wizard.

followed for data entry, and the Input Mask Wizard only works with text and date/time fields.

To use the Input Mask Wizard, your cursor must be in the Input Mask property for a field before you invoke the Wizard. As soon as you place your cursor in the edit box, the Build button appears to its right (the button with the ellipsis). Then there are three ways to invoke the Input Mask Wizard:

- The Build button next to the Input Mask field.
- The Build button on the toolbar.
- The Build command from the Table Design Shortcut menu.

Figure 5.12 illustrates the first screen of the Input Mask Wizard. Depending on the datatype of the field you are working with, different mask options will appear. Likewise, depending on the input mask you select, the subsequent number of steps will vary slightly. All you need to do is to select an input mask from the list box. If you would like to see how the mask works in a control, place your cursor in the Try it text box. As soon as you do, the Input Mask you have selected is applied to the control. When you are happy with you choice, select Next >. Unless you selected the Password mask, the Input Mask Wizard will change, as illustrated in Figure 5.13. If you selected the Password mask, you will move to the last screen of the Input Mask Wizard, which is illustrated in Figure 5.14.

This screen allows you to alter the format or change the placeholder character. You can select either a placeholder from the drop-down list of common placeholders or type in another character. Like the first screen, you can use the Try it edit box to see the results of your selections. When you are happy with your choice, select Next >. If you have selected the Phone Number, Social

Figure 5.13 Second screen of the Input Mask Wizard.

Security Number, Zip Code masks, the Input Mask Wizard will change, as illustrated in Figure 5.14. Otherwise, the last screen of the Input Mask Wizard will be displayed, as shown in Figure 5.15.

If you want to store the character formatting and the entered data, select the option button that says, "With the symbols in the mask...." If you want to store only the entered data, select the button that reads, "Without the symbols in the mask...." After you have made this selection, select Next >. The last screen of the Input Mask Wizard will be displayed, as illustrated in Figure 5.15.

Expression Builder

An expression is any combination of operators, identifiers (references to the value of a field, control, or property), constants, or literals that evaluate to a single value. Expressions can be used for many things, including to define validation rules and default values.

Figure 5.14 Third screen of the Input Mask Wizard.

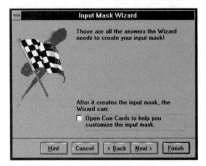

Figure 5.15 Final screen of the Input Mask Wizard.

The easiest way to create expressions is to use the Expression Builder. The Expression Builder, which is illustrated in Figure 5.16, is a tool that allows you to navigate through the various Access objects (tables, queries, and so on), functions (both user-defined and built-in), constants, operators, and common expressions. These are referred to as elements. Not all properties with which you can use the Expression Builder support all of these elements, however. Because validation rules and default values cannot reference forms, queries, reports, or the other items listed in Table 5.2, these elements are not available for validation rules or default values.

The Expression Builder works quite simply. Although you are free to type in the Expression box (and actually must in order to set the values of arguments),

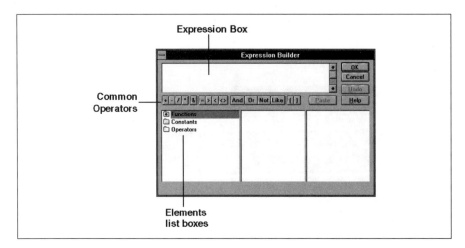

Figure 5.16 The Expression Builder.

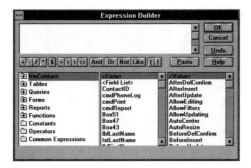

Figure 5.17 Expression Builder for a form.

the whole idea of the Expression Builder is to build your expression by selecting operators and elements from the Element list boxes and pasting them into the Expression box. To paste one of the common operators, click on the appropriate button. To paste an element, select it using the three element boxes, and then double-click on it or select Paste. The three element list boxes are hierarchically linked, from left to right. In other words, as you select a folder in the leftmost box, the middle box displays a list of corresponding elements. When you select an element from the middle box, the rightmost box then displays another list of elements. You make your final selection from the rightmost box, but the combination of all three is what really identifies the element you have selected.

Examine Figure 5.17, which shows the Expression Builder when invoked from a form. Because this chapter focuses on creating tables, Figure 5.18 illustrates the Expression Builder after the Tables folder has been selected. Notice that the middle and right boxes are empty. This is because Tables represents the collection of all tables (the Table Defs collection). You can tell easily that a collection

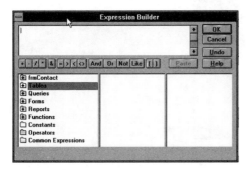

Figure 5.18 Expression Builder with the Tables tree collapsed.

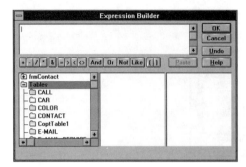

Figure 5.19 Expression Builder with the Tables tree expanded.

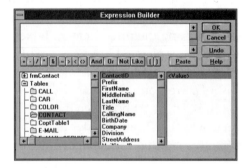

Figure 5.20 Expression Builder with a table selected.

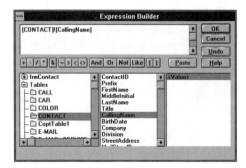

Figure 5.21 Expression Builder with the element pasted into the
Expression Box.

is represented by the presence of a plus sign in the folder (just like File Manager). Double-clicking on the Tables folder will expand the tree to display the names of all of the tables in the current database, as illustrated in Figure 5.19. Notice that there is still nothing in the middle and right fields. When you select a table, the middle box is filled with the fields that belong to the table, and the right box shows the only element that is available: <Value>. This is shown in Figure 5.20. When you double-click on an element in the rightmost box, it is pasted into the Expression box with the correct syntax, as in Figure 5.21.

Your Turn: Building a Validation Rule

Earlier, a validation rule was defined for the State field in the CONTACT table.

To use the Expression Builder to build this validation rule:

1. Open the CONTACT table in Design Mode, if it is not already open.
2. Select the State field.
3. Select the Validation Rule property.
4. Select the Build button. The Expression Builder will be displayed.
5. Double-click on the Functions folder, in the leftmost box. The tree will be expanded one level, and the Built-In Functions folder will become visible.
6. Click on the Built-In Functions folder. Notice that the middle and right element boxes are now filled.
7. Select General from the middle element list box. Notice that the right-most list box changes.
8. Select In from the rightmost list box. Notice that the full syntax for the function appears in the lower left-hand corner of the Expression Builder.

Hint

If you press F1 or select Help, context-sensitive help will be displayed for the element that is selected. This is the best way to find out more information, including the syntax, for an element.

9. Double-click on In or select the Paste button. Notice that the In function is pasted in the Expression box, and that the cursor is to the right of the parenthesis.
10. Move the cursor between the two parentheses.

11. Type "CT", "NY", "MA", "NJ". The quotes are required because the list contains text; if you omit them, Access will automatically add them for you.

12. Select OK. The expression is copied to the validation rule property.

The Table Wizard

The Table Wizard is a tool that allows you to build tables by responding to a series of prompts. The process starts with a variation of the Field Builder, which allows you to add various predefined fields. It then prompts you for a name for the table and asks whether you want Access to automatically create the primary key, or whether you want to do it yourself. If you opt to do it yourself, Access prompts you to choose a field, and define how the key will be maintained. It will then search through all existing tables and try to create relationships, if possible. You are then prompted to accept these relationships or modify them. Finally, you are presented with these options:

- Switch to Table Design mode to modify the table's design.
- Switch to Table Datasheet mode to enter data.
- Switch to Form view, and input data through a new form that the Table Wizard creates.

When you select the Finish button, Access will create the new table and any necessary relationship, and will then leave you in the mode you chose.

To build a table using the Table Wizard:

1. Select the Table tab in the Database window.

2. Select New.

3. Select Table Wizard. The first screen of the Table Wizard, illustrated in Figure 5.22, will be displayed.

4. Select the option button for the kind of table you would like to choose a field from (Business or Personal).

5. Select the table from which you would like to select a field from the Sample Tables list box.

6. Select the field that you would like to add from the Sample Fields list box.

7. Double-click on the field name or press the > button (the add button) to add the field to your table. The field will be added to your table. Note that,

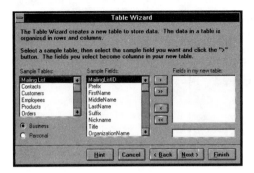

Figure 5.22 First screen of the Table Wizard.

if you use the add button, the selection moves to the next item in the
Sample Fields list box.

> ### Hint
>
> You can also use the >> button (add all button) to add fields from the
> selected table. Once you have added fields to your table, the < (remove)
> and << (remove all) buttons become active, so that you can remove
> fields from your table.

8. You can change the name of a field by altering the text in the edit box
    below the listbox that reads "Fields in my new Table."
9. Repeat steps 4 through 8 until you have added all of the fields that you
    want in your table.
10. Select Next >. The second screen of the Table Wizard, shown in Figure
    5.23, will be displayed.

Figure 5.23 Second screen of the Table Wizard.

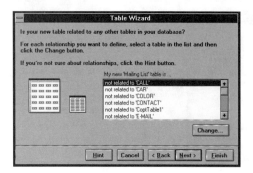

Figure 5.24 Table Wizard Relationship screen.

11. If you do not want to use the default name (the first table from which you added a field in the first screen), type a name for your new table in the edit box (it is selected by default).

12. Select the option button that indicates whether you want Access to create the primary key for you.

13. Select Next >. If you selected the button that reads "Let Microsoft Access set a primary key for me," the Table Wizard changes as you can see in Figure 5.24. Jump to step 16. If you selected the "Set the primary key myself" option button, the Table Wizard changes as illustrated in Figure 5.25, and you should continue with step 14.

14. Select the fields that will be used as the primary key from the drop-down list box.

15. Select the option button that corresponds to the data you want your primary key to contain.

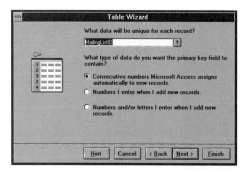

Figure 5.25 Table Wizard Define Primary Key screen.

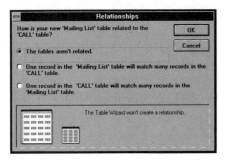

Figure 5.26 Relationships dialog box.

16. Select Next >. The Table Wizard changes as was illustrated in Figure 5.25.

17. Scroll through the list box of relationships. If you do not agree with a choice, double-click on it (or select it and then select Change). The dialog box illustrated in Figure 5.26 will be displayed.

18. Select the option button that corresponds to the relationship you want. (Relationships are covered in greater detail later in this chapter.)

19. Select OK.

20. When you are satisfied with the relationships, select Next >. The final screen of the Table Wizard, illustrated in Figure 5.27, will be displayed.

21. Select the option button that corresponds with what you would like to do when the Table Wizard is finished creating your new table.

22. If you would like the Cue Cards displayed, select the button that reads, "Open Cue Cards to help you modify the Table design or begin entering."

23. Select Finish.

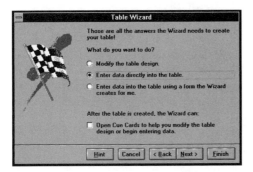

Figure 5.27 Final screen of the Table Wizard.

Your Turn: Building the Rest of the Tables

Now you can build the rest of the tables on your own. It is up to you whether you want to create the tables from scratch, use the Field Builder to help you, or to start with the Table Wizard and then modify the fields. Use the information in Tables 5.13 through 5.55 to create the CONTACT, E_MAIL, E_MAIL_SERVICE, LEAD_SOURCE, PHONE, PHONE_TYPE, RELATIONSHIP, and STATE tables, and define their fields and properties. Remember that the Relationship and Lead Source fields in the CONTACT table are going to store pointers to values in the lookup tables RELATIONSHIP and LEAD_SOURCE. As such, they must be long integers. Also, PHONE and E_MAIL contain fields that refer to the PHONE_TYPE and E_MAIL_SERVICE lookup tables, respectively.

Table 5.13 CONTACT.ContactID

Property	Value
FieldName	ContactID
DataType	Counter
Description	Contact's ID number
Format	
Caption	First Name
Indexed	No

Table 5.14 CONTACT.Prefix

Property	Value
FieldName	Prefix
DataType	Text
Description	Contact's name prefix
Field Size	5
Format	
Input Mask	
Caption	
Default Value	
Validation Rule	
Validation Text	
Required	No
Allow Zero Length	No
Indexed	No

Table 5.15 CONTACT.FirstName

Property	Value
FieldName	FirstName
DataType	Text
Description	Contact's first name
Field Size	15
Format	
Input Mask	
Caption	First Name
Default Value	
Validation Rule	
Validation Text	
Required	Yes
Allow Zero Length	No
Indexed	No

Table 5.16 CONTACT.MiddleInitial

Property	Value
FieldName	MiddleInitial
DataType	Text
Description	Contact's middle initial
Field Size	1
Format	
Input Mask	
Caption	MI
Default Value	
Validation Rule	
Validation Text	
Required	No
Allow Zero Length	No
Indexed	No

Table 5.17 CONTACT.LastName

Property	Value
FieldName	LastName
DataType	Text
Description	Contact's last name
Field Size	25
Format	
Input Mask	
Caption	Last Name
Default Value	
Validation Rule	
Validation Text	
Required	Yes
Allow Zero Length	No
Indexed	No

Table 5.18 CONTACT.Title

Property	Value
FieldName	Title
DataType	Text
Description	Contact's title
Field Size	15
Format	
Input Mask	
Caption	
Default Value	
Validation Rule	
Validation Text	
Required	No
Allow Zero Length	No
Indexed	No

Table 5.19 CONTACT.CallingName	
Property	**Value**
FieldName	CallingName
DataType	Text
Description	Contact's calling name (Robert might be Bob, for example)
Field Size	50
Format	
Input Mask	
Caption	Calling Name
Default Value	
Validation Rule	
Validation Text	
Required	No
Allow Zero Length	No
Indexed	No

Table 5.20 CONTACT.BirthDate	
Property	**Value**
FieldName	BirthName
DataType	Date/Time
Description	Contact's birthdate
Format	Short Date
Input Mask	
Caption	Birth Date
Default Value	
Validation Rule	
Validation Text	
Required	No
Indexed	No

Table 5.21 CONTACT.Company

Property	Value
FieldName	Company
DataType	Text
Description	Contact's company
Field Size	50
Format	
Input Mask	
Caption	
Default Value	
Validation Rule	
Validation Text	
Required	No
Allow Zero Length	No
Indexed	No

Table 5.22 CONTACT.Division

Property	Value
FieldName	Division
DataType	Text
Description	Contact's company division
Field Size	50
Format	
Input Mask	
Caption	
Default Value	
Validation Rule	
Validation Text	
Required	No
Allow Zero Length	No
Indexed	No

Table 5.23 CONTACT.StreetAddress

Property	Value
FieldName	StreetAddress
DataType	Text
Description	Contact's street address
Field Size	50
Format	
Input Mask	
Caption	Street Address
Default Value	
Validation Rule	
Validation Text	
Required	No
Allow Zero Length	No
Indexed	No

Table 5.24 CONTACT.MailStop/Box

Property	Value
FieldName	MailStop/Box
DataType	Text
Description	Contact's mail stop or P.O. Box
Field Size	50
Format	
Input Mask	
Caption	Mail Stop/Box
Default Value	
Validation Rule	
Validation Text	
Required	No
Allow Zero Length	No
Indexed	No

Table 5.25 CONTACT.City

Property	Value
FieldName	City
DataType	Text
Description	Contact's city
Field Size	15
Format	
Input Mask	
Default Value	
Validation Rule	
Validation Text	
Required	No
Allow Zero Length	No
Indexed	No

Table 5.26 CONTACT.State

Property	Value
FieldName	State
DataType	Text
Description	Contact's state
Field Size	2
Format	
Input Mask	
Default Value	
Validation Rule	In ("CT","NY","MA","NJ")
Validation Text	The state must be CT
Required	No
Allow Zero Length	No
Indexed	No

Table 5.27 CONTACT.ZipCode

Property	Value
FieldName	ZipCode
DataType	Number
Description	Contact's postal code
Field Size	Long integer
Format	Short date
Decimal Places	0
Input Mask	
Caption	Zip
Default Value	0
Validation Rule	
Validation Text	
Required	No
Indexed	No

Table 5.28 CONTACT.FirstDateContacted

Property	Value
FieldName	FirstDateContacted
DataType	Date/Time
Description	Date of first contact
Format	Short Date
Input Mask	
Caption	First Contact Date
Default Value	=Now( )
Validation Rule	
Validation Text	
Required	No
Indexed	No

Table 5.29 CONTACT.LastDateContacted

Property	Value
FieldName	LastDateContacted
DataType	Date/Time
Description	Date of most recent contact
Format	Short date
Input Mask	
Caption	Most Recent Contact Date
Default Value	=Now( )
Validation Rule	
Validation Text	
Required	No
Indexed	No

Table 5.30 CONTACT.FollowUpDate

Property	Value
FieldName	FollowUpDate
DataType	Date/Time
Description	Date for follow-up contact
Format	Short date
Input Mask	
Caption	Follow-Up Contact Date
Default Value	=Now( )+14
Validation Rule	
Validation Text	
Required	No
Indexed	No

Table 5.31   CONTACT.Relationship

Property	Value
FieldName	Relationship
DataType	Number
Description	Contact's relationship
Field Size	Long integer
Format	
Decimal Places	0
Input Mask	
Caption	Relationship of Contact
Default Value	
Validation Rule	
Validation Text	
Required	No
Indexed	No

Table 5.32   CONTACT.LeadSource

Property	Value
FieldName	Lead Source
DataType	Number
Description	Source of lead
Field Size	Long integer
Format	
Decimal Places	0
Input Mask	
Caption	Lead Source
Default Value	
Validation Rule	
Validation Text	
Required	No
Indexed	No

Table 5.33 CONTACT.Notes

Property	Value
FieldName	Notes
Data Type	Memo
Description	Notes
Format	
Caption	Other Notes
Default Value	
Validation Rule	
Validation Text	
Required	No
Allow Zero Length	No

Table 5.34 CALL.CallID

Property	Value
FieldName	CallID
DataType	Counter
Description	Call ID
Format	
Caption	
Indexed	No

Table 5.35 CALL.ContactID

Property	Value
FieldName	ContactID
DataType	Number
Description	Contact ID (Must exist in CONTACT table.)
Field Size	Long integer
Format	
Decimal Places	0
Input Mask	
Caption	
Default Value	

Table 5.35 (*Continued*)

Property	Value
Validation Rule	
Validation Text	
Required	No
Indexed	No

Table 5.36 CALL.StartTime

Property	Value
FieldName	StartTime
DataType	Date/Time
Description	Call start time
Format	General date
Input Mask	
Caption	Start
Default Value	
Validation Rule	
Validation Text	
Required	No
Indexed	No

Table 5.37 CALL.EndTime

Property	Value
FieldName	EndTime
DataType	Date/Time
Description	Call end time
Format	General date
Input Mask	
Caption	End
Default Value	
Validation Rule	
Validation Text	
Required	No
Indexed	No

Table 5.38 CALL.Notes

Property	Value
FieldName	Notes
Data Type	Memo
Description	Call notes
Format	
Caption	
Default Value	
Validation Rule	
Validation Text	
Required	No
Allow Zero Length	No

Table 5.39 E_MAIL.ContactID

Property	Value
FieldName	ContactID
DataType	Number
Description	Contact ID (Must exist in CONTACT table.)
Field Size	Long integer
Format	
Decimal Places	0
Input Mask	
Caption	
Default Value	
Validation Rule	
Validation Text	
Required	No
Indexed	No

Table 5.40 E_MAIL.Address

Property	Value
FieldName	Address
DataType	Text
Description	E-mail address
Field Size	25
Format	
Input Mask	
Default Value	
Validation Rule	
Validation Text	
Required	No
Allow Zero Length	No
Indexed	No

Table 5.41 E_MAIL.Service

Property	Value
FieldName	Address
DataType	Number
Description	E-mail service
Field Size	Long integer
Format	
Input Mask	
Default Value	
Validation Rule	
Validation Text	
Required	No
Allow Zero Length	No
Indexed	No

Table 5.42 PHONE.ContactID

Property	Value
FieldName	ContactID
DataType	Number
Description	Contact ID (Must exist in CONTACT table.)
Field Size	Long integer
Format	
Decimal Places	0
Input Mask	
Caption	
Default Value	
Validation Rule	
Validation Text	
Required	No
Indexed	No

Table 5.43 PHONE.Number

Property	Value
FieldName	Number
DataType	Text
Description	Phone number
Field Size	11
Format	!\(999“) ”000\-0000;;“”
Input Mask	
Default Value	
Validation Rule	
Validation Text	
Required	No
Allow Zero Length	No
Indexed	No

Table 5.44 PHONE.Extensions

Property	Value
FieldName	ContactID
DataType	Number
Description	Phone extension
Field Size	Long integer
Format	
Decimal Places	0
Input Mask	
Caption	
Default Value	
Validation Rule	
Validation Text	
Required	No
Indexed	No

Table 5.45 PHONE.Type

Property	Value
FieldName	ContactID
DataType	Number
Description	Type of phone (Code)
Field Size	Long integer
Format	#
Decimal Places	0
Input Mask	
Caption	
Default Value	
Validation Rule	
Validation Text	
Required	No
Indexed	No

Table 5.46 STATE.Abbreviation

Property	Value
FieldName	Abbreviation
DataType	Text
Description	State's abbreviation
Field Size	2
Format	
Input Mask	
Caption	
Default Value	
Validation Rule	
Validation Text	
Required	No
Allow Zero Length	No
Indexed	No

Table 5.47 STATE.FullName

Property	Value
FieldName	FullName
DataType	Text
Description	State's full name
Field Size	20
Format	
Input Mask	
Default Value	
Validation Rule	
Validation Text	
Required	No
Allow Zero Length	No
Indexed	No

Table 5.48 E_MAIL_SERVICE.ServiceID

Property	Value
FieldName	ServiceID
DataType	Counter
Description	Service ID
Format	
Caption	Service ID
Indexed	No

Table 5.49 E_MAIL_SERVICE.Service

Property	Value
FieldName	Prefix
DataType	Text
Description	E-mail service
Field Size	25
Format	
Input Mask	
Caption	
Default Value	
Validation Rule	
Validation Text	
Required	No
Allow Zero Length	No
Indexed	No

Table 5.50 PHONE_TYPE.TypeID

Property	Value
FieldName	TypeID
DataType	Counter
Description	Phone type ID
Format	
Caption	
Indexed	No

Table 5.51 PHONE_TYPE.Type

Property	Value
FieldName	Type
DataType	Text
Description	Type of phone number
Field Size	25
Format	
Input Mask	
Caption	Type of phone
Default Value	
Validation Rule	
Validation Text	
Required	No
Allow Zero Length	No
Indexed	No

Table 5.52 LEAD_SOURCE.LeadSourceID

Property	Value
FieldName	LeadSourceID
DataType	Counter
Description	Lead source ID
Format	
Caption	
Indexed	No

Table 5.53 LEAD_SOURCE.LeadSource

Property	Value
FieldName	LeadSource
DataType	Text
Description	Lead source
Field Size	50
Format	

Table 5.53 (*Continued*)

Property	Value
Caption	Lead Source
Default Value	
Validation Rule	
Validation Text	
Required	No
Allow Zero Length	No
Indexed	No

Table 5.54 RELATIONSHIP.RelationshipID

Property	Value
FieldName	RelationshipID
DataType	Counter
Description	Relationship ID
Format	
Caption	
Indexed	No

Table 5.55 RELATIONSHIP.Relationship

Property	Value
FieldName	Relationship
DataType	Text
Description	Relationship of contact
Field Size	25
Format	
Input Mask	
Caption	Relationship
Default Value	
Validation Rule	
Validation Text	
Required	No
Allow Zero Length	No
Indexed	No

Figure 5.28 Access reminds you to create a primary key.

Defining the Primary Key

As defined in Chapter 4, Information Modeling, a primary key is used to uniquely identify an instance of an entity. As a rule, you should never create a table that does not have a primary key. Whenever you create a table (actually, whenever you save the table for the first time after creating it), Access checks to see if you have defined a primary key. If you have not, Access reminds you to create one by displaying the dialog box illustrated in Figure 5.28.

If you do not want a primary key in your table, select No; if you want Access to create a primary key for you, select Yes. If you already have a field with a counter datatype, Access makes it the primary key; if you do not have a field with a counter datatype, Access adds a new field called ID with a counter datatype, and makes it the primary key. This method is useful, but it is not very flexible. First, it assumes that you want your primary key to be a counter datatype. To be sure, counter datatypes are frequently used, but there are often reasons for using other datatypes (particularly text and number) as primary keys. Second, this method provides no way to create a *composite key*. If you would like to create a primary key for other datatypes or a composite primary key, you must create them manually, and there are two ways to do this:

- Use the Set Primary Key button.
- Invoke the Primary property of an Index (in the Indexes window).

The Set Primary Key Button

The Set Primary Key button on the Table Design Toolbar makes it possible to quickly create a primary key by selecting one or more fields; you then define the key by selecting the button. To use the Set Primary Key button to create a primary (not composite) key, follow these steps:

To create a noncomposite key using the Set Primary Key button:

1. Select the field you want to use as the primary key by clicking on the field's record selector.
2. Select the Set Primary Key button. Notice the Key icon that appears in the record selector.

To create a composite key using the Set Primary Key button:

1. Select the first field you want to use as the primary key by clicking on the field's record selector.
2. Hold down the [Ctrl] key and simultaneously select any additional fields that you want as part of the primary key.
3. Release the [Ctrl] key. The multiple fields you selected should still be highlighted.
4. Select the Set Primary Key button. Notice the Key icon that appears in the record selector of every field you selected.

Hint

This method assumes that you want to select discontinuous fields for the primary key. If you would like to select continuous fields, when the cursor turns into a right arrow, drag it across the record selectors of all of the fields you would like to include. The selection will change as you drag. Be careful not to move the rows, though, because if the cursor is not a right arrow and you drag on a record selector, you will move the row's location. You can also create a primary key by selecting the candidate row(s), and then selecting Set Primary Key from the Table Design window's Shortcut menu, which is illustrated in Figure 5.29.

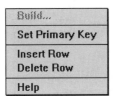

Figure 5.29 The Table Design window Shortcut menu.

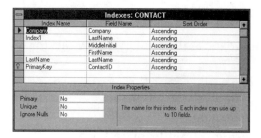

Figure 5.30 The Indexes window.

The Indexes Window

Although you might not have noticed it, when you use the Set Primary Key button to define the primary key for a table, a special index called PrimaryKey is created. If the primary key consists only of a single field, the field's Indexed property is automatically changed to Yes (No Duplicates) and a new index, called PrimaryKey, is added to the table. If the primary key is a composite key, then each field's Indexed property remains as it was, but a new index called PrimaryKey is added to the table. To determine if this was done, simply display the table's Indexes window, which is shown in Figure 5.30.

In addition to viewing the indexes of a table (which is covered in greater detail in the next section), you can create and/or modify the PrimaryKey index. Although the upcoming examples use PrimaryKey because this is the default name Access uses, you can use any name you like.

To create a noncomposite primary key using the Index window:

1. Select the Indexes button from the toolbar. The Indexes window will be displayed.

2. Type PrimaryKey in the Index Name column.

3. Select the adjacent cell in the Field Name column. Notice that an arrow appears on the right side of the cell.

4. Click on the arrow on the right side of the cell. A drop-down list with all of the fields in the table is displayed.

5. Select the field on which you like to create the primary key.

6. Change the Sort Order if you are not satisfied with the default.

7. Change the Primary property to Yes. Notice the key icon that appears in the record selector in both the Indexes window and the Table Design window.

8. Change the Unique property to Yes.

To create a composite primary key using the Index window:

1. Select the Indexes button from the toolbar. The Indexes window will be displayed.
2. Type PrimaryKey in the Index Name column.
3. Select the first field that you would like to create the primary key on from the Field Name column.
4. Change the Sort Order if you are not satisfied with the default.
5. Change the Primary property to Yes. Notice the key icon that appears in the record selector in both the Indexes window and the Table Design window.
6. Change the Unique property to Yes.
7. Select the next field that you like to create the primary key on from the next row of the Field Name column. Make sure that the Index Name column of the new row remains blank.
8. Repeat step 7 as necessary, until the key is complete.

Your Turn: Creating the Primary Keys

Using what you have learned and the information presented in Table 5.56, you are ready to create the required primary keys for all of the tables. Use whichever method or combination of methods you feel comfortable with.

Table 5.56 Tables and Their Primary Keys	
Table	**Primary Key**
CALL	CallID
CONTACT	ContactID
E-MAIL	ContactID; Address
E_MAIL-SERVICE	ServiceID
LEAD_SOURCE	LeadSourceID
PHONE	ContactID; Number
PHONE_TYPE	TypeID
RELATIONSHIP	RelationshipID
STATE	Abbreviation

Creating Indexes

As defined in Chapter 4, Information Modeling, an index is a list that helps speed data access. However, there is also a price you pay for every index you create. Every time a record is updated, inserted, or deleted, every index on the table must also be updated. Imagine that you are writing a book, and every time you add or delete a word to the book during the revision process, you have to modify the book's index to reflect the changes. Likewise, if you change an occurrence of a word (but not all occurrences), you must modify the index to reflect this. At some point, the time it takes to update the index exceeds the amount of time potentially saved using the index to access data. This is why book indexes do not contain a reference to every word. A well-written index contains all of the words or topics of major interest, and their most important locations within the book.

Likewise, an index on an Access table takes time to update. Obviously, the more indexes you have, the longer it will take to update them. So, how do you decide what to index? Since an index is used to speed up data searches, it makes sense to place them on fields that will be frequently searched and sorted. Look at the reports that you plan on running to help you identify your indexes, and use them sparingly. Remember that you can go back and add or remove indexes at any time. Therefore, if your queries and reports are taking longer to run than you would like, you might want to see if an index helps their performance. Likewise, if your response time is slower than acceptable when performing updates, deletions, and insertions, an index might be the culprit. Try removing the index, and note any performance changes.

Note
There are three datatypes that can't be indexed: OLE object, Yes/No, and Memo.

There are two ways to create an index:

- Use a field's Indexed property.
- Use a table's Indexes window.

Using the Indexed Property

The easiest way to create an index on a field is to use the field's Indexed property. By default, the Index property is set to No; in other words, there is no index.

Table 5.57 Valid Settings for the Indexed Property	
Setting	**Description**
No	(Default) No index.
Yes (Duplicates OK)	The index allows duplicates.
Yes (No Duplicates)	The index doesn't allow duplicates.

As illustrated, when you add a single field primary key, Access automatically changes the Indexed property to Yes (No Duplicates). Table 5.57 lists the possible values for the Indexed property. To add an index to a field, use the following steps:

To add an index to a field, using the field's Indexed property:

1. Select the field that you want to add an index to.
2. Select the desired type of index from the Indexed property's drop-down list.

When you do this, Access creates an index that has the same name as the field. Although this method is quick and simple, you can only use it to create indices on single fields.

Indexes Window

What if you want see all of the indexes on a table, create an index with a name other than the field name, or create a composite index? You must use the Indexes window, which is illustrated in Figure 5.31, for all of these tasks. There are two ways to display the Indexes window:

- Select the Indexes window button on the Table Design view toolbar.
- Select View → Indexes.

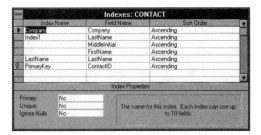

Figure 5.31 Indexes window.

The Indexes window behaves like a mini Table design window. Each index has one or more rows, each containing several columns of data. In addition, the index you have selected has three properties.

Indexes have six properties:

- Index name
- Field name(s)
- Sort order
- Primary
- Unique
- Ignore nulls

An index name is a unique title that you give to an index. Although Access will allow you to enter two indexes with the same name (for the same table), when you try to save the table, Access will display the message box illustrated in Figure 5.32. If you want to create a composite index, you type the name in the first row, and leave the Index Name column blank for the rows for other fields. The field name is the name of the field being indexed. For a composite key, one row is required for each field in the index, and the index name is left blank for all but the first field. Sort order determines the order in which records are displayed. The default is Ascending. The Primary property determines whether an index is a primary key. Valid values are Yes and No. A table cannot be used in a relationship if there is no primary key defined. If you already have a primary key defined, and change the Primary property of another index to Yes, the original primary key's Primary value will be set to No—without warning. The Unique property determines whether you can have duplicate values within the field(s) that constitute the key. Valid values are Yes and No. When you set an indexes Primary property to Yes, Access automatically changes the indexes Unique property to Yes. The Ignore Nulls property determines whether a record that contains null values in the index fields is included in the index. Valid values

Figure 5.32 Duplicate index name message box.

are Yes and No. If you select Yes, records that contain null values in the index fields are left out of the index. If you select No, records with null values in the indexes fields are included in the index. If the fields in your index contain many nulls, setting this property to Yes will improve your system's performance.

To create a noncomposite index using the Indexes window:

1. Select the Indexes button from the toolbar. The Indexes window will be displayed.
2. Type the name of your key in the Index Name column.
3. Select the field that you like to create an index on from the Field Name column.
4. Change the Sort Order if you are not satisfied with the default.

To create a composite primary key using the Indexes window:

1. Select the Indexes button from the toolbar. The Indexes window will be displayed.
2. Type the name of your key in the Index Name column.
3. Select the first field that you like to include in your index from the Field Name column.
4. Change the Sort Order if you are not satisfied with the default.
5. Change the Primary, Unique, and Ignore Nulls properties if you are not satisfied with the defaults.
6. Select the next field that you like to create the primary key on from the next row of the Field Name column. Make sure that the Index Name column of the new row remains blank.
7. Repeat step 6 as necessary until the key is complete.

Your Turn: Creating the Indexes

Use the information presented in Table 5.58 to create required indexes for the CONTACT table. Note that you should have already created the primary keys for all of the tables. Be careful not to overwrite them. The rest of the tables are not included here because their primary keys are the only indexes required. Use whichever method or combination of methods you feel comfortable with.

Table 5.58 Tables and Their Indexes		
Table	Index Name	Indexed Field(s)
CONTACT	ContactLastName	LastName
	ContactZipCode	ZipCode
	ContactCompany	Company
	ContactFullName	LastName; FirstName; MiddleInitial
	ContactLastDateContacted	LastDateContacted

Defining Relationships

Remember, cardinality is defined as *the number of instances expected on each side of a relationship*, which may be one of three kinds: one-to-one, one-to-many, and many-to-many. In many database systems, relationships are purely logical. In other words, although you can define relationships between tables, if you would like to maintain referential integrity, you must write the code in your application to do it. For example, if you were going to insert a record in the PHONE table, and try to use a ContactID that doesn't exist in the CONTACT table, many database systems will not give you an error message.

Access, on the other hand, directly supports one-to-one and one-to-many relationships. Once you define a relationship, Access maintains the referential integrity for you. If you tried to do the previous example in Access, and defined a one-to-many relationship between these two tables (based on ContactID), when you tried to save the record, Access would display the message box illustrated in Figure 5.33. This occurs because CONTACT.ContactID is a foreign key.

Breaking foreign key integrity is obvious when inserting and updating records, but what about when you change foreign keys and/or delete them? Using

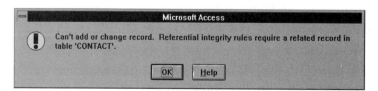

Figure 5.33 Referential integrity rule error message box.

Figure 5.34 Can't change or delete record message box.

the CONTACT and PHONE example again, imagine the following scenario: Jack Jones, whose ContactID is 2222, has four phone numbers. Thus, there are four records in the PHONE table that have the ContactID 2222. Let's say you decide to delete Jack Jones from the CONTACT table. By default, if you had a one-to-many relationship defined, Access would display the message box illustrated in Figure 5.34, and prevents you from performing the deletion. If you perform the deletion in only the CONTACT Table (the parent of the relationship), you would have four "orphan" records in the PHONE table because the parent record (2222) would have been deleted, leaving the records in the PHONE table without a parent. If you really want to delete Jack Jones from the system, the proper way to do it is this:

1. Find all instances of child records in other tables.
2. Delete all child records.
3. Delete the parent record.

This method is traditionally referred to as a cascading delete. Access allows you to override its default behavior, and will transparently perform this series of operations for you if you select the Cascade Delete Related Records option in the Relationships dialog box.

Now let's assume you want to change the primary key in a table. Although you should design your tables so that the primary keys are static (which is one reason counters are great for primary keys), you may run across a situation where a change is required. For instance, say you want to change Jack Jones's ContactID from 2222 in the CONTACT table, to 2222JJ (assuming the datatype would allow the change). By default, if you had a one-to-many relationship defined, Access would display the message box illustrated in Figure 5.35, and prevent you from performing the update. If you perform the update in only the CONTACT table (the parent of the relationship), you would have four orphan records in the PHONE table because the parent record (2222) would have been

Figure 5.35 Can't change or delete record message box.

changed, leaving the records in the PHONE table without a parent. To change Jack Jones's ContactID in the system properly, you would:

1. Find all instances of child records in other tables.
2. Update all child records.
3. Update the parent record.

This is another example of a Cascading Update. Access allows you to override its default behavior, and will transparently perform this series of operations for you, if you select the Cascade Update Related Fields option in the Relationships dialog box.

Note

In the system you are creating here, using the Cascade Update Related Fields option in a relationship with the CONTACT table would not work because CONTACT.ContactID is a counter datatype, which cannot be updated.

Creating Relationships

To build relationships between tables, you use the Relationships window.

To create a relationship:

1. Select Edit → Relationships or the Relationships button on the toolbar. An empty Relationships window will be displayed.
2. Select Relationships → Add Table or the Add Table button. The dialog box illustrated in Figure 5.36 will be displayed.
3. Select the Tables option button in the View option group, if it is not already selected (it is selected by default).

Figure 5.36   Add Table dialog box.

4. Select all of the tables for which you want to define relationships from the Table/Query list box. Note that this list box allows for multiple selections, both contiguous and discontinuous.

5. Select Add. Note that they are added to the Relationships window, even though the Add Table window still has focus.

6. Select Close. Figure 5.37 illustrates the Relationships window for the Contact database before any relationships have been created.

7. Rearrange the tables so that you can see all of their fields. Each table window behaves like any other Access window (except that they can't be

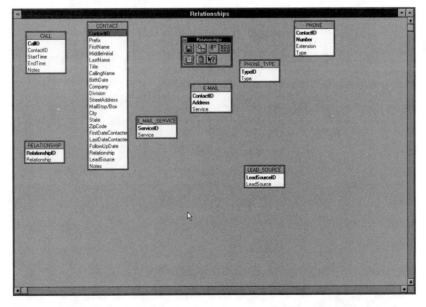

Figure 5.37   Relationships window: no relationships defined.

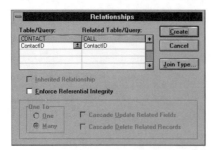

Figure 5.38 Relationships dialog box.

minimized and have no Control menu). You can drag the borders to resize it, and drag the window to a new position via the title bar.

8. Drag the field of the child table (the many side in a one-to-many relationship) over the foreign key of the parent table (often also the primary key). As soon as you release the mouse button, the dialog box illustrated in Figure 5.38 will be displayed.

9. If the fields in the Table/Query and Related Table/Query columns are incorrect, select the correct fields.

10. Select the Enforce Referential Integrity check box if you want Access to manage referential integrity for your application (highly recommended). Notice that the options that pertain to referential integrity become available.

11. Select the right side of the cardinality definition from the One To option group.

12. Select the Cascade Update Related Fields check box, if appropriate.

13. Select the Cascade Delete Related Records check box, if appropriate.

14. Select Create. A join line is created between the two tables, as is shown in Figure 5.39.

Note

If you did not select Enforce Referential Integrity, each end of the join line is a dot. If you selected Enforce Referential Integrity and then selected One-to-One, each end of the join line is bolded and has a 1 appear above it. If you selected Enforce Referential Integrity and then selected One-to-Many, each end of the join line is bolded, and the one side has a 1 appear above it, and the many side has an infinity symbol appear above it.

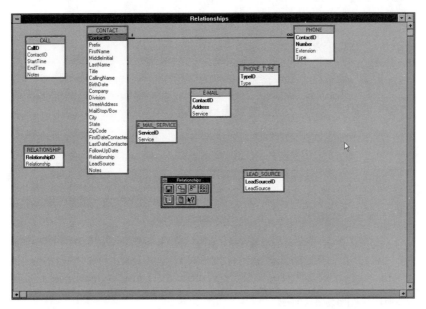

Figure 5.39 Relationships window, with a one-to-many relationship between CONTACT.ContactID and PHONE.ContactID.

15. Repeat steps 8 through 14 until all of your relationships have been defined.

16. Select File → Save Layout or the Save button on the toolbar to save the layout of the Relationships window. Note that the relationships are saved dynamically—this saves the screen layout of your editing session.

17. Select File → Close to close the Relationships window.

Although this process looks lengthy when defined as individual steps, it is really a quick and easy process. Once tables and relationships are added to the Relationships window, you can easily delete tables and delete and edit relationships.

To delete a table from the Relationships window:

1. Make sure that the Relationships window is open.

2. Select the table you would like to delete by clicking on its title bar.

3. Press the Delete key. The table will be removed from the window. Note that if there was a relationship with the removed table, it is still intact. Only the table window is removed from the Relationships window.

Figure 5.40 Delete relationship dialog box.

To delete a relationship:

1. Make sure that the Relationships window is open.
2. Select the relationship that you would like to delete by clicking on it. Notice that the join line becomes bolded.
3. Press the Delete key. The dialog box in Figure 5.40 will be displayed.
4. Select OK. The join line will be removed from the Relationships window, and the relationship will be removed from the database.

To edit a relationship:

1. Make sure that the Relationships window is open.
2. Double-click on the relationship that you would like to edit. The dialog box shown in Figure 5.41 will be displayed.
3. Make your changes to the relationship's definition.
4. Select OK.

Your Turn: Creating the Relationships

Using the information presented in Figure 5.42, you can create required relationships for all of the tables.

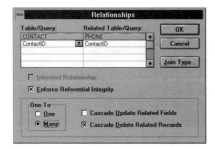

Figure 5.41 Edit Relationships dialog box.

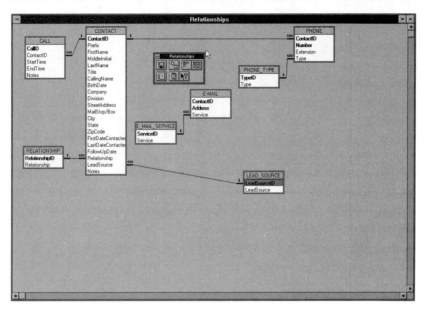

Figure 5.42 All of the relationships.

Testing Your Tables

Now that your tables have been created, test them to make sure they behave properly. To do this, open a table in Datasheet mode and input data. Input sample data that is expected, as well as data that is not expected, and note the results. For example, try adding a record to the CONTACT table that has a value of CA for the State field, and try inputting a text value into one of the Date/Time fields. Note that the Table DataSheet view should not be used for your standard data input vehicle; it should be used only for testing your tables. And only allow users to input data through forms. If you think that a DataSheet view is appropriate for data entry, create a form, and use its DataSheet view.

To open a table in DataSheet view for data entry:

1. Select the Table tab, in the Database window.
2. Double-click on the table you want to open. The table will open in DataSheet view.

Chapter 6

Queries

Microsoft Access has a powerful query feature that makes it possible to select specific data that are needed when performing input or output functions in an application. This chapter discusses these features and utilizes the Win-Contact application to help you create and use queries. You will learn:

- Why you use queries for forms and reports.
- The three types of queries.
- How to apply search criteria for queries.
- How tables are joined.
- How to construct the select queries for the WinContact application.

Note
For purposes of user understanding and to remain consistent with Dranchak's Development Methodology, all queries for this application will be done in this chapter, and will be used as the data sources for the forms and reports described in later chapters.

What Is a Query?

A query is used to ask a question of a table or group of tables. Like any question, the answer you get back will be based on the quality of the question. The more concise the question (query), the more precise the answer. An example of this would be to execute a query for all contacts who live in Connecticut versus executing a query for all contacts who live in Connecticut who have not been called in the last two weeks. Access returns the answer to the user in the form of a results set called a dynaset. The dynaset, or dynamic results set, is displayed via a Datasheet view of the query. A DataSheet view is similar to the row and column layout of a spreadsheet, like Microsoft Excel 5.0. The dynaset is not an actual file of records, but a set of pointers to the actual table(s) against which the query was executed. That said, when should a query be used? Always! Dranchak's Query Rule (DQR) states; Always use a query as the data source of a form or report. It allows more flexibility than a table when manipulating the data, and follows standard systems design theory by maintaining interface layers between the user and the actual data.

Types of Queries

There are three types of queries:

- Select
- Action
- Crosstab

Select queries retrieve data from one or more tables. These queries can be used to display the entire table(s) or just select fields. Selection criteria can also be applied to the query to allow the retrieval of a subset of records. Select queries create a dynaset. Action queries can be used to make changes to the tables of a database. They add, delete, and change groups of records in a table. Action queries can also create a new table from an existing table (or tables). Crosstab queries are used to summarize data in a spreadsheet format. For example, if you wanted to analyze the sales of meat, produce, and dairy products for each grocery store in a chain and compare the results, the easiest way would be to create a column heading for each department and a row for each store. Essentially, that is what a Crosstab query will do. The Access Query Wizard is excellent for experimenting with this function. It is important to be familiar with all three types of queries, but because of the nature of the WinContact application, it only utilizes Select queries.

Building Queries

In this section, you will learn how to build queries that utilize single and multiple tables, determine sort orders for tables, and use selection criteria to build concise dynasets. You will also go through the creation of all the queries in the application, which is a seven-step process as described here:

1. Open a new query in Design mode.
2. Select the tables against which you want the query to execute and place them in the table pane.
3. Select the fields from each table and place them in the Criteria pane.
4. Establish the necessary table relationships by joining any related fields, if relationships do not already exist.
5. Modify the display and selection criteria to meet the design needs of the query.
6. Save the query.
7. Test the query.

The Query Design Window

The Query Design window (Figure 6.1) is broken down into two panes: the table pane and the criteria pane. The top section of the screen is called the table pane. The table pane shows any tables that were selected from the Add Table dialog box. If multiple tables were selected, each would be displayed and a line would appear between any related fields, provided you set up your relationships correctly, (as covered in Chapter 5.) These names can be selected into the query. The bottom section of the screen is called the criteria pane, where the query's criteria is viewed and edited. The interface that Access uses is known as a Query by Example (QBE) grid. The criteria pane is broken down into columns and rows, and each column represents a selected field from the table that will be used in the query. Each of the four rows represent an attribute of the field. These attributes are:

- Field name
- Sort
- Show
- Criteria

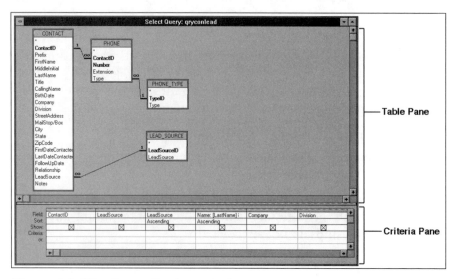

Figure 6.1 The Query Design window.

The field is where you specify the name of the fields from the selected tables that you want in your dynaset. Sort determines the order of the records. Valid values are Ascending (A–Z, 0–9), Descending (Z–A, 9–0), and Not Sorted. Show determines whether the field will be displayed in the output. Criteria is used to create a dynaset that is a subset of the underlying data table(s). This subset contains an expression that matches the criteria expression input by the user. Some examples of criteria are shown in Table 6.1.

Note

When the Show check box is checked, the field is displayed; when it is not checked, the field is not displayed. However, the field is still contained in the query.

There are four ways to get from the Design mode to where the dynaset is viewed in the Datasheet mode. These are:

- Select View → Datasheet.
- Select the Datasheet tool on the toolbar.
- Select Query → Run.
- Select the Run tool (also referred to as the Bang! button) from the toolbar.

Table 6.1 Criteria Examples Used in WinContact	
Description	Criteria
Exact Match	"Office"
Date Match	#2/29/94#
Today	Date( )
Tomorrow	Date( )+1
31 days old or more	<Date( )-30
All Names that begin with "A"	Like "A"

Building the WinContact Form Queries

The WinContact application requires 37 queries to produce the forms and reports contained within the application. The sections that follow detail how to build each query, and before the techniques required to build the queries for each form are described, the form is shown to allow the user to see how the query will be used. The results of the query are illustrated at the end of each section.

Show All Query

For the WinContact form in Figure 6.2, you need to build 27 Select queries that will be subdivided into two types. The first type is the default query that will

Figure 6.2 WinContact main window.

Figure 6.3 The New Query dialog box.

display all the records in the list box for the WinContact application. To do this, the user selects the Show All button. The second type of query is a modification of the default query which will allow the user to select a letter of the alphabet and see only the contacts whose last names begin with that letter. In the user's specifications it was requested that only the contact name and the company name be displayed.

To build the Show All query for the Main Menu form:

1. Select the Query tab from the Database window.
2. Select New. The New Query dialog box (Figure 6.3) will be displayed.
3. Select New Query. The Add Table dialog box, shown in Figure 6.4, will be displayed
4. Select CONTACT from the Table/Query list box.
5. Select Add.
6. Select Close. The Add Table dialog box will close and the Query Design window (Figure 6.5) will be displayed.

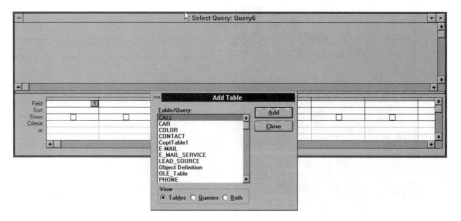

Figure 6.4 The Add Table dialog box.

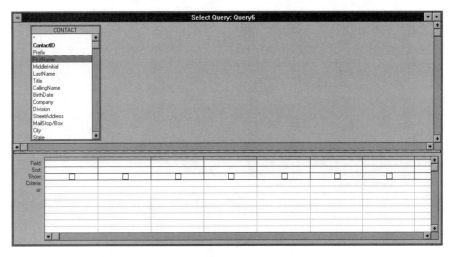

Figure 6.5 The Query Design window.

7. Select the Field Name cell in the first column of the QBE grid. Notice that as soon as you select it, an arrow appears to the right of it.

8. Click on the arrow.

9. Select ContactId from the list box.

Hint

Fields can also be dragged and dropped from the table(s) in the upper portion of the table pane. This is a much faster way of selecting fields when there is more than one table.

---

10. Drag the LastName field from the table pane to the QBE grid and drop it over the second column.

11. In the sort row of the LastName column, choose Ascending to set the sort order of the query.

12. Add Company as the third column in the QBE grid.

13. Select File → Save.

14. Type {qryContactName} in the Save As edit box.

15. Select OK.

16. Test the query by selecting the Run tool form the toolbar.

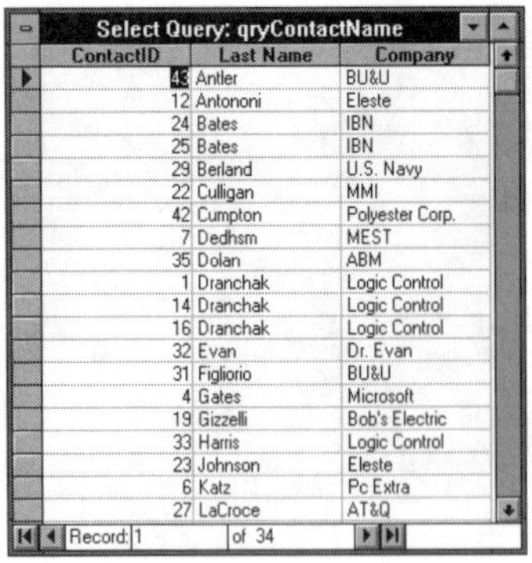

ContactID	Last Name	Company
43	Antler	BU&U
12	Antononi	Eleste
24	Bates	IBN
25	Bates	IBN
29	Berland	U.S. Navy
22	Culligan	MMI
42	Cumpton	Polyester Corp.
7	Dedhsm	MEST
35	Dolan	ABM
1	Dranchak	Logic Control
14	Dranchak	Logic Control
16	Dranchak	Logic Control
32	Evan	Dr. Evan
31	Figliorio	BU&U
4	Gates	Microsoft
19	Gizzelli	Bob's Electric
33	Harris	Logic Control
23	Johnson	Eleste
6	Katz	Pc Extra
27	LaCroce	AT&Q

Figure 6.6 The results of qryContactName.

Figure 6.6 shows the resulting dynaset for qryContactName. The format of the output of this query would be improved if the first name was also displayed. One way to do this is to insert the FirstName field between the LastName and the Company fields. The preferred method is to change the LastName field to a calculated field called Name. Name will be the concatenation (the process of combining text strings) of the LastName and FirstName fields.

To redefine LastName to Name:

1. Open qryContactName in Design mode, if it is not already open.
2. Select the LastName field in the criteria pane.
3. Type the following expression in the Field Name cell of that column:

```
Name:[LastName]&", "&[FirstName]
```

> **Hint**
>
> Press the Shift-F2 to zoom on this cell. This will allow you to see the whole expression at one time.

4. Save the query.
5. Select the Run tool from the toolbar. The result is shown in Figure 6.7.

This query will be the foundation for the next set of queries.

Figure 6.7 The new query for Contact Name.

The Letter Search for Last Name Matches Query

In Figure 6.2, the WinContact main window, there are 26 toggle buttons with the letters A to Z. The user will press a button to view the list of all the contact names for that letter of the alphabet. The object of this query is to retrieve all last names that begin with the letter chosen by the user. You will need to create a separate query for each letter of the alphabet. You will use qryContactName as the model for these queries.

To build the letter search for Last Name matches query:

1. Open the qryContactName query.

2. Select File → Save As.

3. Name the query qryContactName_A.

4. Type {Like "A"} in the criteria cell in the column that has the Name field. This will retrieve all records whose LastName field begins with "A."

5. Save the query.

6. Select the Run tool form the toolbar. The result is shown in Figure 6.8.

Figure 6.8 The results of the Contact Name A query.

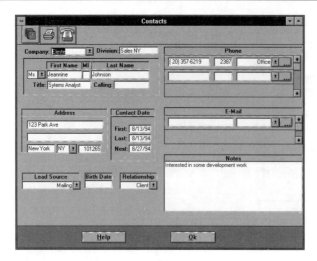

Figure 6.9 The Contacts form.

Your Turn: Building Additional Letter Searches

Repeat the process by changing the search criteria for each letter of the alphabet. Make sure to use the naming convention as shown, taking care to change the last letter of the query name for each query when you state it. For example, the query that would retrieve the last names that begin with the letter "B" should be named qryContactName_B and have a corresponding criteria of Like "B." When you are finished you will have 27 queries.

Your Turn: Building the Contact Query

The Contacts form, which is illustrated in Figure 6.9, is used to add a new contact or edit an existing contact if a contact is selected from the main window. A query is needed to bring up the fields for this screen. This is a basic query with no search criteria. Follow the previous instructions for building a new query, using the CONTACT table and all of the fields listed in Table 6.2. Name the query "qryContacts." Remember to test the query using the methods previously discussed.

Building the WinContact Report Queries

The WinContact application will have three types of contact reports:

Table 6.2 Fields for qryContacts
Fields
CONTACT.LastName
CONTACT.FirstName
CONTACT.MiddleInitial
CONTACT.Prefix
CONTACT.ContactId
CONTACT.Title
CONTACT.CallingName
CONTACT.BirthDate
CONTACT.Company
CONTACT.Division
CONTACT.StreetAddress
CONTACT.MailStopBox
CONTACT.City
CONTACT.State
CONTACT.ZipCode
CONTACT.FirstDateContacted
CONTACT.LastDateContacted
CONTACT.FollowUpDate
CONTACT.Relationship
CONTACT.LeadSource
CONTACT.Notes

- Mailing list reports
- Contact follow-up reports
- Customer contact history reports

You will need to build a query for each type, and then manipulate the queries, using various data sorts to complete the required report queries which were specified in Chapter 2.

To complete WinContact, five Mail List queries are necessary. They are distinguished by their sort patterns, of which the following types will be used:

- Contacts sorted by name and phone type.
- Contacts sorted by zip code, name, and phone type.

- Contacts sorted by state, name, and phone type.
- Contacts sorted by lead source, name, and phone type.
- Contacts sorted by relationship, name, and phone type.

Contacts Sorted by Name and Phone Type

The contacts sorted by name and phone type query is used to produce a report that will display each contact, his or her company name, company address, and various phone numbers. One of the strengths of WinContact is that it is created with a separate table for handling multiple phone numbers for each contact. This report will display each phone number, referenced by type (office, home, fax, or beeper) for a given contact. This part of the query varies since some contacts may have only one phone number and some may have more. The report is sorted by last name, first name, and phone type.

This query uses multiple tables related by joins. Figure 6.10 illustrates table joins. Joining is the process of linking two tables via a common data element, often a common field like ContactId. An equi-join refers to two tables that have a one-to-one matching relationship for each table; in other words, there are no records in either table that do not have a match in the other table. This is also commonly referred to as an inner join. An outer join is when one table may have no matching records, one matching record, or more than one matching

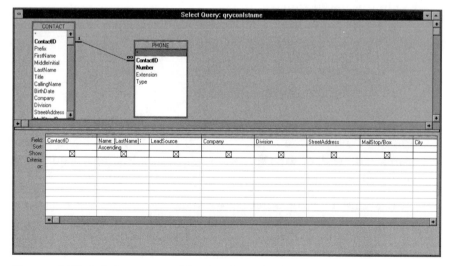

Figure 6.10 Joining two tables in the WinContact application.

Table 6.3 Fields for the qryContactLastName Query
Fields
CONTACT.ContactId CONTACT.Company CONTACT.Division CONTACT.StreetAddress CONTACT.MailStopBox CONTACT.City CONTACT.State CONTACT.ZipCode PHONE.Number PHONE.Extension PHONE.Type PHONE_TYPE.Type

record in the other table, but you still want to see all the records even those for which there is no match in the results. An example of this in WinContact would be the relationship of ContactId in the CONTACT table to ContactId in the CALL table: There either can be no calls, one call, or many calls to a contact.

To create a join, in the table pane drag and drop a field from one table to the field in the other table that you want to join. To delete a join, select the join line and press the Delete key.

To add fields to the contacts sorted by name and phone type query:

1. Create a new query.
2. Add the CONTACTS, PHONE, and PHONE_TYPE tables to the query.
3. Add the fields from Table 6.3 to the criteria pane.
4. Select the second column.
5. Select Edit → Insert Column. Notice that the cursor is in the field name row of the new column.
6. Add the Name expression as in past queries.
7. Set the sort order of the Name field to Ascending.
8. Highlight the column that contains the Type field from the Phone table.
9. Set the sort order of the Type field to Ascending.

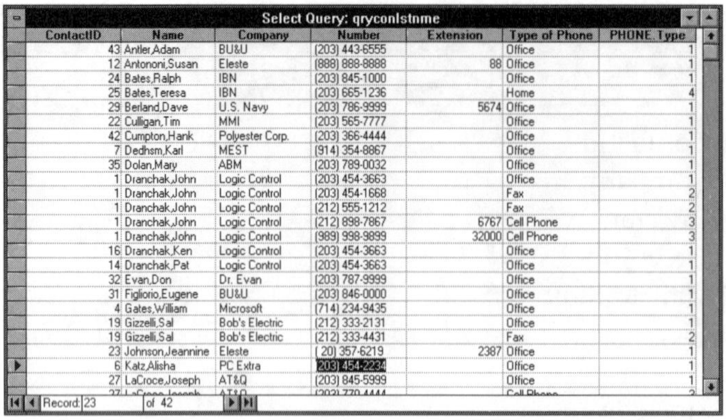

Select Query: qryconlstnme

ContactID	Name	Company	Number	Extension	Type of Phone	PHONE.Type
43	Antler,Adam	BU&U	(203) 443-6555		Office	1
12	Antononi,Susan	Eleste	(888) 888-8888	88	Office	1
24	Bates,Ralph	IBN	(203) 845-1000		Office	1
25	Bates,Teresa	IBN	(203) 665-1236		Home	4
29	Berland,Dave	U.S. Navy	(203) 786-9999	5674	Office	1
22	Culligan,Tim	MMI	(203) 565-7777		Office	1
42	Cumpton,Hank	Polyester Corp.	(203) 366-4444		Office	1
7	Dedhsm,Karl	MEST	(914) 354-8867		Office	1
35	Dolan,Mary	ABM	(203) 789-0032		Office	1
1	Dranchak,John	Logic Control	(203) 454-3663		Office	1
1	Dranchak,John	Logic Control	(203) 454-1668		Fax	2
1	Dranchak,John	Logic Control	(212) 555-1212		Fax	2
1	Dranchak,John	Logic Control	(212) 898-7867	6767	Cell Phone	3
1	Dranchak,John	Logic Control	(989) 998-9899	32000	Cell Phone	3
16	Dranchak,Ken	Logic Control	(203) 454-3663		Office	1
14	Dranchak,Pat	Logic Control	(203) 454-3663		Office	1
32	Evan,Don	Dr. Evan	(203) 787-9999		Office	1
31	Figliorio,Eugene	BU&U	(203) 846-0000		Office	1
4	Gates,William	Microsoft	(714) 234-9435		Office	1
19	Gizzelli,Sal	Bob's Electric	(212) 333-2131		Office	1
19	Gizzelli,Sal	Bob's Electric	(212) 333-4431		Fax	2
23	Johnson,Jeannine	Eleste	(20) 357-6219	2387	Office	1
6	Katz,Alisha	PC Extra	(203) 454-2234		Office	1
27	LaCroce,Joseph	AT&Q	(203) 845-5999		Office	1

Record: 23 of 42

Figure 6.11 The results for qryContactLastName.

10. Save the query as qryContactLastName.
11. Select the Run tool from the toolbar. The result is shown in Figure 6.11.

You have now created a query sorted first by name and then by phone type. This means that for each contact the phone numbers will be listed in a consistent manner (office, fax, home, and cellular). You will use this query as the starting point for the next four queries. The concept for building the additional queries is simply to add another sort column to the query.

Contacts Sorted by Zip Code and Name Query

The contacts sorted by zip code and name query is used to create a report that lists each contact name along with his or her company, company address, and office phone number. This report will be sorted by zip code in ascending order and then by last name and first name for those contacts who have the same zip code. This report requires only the contact's office phone number, and should not include any of the other types of phone numbers (fax or cellular) a contact might have. Since this query uses multiple tables, it will be necessary to limit the records from the PHONE table to those that have a Phone_Type equal to the word "office." This will be accomplished by adding a criterion to the Phone_Type column of the query.

To add a criterion to a field, select the first Criteria cell of the corresponding column in the QBE grid, and type the expression that you wish to use for your criterion. As discussed earlier, criteria matches can be based on text, numeric values, or expressions.

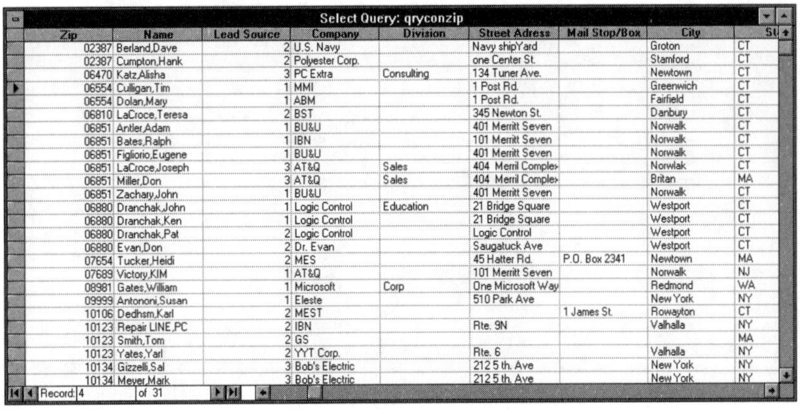

Select Query: qryconzip

Zip	Name	Lead Source	Company	Division	Street Adress	Mail Stop/Box	City	St
02387	Berland,Dave	2	U.S. Navy		Navy shipYard		Groton	CT
02387	Cumpton,Hank	2	Polyester Corp.		one Center St.		Stamford	CT
06470	Katz,Alisha	3	PC Extra	Consulting	134 Tuner Ave.		Newtown	CT
06554	Culligan,Tim	1	MMI		1 Post Rd.		Greenwich	CT
06554	Dolan,Mary	1	ABM		1 Post Rd.		Fairfield	CT
06810	LaCroce,Teresa	2	BST		345 Newton St.		Danbury	CT
06851	Antler,Adam	1	BU&U		401 Merritt Seven		Norwalk	CT
06851	Bates,Ralph	1	IBN		101 Merritt Seven		Norwalk	CT
06851	Figliorio,Eugene	1	BU&U		401 Merritt Seven		Norwalk	CT
06851	LaCroce,Joseph	3	AT&Q	Sales	404 Merril Comple›		Norwlak	CT
06851	Miller,Don	3	AT&Q	Sales	404 Merril Comple›		Britan	MA
06851	Zachary,John	1	BU&U		401 Merritt Seven		Norwalk	CT
06880	Dranchak,John	1	Logic Control	Education	21 Bridge Square		Westport	CT
06880	Dranchak,Ken	1	Logic Control		21 Bridge Square		Westport	CT
06880	Dranchak,Pat	2	Logic Control		Logic Control		Westport	CT
06880	Evan,Don	2	Dr. Evan		Saugatuck Ave		Westport	CT
07654	Tucker,Heidi	2	MES		45 Hatter Rd.	P.O. Box 2341	Newtown	MA
07689	Victory,KIM	1	AT&Q		101 Merritt Seven		Norwalk	NJ
08981	Gates,William	1	Microsoft	Corp	One Microsoft Way		Redmond	WA
09999	Antononi,Susan	1	Eleste		510 Park Ave		New York	NY
10106	Dedhsm,Karl	2	MEST			1 James St.	Rowayton	CT
10123	Repair LINE,PC	2	IBN		Rte. 9N		Valhalla	NY
10123	Smith,Tom	2	GS					MA
10123	Yates,Yarl	2	YYT Corp.		Rte. 6		Valhalla	NY
10134	Gizzelli,Sal	3	Bob's Electric		212 5 th. Ave		New York	NY
10134	Meyer,Mark	3	Bob's Electric		212 5 th. Ave		New York	NY

Record: 4 of 31

Figure 6.12 The results of qryContactZip.

To build the contacts sorted by zip code and name query:

1. Open the qryContactLastName query in Design mode.
2. Save it as qryContactZip.
3. Drag and drop ZipCode over the second column. Access automatically inserts a new column for ZipCode.
4. Set the sort order of the ZipCode field to Ascending.
5. Select the column that contains the Phone_Type field.
6. Type {Office} in the criteria cell. Note that "Office" is typed here to limit the query to just the office phone number of a contact.
7. Save the query.
8. Select the Run tool from the toolbar. The result is shown in Figure 6.12.

Note

Refer to Microsoft Access's on-line help for a complete explanation of syntax of criteria.

Contacts Sorted by State and Name Query

The contacts sorted by state and name query is a modification of the preceding query. It is the data source for a report that allows the user to view his or her contacts by state. This query will be sorted by state and then by last name for those contacts in the same state.

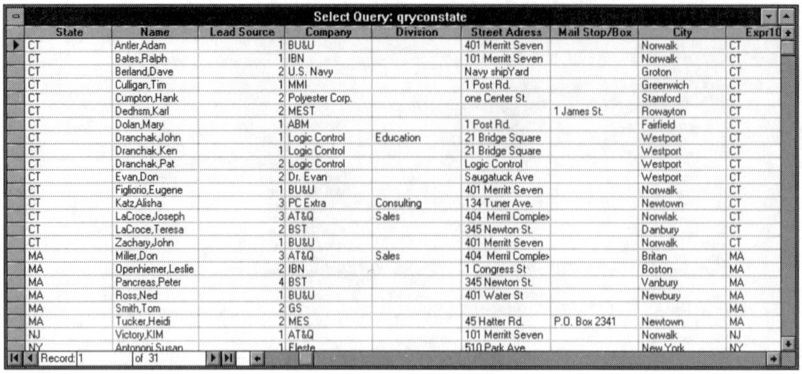

Select Query: qryconstate

State	Name	Lead Source	Company	Division	Street Adress	Mail Stop/Box	City	Expr10
CT	Antler,Adam	1	BU&U		401 Merritt Seven		Norwalk	CT
CT	Bates,Ralph	1	IBN		101 Merritt Seven		Norwalk	CT
CT	Berland,Dave	2	U.S. Navy		Navy shipYard		Groton	CT
CT	Culligan,Tim	1	MMI		1 Post Rd.		Greenwich	CT
CT	Cumpton,Hank	2	Polyester Corp.		one Center St.		Stamford	CT
CT	Dedhsm,Karl	2	MEST			1 James St.	Rowayton	CT
CT	Dolan,Mary	1	ABM		1 Post Rd.		Fairfield	CT
CT	Dranchak,John	1	Logic Control	Education	21 Bridge Square		Westport	CT
CT	Dranchak,Ken	1	Logic Control		21 Bridge Square		Westport	CT
CT	Dranchak,Pat	2	Logic Control		Logic Control		Westport	CT
CT	Evan,Don	2	Dr. Evan		Saugatuck Ave		Westport	CT
CT	Figliorio,Eugene	1	BU&U		401 Merritt Seven		Norwalk	CT
CT	Katz,Alisha	3	PC Extra	Consulting	134 Tuner Ave.		Newtown	CT
CT	LaCroce,Joseph	3	AT&Q	Sales	404 Merril Comple›		Norwlak	CT
CT	LaCroce,Teresa	2	BST		345 Newton St.		Danbury	CT
CT	Zachary,John	1	BU&U		401 Merritt Seven		Norwalk	CT
MA	Miller,Don	3	AT&Q	Sales	404 Merril Comple›		Britan	MA
MA	Openhiemer,Leslie	2	IBN		1 Congress St		Boston	MA
MA	Pancreas,Peter	4	BST		345 Newton St.		Vanbury	MA
MA	Ross,Ned	1	BU&U		401 Water St		Newbury	MA
MA	Smith,Tom	2	GS					MA
MA	Tucker,Heidi	2	MES		45 Hatter Rd.	P.O. Box 2341	Newtown	MA
NJ	Victory,KIM	1	AT&Q		101 Merritt Seven		Norwalk	NJ
NY	Antononi,Susan	1	Fleste		510 Park Ave		New York	NY

Record: 1 of 31

Figure 6.13 The results of qryContactState.

To build the contacts sorted by state and name query:

1. Open qryContactLastName in Design mode.
2. Save the file as qryContactState.
3. Select the second column.
4. Drag and drop State into the second column. Access automatically inserts a new column.
5. Set the sort order of the State field to Ascending.
6. Select the column that contains the PhoneType field.
7. Type {Office} in the criteria cell.
8. Save the query.
9. Select the Run tool from the toolbar. The result is shown in Figure 6.13.

Contacts Sorted by Lead Source and Name Query

This query is used to list the contact names by lead source. It is also based on the contacts by Zip code and name query.

To build the contacts sorted by lead source and name query:

1. Open qryContactLastName query in Design mode.
2. Save the query as qryContactLeadSource.
3. Select the Add Table tool.
4. Select LEAD_SOURCE from the Table/Query list box.

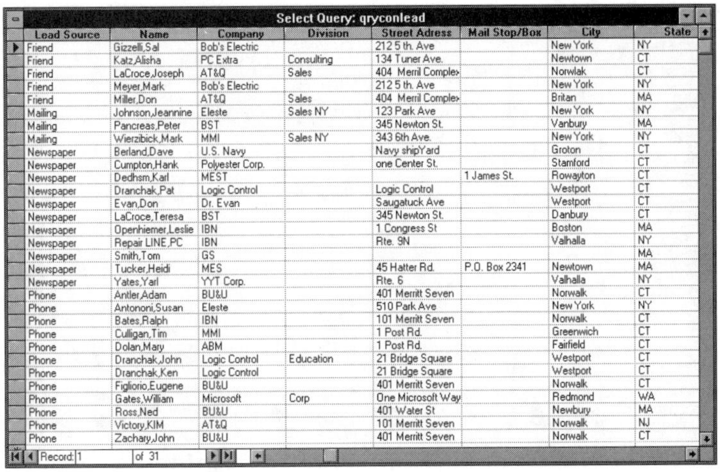

Select Query: qryconlead

Lead Source	Name	Company	Division	Street Adress	Mail Stop/Box	City	State
Friend	Gizzelli,Sal	Bob's Electric		212 5 th. Ave		New York	NY
Friend	Katz,Alisha	PC Extra	Consulting	134 Tuner Ave.		Newtown	CT
Friend	LaCroce,Joseph	AT&Q	Sales	404 Merril Comple›		Norwlak	CT
Friend	Meyer,Mark	Bob's Electric		212 5 th. Ave		New York	NY
Friend	Miller,Don	AT&Q	Sales	404 Merril Comple›		Britan	MA
Mailing	Johnson,Jeannine	Eleste	Sales NY	123 Park Ave		New York	NY
Mailing	Pancreas,Peter	BST		345 Newton St.		Vanbury	MA
Mailing	Wierzibick,Mark	MMI	Sales NY	343 6th Ave.		New York	NY
Newspaper	Berland,Dave	U.S. Navy		Navy shipYard		Groton	CT
Newspaper	Cumpton,Hank	Polyester Corp.		one Center St.		Stamford	CT
Newspaper	Dedhsm,Karl	MEST			1 James St.	Rowayton	CT
Newspaper	Dranchak,Pat	Logic Control		Logic Control		Westport	CT
Newspaper	Evan,Don	Dr. Evan		Saugatuck Ave		Westport	CT
Newspaper	LaCroce,Teresa	BST		345 Newton St.		Danbury	CT
Newspaper	Openhiemer,Leslie	IBN		1 Congress St		Boston	MA
Newspaper	Repair LINE,PC	IBN		Rte. 9N		Valhalla	NY
Newspaper	Smith,Tom	GS					MA
Newspaper	Tucker,Heidi	MES		45 Hatter Rd.	P.O. Box 2341	Newtown	MA
Newspaper	Yates,Yarl	YYT Corp.		Rte. 6		Valhalla	NY
Phone	Antler,Adam	BU&U		401 Merritt Seven		Norwalk	CT
Phone	Antononi,Susan	Eleste		510 Park Ave		New York	NY
Phone	Bates,Ralph	IBN		101 Merritt Seven		Norwalk	CT
Phone	Culligan,Tim	MMI		1 Post Rd.		Greenwich	CT
Phone	Dolan,Mary	ABM		1 Post Rd.		Fairfield	CT
Phone	Dranchak,John	Logic Control	Education	21 Bridge Square		Westport	CT
Phone	Dranchak,Ken	Logic Control		21 Bridge Square		Westport	CT
Phone	Figliorio,Eugene	BU&U		401 Merritt Seven		Norwalk	CT
Phone	Gates,William	Microsoft	Corp	One Microsoft Way		Redmond	WA
Phone	Ross,Ned	BU&U		401 Water St		Newbury	MA
Phone	Victory,KIM	AT&Q		101 Merritt Seven		Norwalk	NJ
Phone	Zachary,John	BU&U		401 Merritt Seven		Norwalk	CT

Record: 1 of 31

Figure 6.14 The results of qryContactLeadSource.

5. Select Add.
6. Select Close.
7. Drag and drop LeadSource from the LEAD_SOURCE table in the table pane into the second column of the QBE grid. Access automatically inserts a new column for LeadSource.
8. Set the sort order of the LeadSource column to Ascending.
9. Select the column that contains the PhoneType field.
10. Type {Office} in the criteria cell.
11. Save the query.
12. Run the query. The result is shown in Figure 6.14.

Contacts Sorted by Relationship and Name Query

This query is used to list contact names by relationship, and it is based on the contacts by zip code and name query.

To build the contacts sorted by relationship and name query:

1. Open qryContactLastName in Design view.
2. Save As qryContactRelationship.
3. Select the Add Table tool.

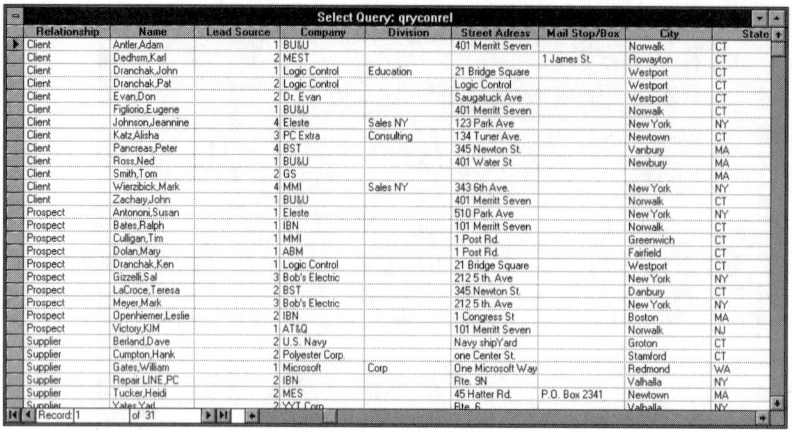

Select Query: qryconrel

Relationship	Name	Lead Source	Company	Division	Street Adress	Mail Stop/Box	City	State
Client	Antler,Adam	1	BU&U		401 Merritt Seven		Norwalk	CT
Client	Dedhsm,Karl	2	MEST			1 James St.	Rowayton	CT
Client	Dranchak,John	1	Logic Control	Education	21 Bridge Square		Westport	CT
Client	Dranchak,Pat	2	Logic Control		Logic Control		Westport	CT
Client	Evan,Don	2	Dr. Evan		Saugatuck Ave		Westport	CT
Client	Figliorio,Eugene	1	BU&U		401 Merritt Seven		Norwalk	CT
Client	Johnson,Jeannine	4	Eleste	Sales NY	123 Park Ave		New York	NY
Client	Katz,Alisha	3	PC Extra	Consulting	134 Tuner Ave.		Newtown	CT
Client	Pancreas,Peter	4	BST		345 Newton St.		Vanbury	MA
Client	Ross,Ned	1	BU&U		401 Water St		Newbury	MA
Client	Smith,Tom	2	GS					MA
Client	Wierzibick,Mark	4	MMI	Sales NY	343 6th Ave.		New York	NY
Client	Zachary,John	1	BU&U		401 Merritt Seven		Norwalk	CT
Prospect	Antononi,Susan	1	Eleste		510 Park Ave		New York	NY
Prospect	Bates,Ralph	1	IBN		101 Merritt Seven		Norwalk	CT
Prospect	Culligan,Tim	1	MMI		1 Post Rd.		Greenwich	CT
Prospect	Dolan,Mary	1	ABM		1 Post Rd.		Fairfield	CT
Prospect	Dranchak,Ken	1	Logic Control		21 Bridge Square		Westport	CT
Prospect	Gizzelli,Sal	3	Bob's Electric		212 5 th. Ave		New York	NY
Prospect	LaCroce,Teresa	2	BST		345 Newton St.		Danbury	CT
Prospect	Meyer,Mark	3	Bob's Electric		212 5 th. Ave		New York	NY
Prospect	Openhiemer,Leslie	2	IBN		1 Congress St		Boston	MA
Prospect	Victory,KIM	1	AT&Q		101 Merritt Seven		Norwalk	NJ
Supplier	Berland,Dave	2	U.S. Navy		Navy shipYard		Groton	CT
Supplier	Cumpton,Hank	2	Polyester Corp.		one Center St.		Stamford	CT
Supplier	Gates,William	1	Microsoft	Corp	One Microsoft Way		Redmond	WA
Supplier	Repair LINE,PC	2	IBN		Rte. 9N		Valhalla	NY
Supplier	Tucker,Heidi	2	MES		45 Hatter Rd.	P.O. Box 2341	Newtown	MA
Supplier	Yates,Yarl	2	YYT Corp		Rte. 6		Valhalla	NY

Record: 1 of 31

Figure 6.15 The results of qryContactRelationship.

4. Select Relationship from the Table/Query list box.
5. Select Add.
6. Select Close.
7. Drag and drop Relationship from the RELATIONSHIP table over the second column. Access automatically inserts a new column for Relationship.
8. Set the sort order of the Relationship field to Ascending.
9. Select the column that contains the PhoneType field.
10. Type {Office} in the criteria cell.
11. Save the query.
12. Select the Run tool from the toolbar. The result is shown in Figure 6.15.

To complete WinContact you also must build four contact follow-up queries, which are distinguished by their date criteria. These are the follow-up queries that will be built:

- Company and contacts who have not been contacted in the last 30 days.
- Company and contacts who have not been contacted in the last 60 days.
- Company and contacts who have follow-up calls scheduled for the present day.
- Company and contacts who have follow-up calls scheduled for the next day.

Table 6.4 Fields for the Contacts Not Contacted in the Last 30 Days Query
Fields
CONTACT.Company
CONTACT.LastDateContacted
PHONE.Number
PHONE.Extension
PHONE.Type
PHONE_TYPE.Type

Contacts Not Called in the Last 30 Days Query

This query is designed to select the contacts who have not been called in the last 30 days. The query uses the current date from the system and subtracts 30 calendar days from it. Any contacts who have not been called since that calculated date will be selected by the query. The query displays the name of the contact, his or her company, the office phone number, and the date on which he or she was last contacted.

To build the contacts not contacted in the last 30 days query:

1. Open a new query.
2. Add the CONTACTS, PHONE, and PHONE_TYPE tables to the table pane of the query.
3. Add the fields listed in Table 6.4 to the query.
4. Type {Office} in the criteria cell of the Phone_Type column.
5. Create a column for Name using the expression you created earlier.
6. Set the sort order of the LastDateContacted column to Ascending.
7. Enter the following expression into the criteria field of LastDateContacted:

```
<Date()-30 and > Date()-61
```

Note
This expression selects records that have a date value less than 30 days prior to the present day and greater than 60 days prior to the present day.

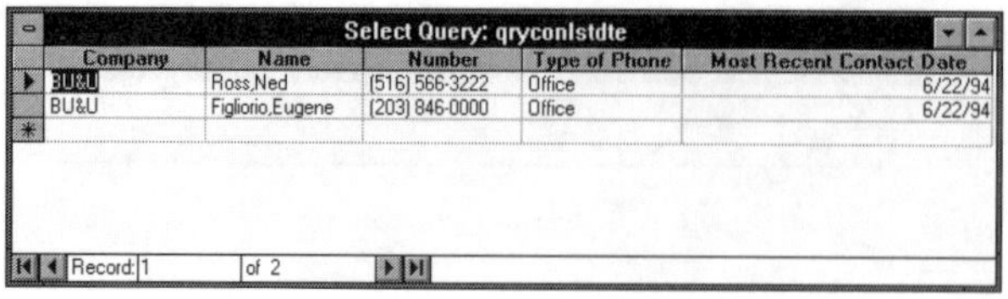

Select Query: qryconlstdte

Company	Name	Number	Type of Phone	Most Recent Contact Date
BU&U	Ross,Ned	(516) 566-3222	Office	6/22/94
BU&U	Figliorio,Eugene	(203) 846-0000	Office	6/22/94

Record: 1 of 2

Figure 6.16 The results of qryContactLastDate.

8. Save the query as qryContactLastDate.
9. Select the Run tool from the toolbar. The result is shown in Figure 6.16.

Contacts Not Called in the Last 60 Days Query

This query selects those contacts who have not been called in the last 60 days. It is based on the preceding query. The only distinction is that the selection criterion for the LastContactDate has been changed to "greater than 60 days."

To build the contacts not identified in the last 60 days query:

1. Open qryContactLastDate.
2. Save the query as qryContactLastDate60.
3. Select the column for LastDateContacted.
4. Type the following expression in the criteria cell:

```
<Date()-60
```

5. Save the query.
6. Select the Run tool from the toolbar. The result is shown in Figure 6.17.

Contacts with Follow-Up Calls Scheduled for Present Day Query

This query finds those contacts who are scheduled to be called on a specified day. It too is built from the contacts not identified in the last 30 days query and is modified to utilize the FollowUpDate field in the CONTACTS table.

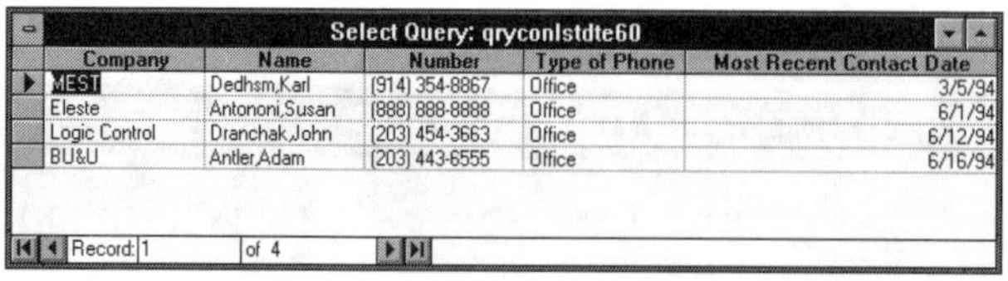

Select Query: qryconlstdte60

Company	Name	Number	Type of Phone	Most Recent Contact Date
MEST	Dedhsm,Karl	(914) 354-8867	Office	3/5/94
Eleste	Antononi,Susan	(888) 888-8888	Office	6/1/94
Logic Control	Dranchak,John	(203) 454-3663	Office	6/12/94
BU&U	Antler,Adam	(203) 443-6555	Office	6/16/94

Record: 1 of 4

Figure 6.17 The results of qryContactLastDate60.

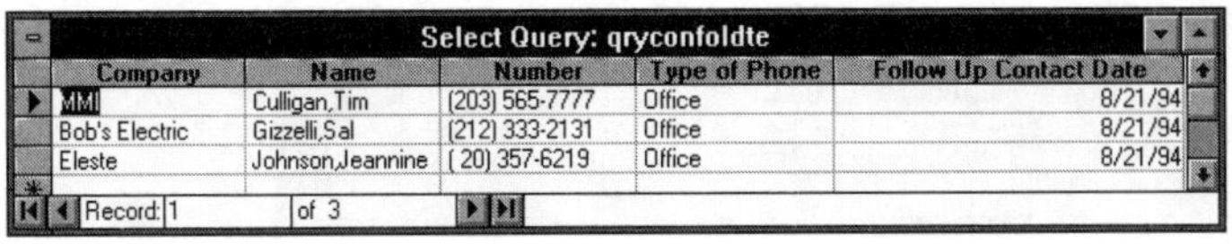

Figure 6.18 The results of qryContactToday.

To build the contacts with follow-up calls scheduled today query:

1. Open qryContactLastDate.
2. Save the query as qryContactToday.
3. By dragging and dropping, insert the FollowUpDate field over the Last-DateContacted column. Notice that the LastDateContacted field has moved one column to the right to allow for this insertion.
4. Set the sort order of the FollowUpDate field to Ascending.
5. Type the following expression in the FollowUpDate column's criteria cell.

   `=Date()`

6. Select the column for LastDateContacted.
7. Select Edit → Delete Column.
8. Save the query.
9. Select the Run tool from the toolbar. The result is shown in Figure 6.18.

Contacts with Follow-Up Calls Scheduled for Next Day Query

This query is designed to select those contacts who need to be called tomorrow. This query is based on the preceding one, but modified in the FollowUpDate field selection criteria.

To build the contacts with follow-up calls scheduled for tomorrow query:

1. Open qryContactToday.
2. Save the query as qryContactTomorrow.
3. Select the column for FollowUpDate.
4. Type the following expression in the FollowUpDate column's criteria cell:

   `=Date()+1`

5. Save the query.
6. Select the Run tool from the toolbar. The result is shown in Figure 6.19.

Company	Name	Number	Type of Phone	Follow Up Contact Date
BN	Bates,Ralph	(203) 845-1000	Office	8/22/94
MMI	Culligan,Tim	(203) 565-7777	Office	8/22/94
BU&U	Figliorio,Eugene	(203) 846-0000	Office	8/22/94
Eleste	Johnson,Jeannine	(20) 357-6219	Office	8/22/94

Record: 1   of 4

Figure 6.19 The results of qryContactTomorrow.

Customer Contact History Selection Query

The customer contact history selection query is used in the list box on the report selection form so that the user can select the last name of the contact for whom they want a history.

To build the customer contact history selection query:

1. Open a new query.
2. Add the CONTACTS table to the table pane of the query.
3. Add the ContactId field to the query.
4. Select the second column. Use the Name expression as in previous queries.
5. Set the sort order of the Name field to Ascending.
6. Save the query as qryReportLastName.
7. Select the Run tool from the toolbar. The result is shown in Figure 6.20.

Customer Contact History Query

The customer contact history query will provide a listing of all the calls placed to a particular contact, and include the start time of the call, length of the call,

Figure 6.20 The results of qryReportLastName.

Table 6.5 Fields for the Customer Contact History Query
Fields
CONTACT.LastName
CONTACT.FirstName
CONTACT.MiddleInitial
CONTACT.Prefix
CONTACT.ContactId
CONTACT.Company
CONTACT.Title
CONTACT.Division
CONTACT.StreetAddress
CONTACT.MailStopBox
CONTACT.City
CONTACT.State
CONTACT.ZipCode
CONTACT.FollowUpDate
CALL.StartTime
CALL.EndTime
CALL.Notes
PHONE_TYPE.Type

and any notes. The unique characteristic of this query is that its selection criteria is based on input from a contact list box on the report selection form.

To build the customer contact history query:

1. Open a new query in Design mode.
2. Add the CONTACTS and CALL tables to the table pane of the query.
3. Place the fields shown in Table 6.5 in the query.
4. Set the sort order of the StartTime field to Ascending.
5. Enter a test data such as {Antononi} in the criteria cell of the LastName field.

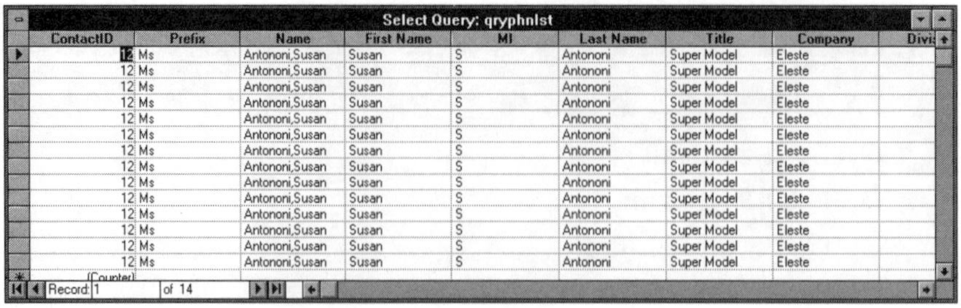

Figure 6.21 The results of qryPhoneList.

Note

The selection criteria for this query will be input from a form which is not built yet. You will use a test record to check the results of the query. Make sure you have a CONTACT record built which has some associated CALL records built also.

---

6. Save the query as qryPhoneList.

7. Run the query. The result is shown in Figure 6.21.

8. Remove the test criteria.

Using Values from a Form as Criteria for a Macro

Sometimes the selection criteria for a macro is not known until a user inputs it to a control on a form. This is known as dynamic selection. Access allows the user to select a data field and then use that selection to produce a query and, in this case, a report. The following expression is an example of using input from a form to select criteria for a query:

```
[Forms]![frmReport]![lstRepName]
```

Here, lstRepName is the list box from the form frmReport. When the user selects an entry from the list box, it is read by the query and used to select only calls that match the name of the contact.

To modify the customer contact history query for dynamic selection:

1. Open the qryPhoneList query in Design mode.

2. Enter the following expression into the criteria cell of the Name column:

   ```
   [Forms]![frmReport]![lstRepName]
   ```

> **Note**
>
> The form frmReport that will be used in dynamic selection has not been created yet. As such, the lstRepName list box does not exist. Thus, you cannot test this query.

3. Save the query.

You have now completed the application queries. In Chapters 7 and 8, you will use these queries as the data sources for various forms and reports.

Chapter 7

Forms

Microsoft Access has many form creation features that may encourage a user to choose a form to view data rather than a report. Developing powerful and user-friendly forms is a very straightforward process. Access provides a developer with a graphical interface that allows direct placement and formatting of controls on the screen, which is called direct manipulation. By utilizing direct manipulation techniques such as drag and drop, changes to a form occur rapidly and in an interactive mode. The primary benefits of this are reduction in development time and a better user interface. This chapter discusses the features and uses of the Microsoft Access Form Design window to create forms. You will learn:

- What a form is and when to use it.
- How to use the Form Design window.
- Form properties.
- How to create, save, and view a form.
- How to use command buttons.
- How to use option groups.
- How to use the Picture Builder.

What Is a Form?

A form is a method of viewing data on the screen. Data resides in table format within an Access database. Although these tables can be viewed or modified directly in Datasheet view, there are many benefits to using forms, some of which are that:

- Data can be formatted and grouped to provide more meaningful and understandable information.
- Rules for data entry can be built into the form to allow for greater data accuracy.
- Users can be protected from accidentally changing or deleting data.

Forms are used for adding, editing, viewing data, and navigating the application.

Building Forms

There are two ways to build forms: utilizing the Form Wizard or building the form from scratch. Simple forms can be built using the Form Wizard, but complex forms will have to be built from scratch in the Form Design window. Both of these processes are called constructive editing, which means building a finished product from the ground up. Conversely, using Wizard to build a form that is similar to what you want and then modifying it is called deconstructive editing, which provides both speed and flexibility for form creation. Although the Form Wizard provides a quick and easy way to create forms, the style of the forms you can create is not consistent with Sangatuck Marketing Group's interface requirements.

Building a form from scratch is a six-step process:

1. Create a new form based on the correct table or query.
2. Add the required sections to the form.
3. Add the required controls via drag and drop.
4. Format the form by moving and sizing the controls for consistency and setting the properties that affect the form and each control's appearance.
5. View the form.
6. Save the form.

It is important to be aware that steps 3 and 4 are iterative.

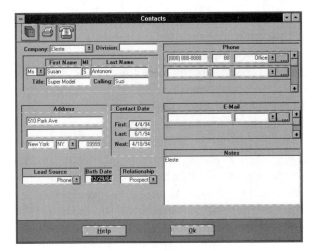

Figure 7.1 The Contacts form.

The objective of good interface design is that it must target the needs of the users (consequently, don't design one form to be used by different types of users). For example, if the user is a data entry person, it is necessary to have the form reflect the media layout from which the user is inputting, so that he or she can navigate it in a natural manner. If the user is entering calls for a customer service application, then the data input process should follow questions being asked of the inquiring customer. And although this same information may be needed by an executive in the marketing department, chances are it would not be a good idea to use the same form layout. In the case of SMG, the Contacts form, which is illustrated in Figure 7.1, was created in a manner that would make it easy for someone to input information from a first contact. There is certain information that can always be obtained from a first contact, such as name, company, address, and phone number. These are positioned in the upper portion of the screen. Other information such as birthdate may not be so readily available, so this was placed in the lower portion of the form.

Good interface design can be achieved by following these five rules:

1. Use group-related controls.
2. Perform only one task on a form.
3. Use space to separate controls.
4. Reduce typing by using list and combo boxes.
5. Navigate the user through data input in the natural order of data reception.

Grouping related controls by drawing rectangles or lines provides a subtle reminder to the user that these controls are related to each other. A rectangle around the parts of an address would be a good example of this. Rule 2, perform only one task on a form, means solve only one objective of the application with that form; for example, don't combine the process of adding contact information and logging calls on the same form. Rule 3, use space to separate controls, is achieved by positioning the controls with as much space as possible between them. It is very hard to be productive when the form is hard to read. Use a multipage form in cases where there is too much data to fit on one form. (But before you use a multipage form, verify that you are not combining separate tasks on the same form.) Rule 4, reduce typing by using list boxes and combo boxes, makes data input quicker and more accurate. The final step, navigate the user through data input in the natural order of data reception, means mimic the input source whether it is a paper document or a phone call.

Sections of a Form

The Form Design window (Figure 7.2) contains five sections:

- Form Header
- Page Header
- Detail
- Page Footer
- Form Footer

The Detail section is typically used to display data that is going to be added, edited, or viewed. The Form Header section provides a nonscrollable region at the top of the form; the Form Footer section provides a nonscrollable region at the bottom of the form. These sections are always visible even in a multipage form; therefore, they are normally used to display objects such as command buttons or graphical controls. The Form Header section is also frequently used to hold a toolbar. The Page Header and Page Footer sections are used only when printing a form since; obviously, they allow you to print a header and footer on every page of your document.

Properties

Properties are used to define attributes, sections, and controls on the form. Every text box, label, button, box, section, and line has certain properties associated

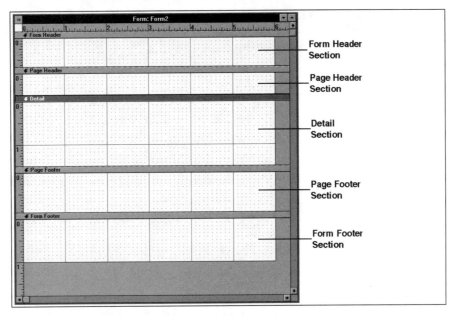

Figure 7.2 Form Design window.

with it. These properties are displayed and edited in a Property Sheet, which is illustrated in Figure 7.3. By modifying properties a designer can change the display, the events or the data associated with a form, section, or control. Table 7.1 lists the most common properties, which are grouped into four logical categories:

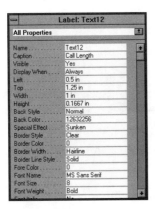

Figure 7.3 A property sheet for a control.

Table 7.1 Control Properties

Property	Description
Name	Identifies the control.
Caption	Text associated with the control.
Visible	Determines whether a control is displayed.
Width	How wide the control is.
Height	How high the control is.
Left	Where the control is positioned relative to the left border of the form.
Top	Where the control is positioned relative to the top border of the form.
Font Name	Font type.
Font Size	Type size.
Default Value	Value that appears as the default (can be modified).
Validation Rule/ Validation Text	Evaluates entered data against an expression and determines if it is valid for the record. If the data is invalid, it displays the text entered in the validation text property.
Input Mask	Specifies how the input will look on the form. A telephone number is the most common. A mask is built to show (000)999-9999.

- Layout properties
- Event properties
- Data properties
- Other properties

Note

Although properties relate to a form, section, or control, from this point on, in this chapter we will generically use the term control.

Layout properties determine how the control will appear on the form. Event properties determine what will happen when the control is selected via a

Table 7.2 Form Properties	
Property	**Description**
Record Source	Identifies the table or query from which the form is based.
Default View	Determines whether the initial view will be a single or continuous form (more than one detail section).
Default Editing	Determines whether the initial editing mode will be data entry
Modal	Determines if the form will retain focus until it is closed.
Width	Width of the form.

keystroke or mouse action, and data properties determine how the actual data will interact with the control. Other properties are miscellaneous properties that could not be grouped in the other three. Properties are set with default values depending on the controls with which they are associated. Therefore, it is not necessary to manually set all properties for a control.

Forms also have properties which control the source of the form's data, the appearance of the form, and the type of form. Five of a form's most common properties are listed in Table 7.2. For a full explanation of all the properties, consult the Access on-line help system.

Event Processing

Access is an event-driven software application, which means that events control the processing of data. This is different from traditional programs, which are procedure-driven. Nothing happens in Access unless an event causes it. For example, if a user clicks the mouse on the OK button, that is an event. As the developer you have to tell Access how to respond when an event occurs. Table 7.3 describes the most common events in Access. For a complete list and explanation of each property, use the Access on-line help system.

Adding Controls to a Form

Adding controls to a form is a four-step process:

Table 7.3 Events

Event	Event Property	Occurrence
Click	On Click	A user clicks a mouse button.
Double-Click	On Dbl Click	A user double-clicks a mouse button.
MouseMove	On Mouse Move	A mouse moves over a control.
MouseDown	On Mouse Down	The down part of a click.
MouseUp	On Mouse Up	The up part of a click.
GotFocus	On Got Focus	An option or toggle button is clicked.
LostFocus	On Lost Focus	A different option or toggle button is clicked, and the original button that had focus now has lost it.
Open	On Open	The form is opened.
Close	On Close	The form is closed.
Updated	On Update	A table is updated.
Print	On Print	The print command is issued.

1. Select the control tool from the toolbox. The cursor changes to reflect the tool selected.
2. Position the cursor in the approximate location on the screen.
3. Click and drag it to the specific size.
4. Make any modifications to the control's property sheet, if necessary.

The two most commonly used controls are Text Box and Label. A Text Box control is used to display data from a table or query or that is calculated from other fields; it is dynamic in nature. The table or query is determined by setting the form's Data Source property. A Label control is used to display some informational text, such as a title of a form or a title of a text box control; it is static in nature. Controls can either be bound or unbound. A bound control is linked to a field in a table or query, and it is used to display fields from a table. An unbound control has no link. They include rectangles, lines, or titles.

Adding a field to a form is done by binding the field to a control. There are two ways to do this:

- Dragging and dropping the field from the Field List window.
- Selecting a control and changing its Control Source property.

To bind a field to a control using drag and drop:

1. Select a control tool from the toolbox.
2. Drag and drop a field from the Field List window onto the form.

To bind a field to a control using the Control Source property:

1. Select a control tool from the toolbox.
2. Draw the control on the form.
3. Set the Control Source property in the property sheet.

Once you have placed controls on a form, you can reposition them in these ways:

- Select the control and move it with the mouse.
- Change the Left and Top properties in the control's property sheet.

To move a control using the mouse:

1. Select the control.
2. Move the mouse around the perimeter of the selected control until the hand cursor, which you can see in Figure 7.4, is displayed.
3. Drag and drop the control to its new location.

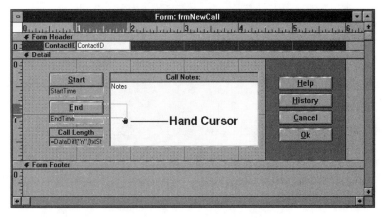

Figure 7.4 Moving a control with the mouse.

Note

To move a control separately from its label, move the mouse to the left-hand corner of the control until the single finger cursor is displayed; then drag and drop the control in its new location.

To move a control by changing its properties:

1. Select the control.
2. Select the Property tool from the toolbar.
3. Set the values of the Left and Top properties to the new location.

There are two ways to size a control:

- Select the control and size it with the mouse.
- Change the Width and Height properties in the control's property sheet.

To size a control by using the mouse:

1. Select the control.
2. Move the mouse around the perimeter of the selected control until the arrow cursor, shown in Figure 7.5, is displayed.
3. Drag the boundary of the control to change its size.

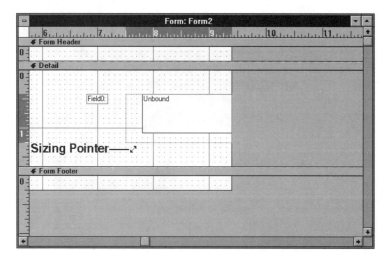

Figure 7.5 Sizing a control with the mouse.

To size a control by changing its properties:

1. Select the control.

2. Select the Property tool from the toolbar.

3. Set the values of the Width and Height properties to the new size.

Rectangle, line, and label controls are often used to assist in control grouping, which is a means of visually grouping like controls on the form. These unbound controls can be added to a form in a manner similar to bound controls.

To add an unbound control to a form using the drag and drop:

1. Select a control tool from the toolbox.

2. Draw the selected control onto the form.

Tab order ensures that a user will progress throughout the form as designated in the design specifications. After all the controls are entered on the form, it is important that the tab order be set. Anytime the form is modified, the tab order should be checked to make sure that it is correct. Poor tab order can make data entry a laborious task.

To set the tab order:

1. Select Edit → Tab_Order. The dialog box in Figure 7.6 will be displayed.

2. Drag and drop the fields in the Tab Order list box to obtain the proper order.

Hint

You can also select AutoArrange to align the fields by their position on the screen in left-to-right order in a downward fashion.

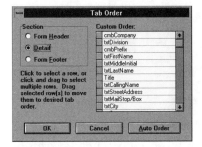

Figure 7.6 The Tab Order dialog box.

Figure 7.7 The New Form dialog box.

The Contact Form

The contact form allows a user to add, edit, and view all data on a contact. The form also lets the user select other forms in the application.

To place controls on the contact form:

1. Open the CONTACTS database and select the Forms tab from the database window.

2. Select New. The dialog box in Figure 7.7 will be displayed.

3. Select Contacts from the Table/Query list box.

4. Select Blank Form. The Report Design window is displayed in Figure 7.8.

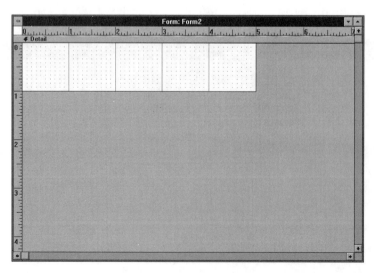

Figure 7.8 The blank Report Design window (no header or footer sections).

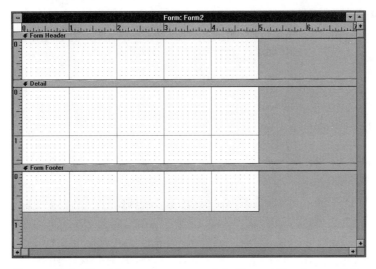

**Figure 7.9 The Design screen with Form Header and Form Footer
sections.**

5. Select Format → Form Header/Footer. The Form Header and Form Footer
   sections will be displayed.

6. Reduce the height of the Header section to .5" by dragging the lower
   border of the section upward.

7. Increase the size of the Detail section to 6.5" wide by 4" high.

8. Increase the height of the Footer section to .5" high. The new section
   dimensions are illustrated in Figure 7.9.

9. Select Edit → Select Form.

Hint

Clicking on the white box in the left-hand corner between the rulers is
another method of selecting the entire form.

---

10. Select the Property tool from the toolbar. The property sheet shown in
    Figure 7.10 will be displayed.

11. Set the form properties to the values listed in Table 7.4.

12. Use the Rectangle tool to place three rectangles in the Detail section using
    the properties listed in Table 7.5.

Figure 7.10 The Contacts Form property sheet.

13. Drag and drop the fields listed in Table 7.6 from the Field List window into the Contacts form. Move and size the controls so that the form looks like the one in Figure 7.11.

14. Select File → SaveAs.

15. Type {frmContact}.

16. Select OK.

Table 7.4 Form Property Values for the Contacts Form	
Property	**Value**
Caption	Contact Form
Default View	Single Form
Scroll Bars	Neither
Record Selectors	No
Navigation Buttons	No

Table 7.5 Grouping Rectangles Dimensions				
Name	**Left**	**Top**	**Width**	**Height**
rctName	.15"	.31"	3.1"	.8"
rctAddress	.1"	1.59 "	1.9"	.94"
rctContactDate	2.15"	1.58"	1"	.96"

Table 7.6 Controls on the Contacts Form

Control Name	Control Type	Left	Top	Width	Height
Company	text box	.78"	.07"	.96"	.078"
Company	label	.15"	.078"	.63"	.167"
Division	text box	2.15"	1.58"	1"	.96"
Division	label	1.78"	.062"	.57"	1.67"
Prefix	text box	.23"	.585"	.4"	.1667"
First Name	label	.67"	.385"	.81"	.167"
FirstName	text box	.69"	.585"	.80"	.167"
MI	label	1.48"	.39"	.20"	.167"
MI	text box	1.51"	.59"	.167"	.167"
Last Name	label	1.7"	.38"	1.32"	.167"
LastName	text box	1.7"	.58"	1.32"	.167"
Title	label	.322"	.81"	.36"	.167"
Title	text box	.69"	.81"	.1"	.167"
Calling	label	1.171"	.81"	.5"	.167"
CallingName	text box	.81"	.81"	.8"	.167"
Address	label	.11"	1.42"	1.95"	.167"
StreetAddress	text box	.23"	1.68"	1.73"	.167"
MailStop/Box	text box	.23"	1.95"	1.73"	.167"
City	text box	.23"	2.2"	.625"	.167"
State	text box	.91"	2.2"	.44"	.167"
ZipCode	text box	1.41"	2.2"	.51"	.167"
Contact Date	label	2.15"	1.4"	1"	.167"
First	label	2.2"	1.7"	.35"	.167"
FirstDate	text box	2.5"	1.7"	.5"	.167"
Last	label	2.2"	1.98"	.35"	.167"
LastDate	text box	2.2"	1.98"	.5"	.167"
Next	label	2.2"	2.2"	.35"	.167"
FollowUp	text box	2.5"	2.2"	.5"	.167"
Lead Source	label	.12"	2.8"	1.3"	.167"
LeadSource	text box	.12"	3"	1.3"	.167"
Birth Date	label	1.5"	2.8"	.62"	.167"
BirthDate	text box	1.5"	3"	.62"	.167"
Relationship	label	2.3"	2.8"	.84"	.167"
Relationship	text box	1.5"	2.8"	.84"	.167"

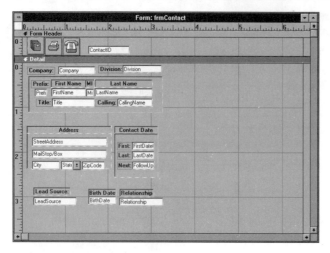

Figure 7.11 The Contacts form in Design mode.

17. Select the Form tool from the toolbar. The Contacts form, which is illustrated in Figure 7.12, will be displayed.

18. Close the form.

The Contacts form is not complete. You will return to building this form later in the chapter after you have learned how to add more controls.

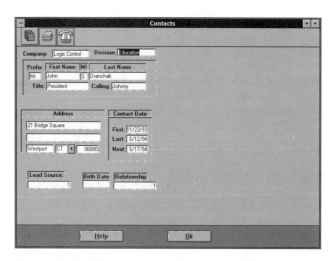

Figure 7.12 The Contacts form in Form view.

Adding Command Buttons to a Form

Command buttons are used to execute commands. When a user a clicks on a command button, an associated macro executes a series of commands. The most common command button is OK. The most common event for a command button is the click event. Command buttons can also be used to open other forms, print reports, and execute Access functions.

To add a command button to a form:

1. Select the Command button tool from the tool box. The cursor will change to a Command button cursor.
2. Draw the button on the form in its approximate position.
3. Size and move the Command button by dragging it.
4. Set the event properties in the Command button's property sheet to execute the desired macro(s).

The Color Palette

The Color Palette tool, shown in Figure 7.13, is used to change the appearance of a form and all of the controls on it. The Color Palette contains special effects for assisting in making the form more pleasing to the eye. It can alter the following properties:

- Foreground color
- Background color
- Border color
- Border special effect
- Border line thickness
- Border line style

Be aware that the Color Palette does not alter the colors of a form; rather, it alters the colors of each section of a form.

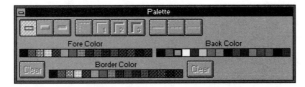

Figure 7.13 The Color Palette tool.

To use the color palette:

1. Select the control or section whose appearance you would like to alter.

2. Select the Color Palette tool from the toolbar.

3. Select a color from one of the three color palettes. For any control you can change the background, foreground, and border; for a form, you can change only the background.

4. Select a special effect, if any.

The System Maintenance Form

The System Maintenance form allows the user to access one of four tables to perform data maintenance. These tables are the data source for the combo boxes and subforms of the Contact form. The System Maintenance form has four command buttons, each of which opens another form. The OK command button is used to exit the form when updating is complete.

To build the System Maintenance form:

1. Open a blank form based on no query.

2. Add Form Header and Form Footer sections by selecting Format → Form Header/Footer.

3. Set the Visible property of the Form Header section to No. This will hide the Form Header section.

4. Increase the size of the Detail section to 3.25" wide by 2.25" high.

5. Increase the height of the Form Footer section to .5" high.

6. Select the form by clicking on the white box in the left-hand corner between the rulers.

7. Select the Property Sheet tool from the toolbar.

8. Set the values of the form properties to those listed in Table 7.7.

9. Select the Command button tool and draw a command button in the Form Footer section.

10. Copy and paste the Command button to obtain another button, and center the two buttons in the Form Footer section.

11. Set the value of the two command button properties to those listed in Table 7.8.

Table 7.7 System Maintenance Form Properties

Property	Value
Caption	System Maintenance
Default View	Single Form
Scroll Bars	Neither
Record Selectors	No
Navigation Buttons	No
AutoCenter	Yes
Autosize	Yes

Table 7.8 Property Values for the System Maintenance Form Footer Section Command Buttons

Control	Property	Value
Help Button	Name	cmdHelp
	Caption	&Help
	On Click	mcrfrmSysMaint.cmdHelp
	Left	.437"
	Top	.125"
	Width	1"
	Height	.25"
OK Button	Name	cmdOk
	Caption	&Ok
	On Click	mcrfrmSysMaint.cmdOk
	Left	1.83"
	Top	.125"
	Width	1"
	Height	.25"

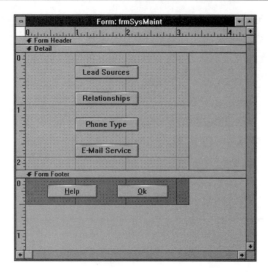

Figure 7.14 The System Maintenance form in Design view.

Note

Since none of the macros have been created, the macro name must be typed into the On Click event property. If the macro were already created, selecting the property would cause an arrow to appear, which, when clicked, would show a drop-down list of all the macros.

12. Create four command button controls and center them vertically underneath one another in the Detail section. Figure 7.14 illustrates the correct placement of the buttons.

13. Set the values for the four button properties to those listed in Table 7.9.

14. Display the Color Palette, if it is not already open.

15. Select each control listed in Table 7.10 and change its appearance to the suggested color and special effect.

16. Save the form as frmSysMaint.

17. Select the Form tool from the toolbar. The System Maintenance form, which is illustrated in Figure 7.15, will be displayed.

18. Close the form.

Table 7.9 Property Values for the System Maintenance Detail Section Command Buttons

Control	Property	Value
Lead Source Button	Name	cmdLeadsources
	Caption	Lead Sources
	On Click	mcrfrm.sysMaint.cmdLeadSources
	Left	1"
	Top	.25"
	Width	1"
	Height	.25"
Relationship Button	Name	cmdRelationships
	Caption	Relationships
	Left	1"
	Top	.75"
	Width	1"
	Height	.25"
	On Click	mcrfrmSysMaint.cmdRelationships
Phone Type Button	Name	cmdPhoneType
	Caption	Phone Type
	Left	1"
	Top	1.25"
	Width	1"
	Height	.25"
	On Click	mcrfrmSysMaint.cmdPhoneType
Email Service Button	Name	cmdEMailService
	Caption	E-Mail Service
	On Click	mcrfrmSysMaint.cmdEMailService
	Left	1"
	Top	1.75"
	Width	1"
	Height	.25"

Table 7.10 Colors of the System Maintenance Form

Control	Appearance	Special Effect
Detail Section Color	Medium Gray	
Footer Section Color	Dark Gray	
Command Button Color	Medium Gray	Raised

Figure 7.15 The System Maintenance form in Form view.

The New Call Form

The New Call form allows a user to log the date and time of a call made to a contact, and record notes from the conversation. The user presses the Start Time command button to record the start time in the call log, and the End Time command button to record the time the call concluded.

To build the New Call form:

1. Open a new form using CALL as the Record Source property of the form.
2. Add Form Header and Footer sections by clicking on Format → Form Header/Footer.
3. Reduce the Header section to .25" by dragging the lower border of the section upward.
4. Set the Form Footer section Visible property to No.
5. Increase the size of the Detail section to 6" wide by 2" high.
6. Create a text box control by dragging a ContactID field 1" from the left and 0" from the top in the Form Header section.
7. Set the value of the Name property to txtContactID.
8. Set the value of the Visible property of the ContactID control to NO.
9. Select the Rectangle tool.
10. Draw a rectangle 4.5" from the left and 0" from the top. Make the rectangle 1.5" wide by 1.83" high. Choose Dark Gray from the Color Palette for the background color .
11. In the Detail section, create six command buttons.
12. Set the values of the six buttons properties to those listed in Table 7.11.

Table 7.11 Values of the New Call Command Button Controls

Control	Property	Value
Start Button	Name	cmdStart
	Caption	&Start
	On Click	mcrfrmNewCall.cmdStart
	Left	.5"
	Top	.25"
	Width	1"
	Height	.25"
End Button	Name	cmdEnd
	Caption	&End
	On Click	mcrfrmNewCall.cmdEnd
	Left	.5"
	Top	.75"
	Width	1"
	Height	.25"
Help Button	Name	cmdHelp
	Caption	&Help
	On Click	Macro2
	Left	4.75"
	Top	.31"
	Width	1"
	Height	.25"
History Button	Name	cmdHistory
	Caption	&History
	On Click	mcrfrmNewCall.cmdHistory
	Left	4.75"
	Top	.62"
	Width	1"
	Height	.25"
Cancel Button	Name	cmdCancel
	Caption	&Cancel
	On Click	mcrfrmNewCall.cmdCancel
	Left	4.75"
	Top	.93"
	Width	1"
	Height	.25"

(continues)

Table 7.11 (*Continued*)

Control	Property	Value
OK Button	Name	cmdOk
	Caption	&Ok
	On Click	mcrfrmNewCall.cmdOk
	Left	4.75"
	Top	1.25"
	Width	1"

Table 7.12 Property Values for the New Call Form Text Box Controls

Control	Property	Value
Start Time text box	Name	txtStart
	Control Source	StartTime
	Left	.5"
	Top	.5"
	Width	1"
	Height	.167"
	Special Effect	Sunken
	Background Color	Medium Gray
End Time text box	Name	txtEnd
	Control Source	EndTime
	Left	.5"
	Top	1"
	Width	1"
	Height	.167"
	Special Effect	Sunken
	Background Color	Medium Gray
Call Length text box	Name	txtCallLength
	Control Source	=DateDiff("n",[txtStartTime], [txtEndTime])
	Left	.5"
	Top	1.41"
	Width	1"
	Height	.167"
	Special Effect	Sunken

Table 7.12 (*Continued*)

Control	Property	Value
Notes text box	Background Color	Medium Gray
	Name	txtNotes
	Control Source	Notes
	Left	1.62"
	Top	4"
	Width	2.75"
	Height	1.25"
	Special Effect	Sunken

13. In the Detail section, create four text box controls using the property values listed in Table 7.12.

14. Delete the corresponding labels.

15. Using the Label tool, create two labels. Set the labels to the properties listed in Table 7.13.

Table 7.13 New Call Label Properties

Control	Property	Value
Call Length label	Name	lblCallLength
	Caption	Call Length
	Special Effect	Sunken
	Left	.5"
	Top	1.25"
	Width	1"
	Height	.167"
	Background Color	Medium Gray
Notes label	Name	lblNotes
	Caption	Call Notes
	Special Effect	Sunken
	Left	1.62"
	Top	.25"
	Width	2.75"
	Height	.167"
	Background Color	Medium Gray

Figure 7.16 The New Call form in Design mode.

16. Compare the form just created to the New Call form in Figure 7.16, making any necessary changes.

17. Set the colors and attributes, which are listed in Table 7.14.

18. Save the file as frmNewCall.

19. Select the Form tool from the toolbar. The Call Log form, which is illustrated in Figure 7.17, will be displayed.

20. Close the form.

Table 7.14 Colors for the New Call Form		
Section	**Color**	**Special Effect**
Detail Section color	Medium Gray	
Footer Section color	Medium Gray	
Command Button color	Medium Gray	Raised
Label color	Medium Gray	Sunken
Text Box color	White	

Figure 7.17 The Call Log form in Form view.

Using a Subform Within a Form

A subform is a form within a form. They are used when there is a one-to-many relationship between tables. For example, in the WinContact application, there is a one-to-many relationship between the CONTACTS table and the CALL table. There are two ways to create a subform:

- Use the Subform tool.
- Drag and drop a form.

When the Subform tool from the toolbox is used, a subform control is drawn on the parent form, and you manually set the links by assigning the control's properties. When the drag and drop method is used, the links are automatically set.

To create a subform with the Subform tool:

1. Select the Subform control tool.
2. Click on the form at the desired location, and drag the new control to the desired size.
3. Move and size the new subform control as required.
4. Set the Name, Source Object, Link Child Fields, and Link Master Fields properties.
5. Build the form that you specified in the Source Object property.

To create a subform using the drag and drop method:

1. Create the form that you will use as the subform and save it.
2. Arrange your windows so that the form to which you want to add the subform is next to the database window, as illustrated in Figure 7.18.
3. Select the Form Tab in the Database window.
4. Drag the form that you want to use as the subform from the Database window to the parent form. Provided that theirs is a compatible field, the Link Child Fields and Link Master Fields properties will be automatically set.

The Call Log History Form

The Call Log History form gives a user the opportunity to view the dates and notes of past calls to a particular client. It contains a subform that displays notes about a particular call.

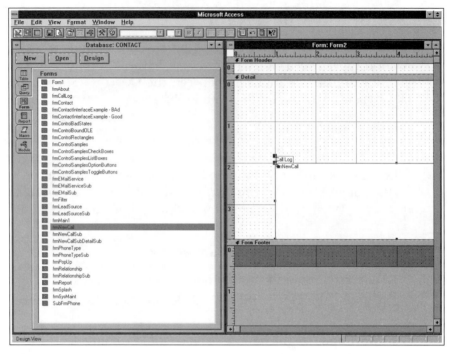

Figure 7.18 Tiled Database and Form windows.

To build the Call Log History form:

1. Open a new blank form with its record source set to CALL.
2. Set the form properties to the values listed in Table 7.15.
3. Add Form Header and Footer sections.
4. Reduce the height of the Form Header section to .31".

Table 7.15 Form Property Values for the Contacts Form	
Property	**Value**
Caption	Call Log History
Default View	Single Form
Scroll Bars	Neither
Record Selectors	No
Navigation Buttons	No

Table 7.16 Property Values for the Call History Form Label Controls

Control	Property	Value
Start Time label	Name	lblStart
	Caption	StartTime
	Left	.25"
	Top	.062"
	Width	1.25"
	Height	.167"
	Special Effect	Sunken
End Time label	Name	lblEndCaptionEndTime
	Left	1.62"
	Top	.062"
	Width	1.25"
	Height	.167"
	Special Effect	Sunken
Call Length label	Name	lblCallLength
	Caption	Length
	Left	3.06"
	Top	.062"
	Width	1.25"
	Height	.167"
	Special Effect	Sunken

5. Reduce the Detail section to .25" wide by 5" high.

6. Increase the height of the Footer section to 1.66".

7. Create three label controls in the Form Header section using the properties are listed in Table 7.16.

8. Create three text box controls in the Detail section using the properties listed in Table 7.17.

9. Delete the corresponding labels.

10. Use a Subform/Subreport tool to create a subform (Figure 7.19) in the Form Footer section using the properties listed in Table 7.18.

Table 7.17 Property Values for the Call History Form Text Box Controls

Control	Property	Value
Start Time text box	Name	txtStart
	Control Source	StartTime
	Left	.25"
	Top	.062"
	Width	1.25"
	Height	.167"
	Special Effect	Sunken
End Time text box	Name	txtEnd
	Control Source	EndTime
	Left	.1.62"
	Top	.062"
	Width	1.25"
	Height	.167"
	Special Effect	Sunken
Call Length text box	Name	txtCallLength
	Control Source	=DateDiff("n",[txtStartTime], [txtEndTime])
	Left	3.06"
	Top	.062"
	Width	1.25"
	Height	.167"
	Special Effect	Sunken

11. Delete the label.

12. Use the Color Palette to change the form and the label controls to Medium Gray.

13. Save the form as frmCallLog.

14. Select the Form tool from the toolbar. A "There is no form" error message, shown in Figure 7.20, will be displayed.

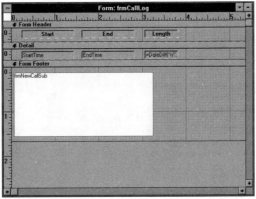

Figure 7.19 The Call Log History form with subform, in Design

Table 7.18 Property Values for the Call History Subform Control

Control	Property	Value
NewCallSubform	Name	NewCall
	Source Object	frmNewCallsub
	Link Parent field	CallID
	Link Child field	CallID
	Border Style	Clear
	Left	.06"
	Top	.125"
	Width	3.18"
	Height	1.43"
	Visible	Yes

Figure 7.20 The no form error message.

The Call Log History Subform

Before you can view the Call Log History form, you must create the subform. The Call Log History subform is used to keep track of the Note fields.

To build the Call Log History subform:

1. Open a new blank form, with a Record Source property of CALL.
2. Add Form Header and Footer sections.
3. Reduce the height of the Header section to .25" by dragging the lower border of the section upward.
4. Increase the size of the Detail section to 1.09" wide by 3.5" high.
5. Set the Form Footer section Visible property to No.
6. Drag and drop the CallID field to 0" from the left and 0" from the top, in the Form Footer section.
7. Set the Visible property to No.
8. In the Detail section, create a text box control for the Notes field.
9. Set the values of the properties of the Notes control to those in Table 7.19.
10. Delete the label.
11. Save the form as frmNewCallSub.
12. Test the Call Log History form by selecting the Form tool. The Call Log form, which is illustrated in Figure 7.21, will be displayed.

Table 7.19 Property Values for the Notes Field

Control	Property	Value
Notes	Name	txtNotes
	Control Source	frmNewCallsub
	Left	.06"
	Top	.03"
	Width	3.1"
	Height	1.03"
	Visible	Yes
	Background Color	Medium Gray
	Special Effect	Sunken

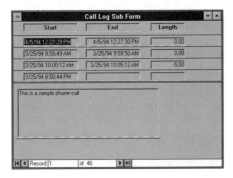

Figure 7.21 The Call Log subform in Form view.

The E-Mail Service Table Update Form

The E-mail Service form lets the user perform maintenance updates to the E-MAIL SERVICET table. It contains a subform and two command buttons.

To build the E-mail Service form:

1. Open a new blank form.
2. Add Form Header and Footer sections.
3. Set the Visible property of the Form Header section to No.
4. Expand the size of the Detail section to 3" wide by 2" high.
5. Expand the height of the Footer section to .5" high.
6. In the Detail section, use a Subform/Subreport tool to create a subform control, whose properties are listed in Table 7.20.

Table 7.20 Property Values for the E-mail Service Table Update Subform Control		
Control	**Property**	**Value**
E-mail Update subform	Name	frmEmailServicesub
	Source Object	frmEmailServicesub
	Border Style	Clear
	Left	.5"
	Top	.5"
	Width	2"
	Height	1"
	Visible	Yes

Table 7.21 Properties of the E-mail Service Form Command Buttons

Control	Property	Value
Help Button	Name	cmdHelp
	Caption	&Help
	On Click	mcrfrmEmailService.cmdHelp
	Left	.3"
	Top	.083"
	Width	1"
	Height	.25"
OK Button	Name	cmdOk
	Caption	&Ok
	On Click	mcrfrmEmailService.cmdOk
	Left	1.7"
	Top	.083"
	Width	1"
	Height	.25"

7. Delete the subform control's label.

8. Create two command buttons in the Form Footer section, using the properties listed in Table 7.21.

9. Select the colors and attributes listed in Table 7.22 from the Color Palette tool.

10. Save the form as frmEMailService.

11. Test the form when the subform is created. The E-mail Service update form, illustrated in Figure 7.22, will be displayed.

Table 7.22 Colors for the E-mail Service Form

Section	Color	Special Effect
Detail section color	Medium Gray	
Footer section color	Medium Gray	
Command button color	Medium Gray	Raised
Label color	Medium Gray	
Subform color	White	

Figure 7.22 The E-mail Service form in Form view.

Your Turn: Building the Lead Source Form

The Lead Source form allows a user to perform maintenance updates to the LEAD SOURCE table. It contains a subform and two command buttons. To build the Lead Source table update form, copy frmEmailService form and save it as frmLeadSource. Modify the control properties listed in Table 7.23. The completed form is illustrated in Figure 7.24.

Table 7.23 Properties of the Lead Source Update Form Controls		
Control	Property	Value
Lead Source subform	Name	frmLeadSourcesub
	Source Object	frmLeadSourcesub
	Border Style	Clear
	Left	.5"
	Top	.5"
	Width	2"
	Height	1"
	Visible	Yes
Help button	Name	cmdHelp
	Caption&Help	
	On Click	mcrfrmLeadSource.cmdHelp
	Left	.3"
	Top	.083"
	Width	1"
	Height	.25"

(continues)

Table 7.23 (*Continued*)

Control	Property	Value
OK button	Name	cmdExit
	Caption	&Ok
	On Click	mcrfrmLeadSource.cmdOk
	Left	1.7"
	Top	.083"
	Width	1"
	Height	.25"

Figure 7.23 The Lead Source Update Form in form view.

Your Turn: Building the Relationship Form

The Relationship form is used to perform maintenance updates to the RELA-TIONSHIP table. It contains a subform and two command buttons. To build the Relationship table update form, copy the frmEmailService form and save it as frmRelationship. Modify the control properties listed in Table 7.24. The completed form is illustrated in Figure 7.24.

Table 7.24 Properties of the Relationship Update Form Controls

Control	Property	Value
Relationship subform	Name	frmRelationshipsub
	Source Object	frmRelationshipsub
	Border Style	Clear
	Left	.5"
	Top	.5"
	Width	2"

Table 7.24 (*Continued*)		
Control	**Property**	**Value**
	Height	1"
	Visible	Yes
Help button	Name	cmdHelp
	Caption	&Help
	On Click	mcrfrm Relationship.cmdHelp
	Left	.3"
	Top	.083"
	Width	1"
	Height	.25"
OK button	Name	cmdExit
	Caption	&Ok
	On Click	mcrfrm Relationship.cmdOk
	Left	1.7"
	Top	.083"
	Width	1"
	Height	.25"

Your Turn: Building the Phone Type Form

The Phone Type Form is for performing maintenance updates to the PHONE TYPE table. It contains a subform and two command buttons. To build the Phone Type table update form, copy the frmEmailService form and save it as frmPhoneType. Modify the control properties listed in Table 7.25. The completed form is in Figure 7.25.

Figure 7.24 The Relationship form in Form view.

Table 7.25 Properties of the Phone Type Form Controls

Control	Property	Value
PhoneType subform	Name	frmPhoneTypesub
	Source Object	frmPhoneTypesub
	Border Style	Clear
	Left	.5"
	Top	.5"
	Width	2"
	Height	1"
	Visible	Yes
Help button	Name	cmdHelp
	Caption	&Help
	On Click	mcrfrm PhoneType.cmdHelp
	Left	.3"
	Top	.083"
	Width	1"
	Height	.25"
OK button	Name	cmdExit
	Caption	&Ok
	On Click	mcrfrmPhoneType.cmdOk
	Left	1.7"
	Top	.083"
	Width	1"

Figure 7.25 The Phone Type form in Form view.

The E-Mail Service Subform

The E-mail Service subform is used to display the actual EMAIL Table for as many records as there are.

To build the E-mail Service subform:

1. Open a new blank form in Design view with the Record Source property set to EMAIL_SERVICE.
2. Add Form Header and Footer sections.
3. Reduce the height of the Header section to .25" by dragging the lower border of the section upward.
4. Reduce the size of the Detail section to 1.5" wide by .25" high.
5. Using the Label control tool, add a label to the Form Header section with a caption of Service Name. Size it the same width as the form.
6. Drag and drop the ServiceID field into the Detail section.
7. Delete the ServiceID Label.
8. Drag and drop the Service field into the Detail section on top of the ServiceID field so that it completely hides it.
9. Delete the Service label.

> **Note**
>
> This keeps the complete table open during the updating process, but it does not appear as though it is.

10. Change the Name properties of both text box controls to reflect correct naming conventions.
11. Save the file as frmEmailServiceSub.
12. Select the Form tool from the toolbar. The E-mail Service subform, which is illustrated in Figure 7.26, will be displayed.

Figure 7.26 The E-mail Service subform in Form view.

Figure 7.27 The Lead Sources subform in Form view.

Your Turn: Building the Lead Sources Subform

The Lead Sources subform is used to display and allow updating of the LEAD SOURCES table. To build the Lead Sources subform, copy the frmEmailService-sub form and save it as frmLeadSourceSub. Set the Record Source property to LEAD_SOURCE. Replace the ServiceID and Service fields with the LeadSourceID and LeadSource fields. The completed form is shown in Figure 7.27.

Your Turn: Building the Relationship Subform

The Relationship subform is used to display and allow updating of the RELA-TIONSHIP table. To build the Relationship subform, copy the frmEmailService-sub form and save it as frmRelationshipSub. Set the Record Source property to RELATIONSHIP. Replace the ServiceID and Service fields with the Relation-shipID and Relationship fields. The completed form is shown in Figure 7.28.

Your Turn: Building the Phone Type Subform

The Phone Type subform displays and allows updating of the PHONE_TYPE table. To build the Phone Type subform, copy the frmEmailServicesub form and save it as frmPhoneTypeSub. Set the Record Source property to PHONE_TYPE. Replace the ServiceID and Service fields with the TypeID and Type fields. The completed form is shown in Figure 7.29.

Figure 7.28 The Relationship subform in Form view.

Figure 7.29 The Phone Type subform in Form view.

Option Groups

An option group, which you can see in Figure 7.30, is used to give the user alternatives. Instead of typing or choosing from a drop-down list, a user can simply click on an option, then click on a command button to execute that option. An option group is a box that surrounds a group of option buttons, check boxes, or toggle buttons. When using an option group all the button controls have an Option Value property associated with them, and each button is assigned a unique value that is utilized in the executed macro.

To build an option group:

1. Select the Option Group tool from the toolbox.
2. Click on the selected field to bind it to the option group.
3. Drag the selected field to the form.
4. Move and size the option group on the form.
5. Select the Option button tool.
6. Draw an Option button control by clicking and dragging the control on the form over an option group. Notice that when you move the cursor over an option group, it is highlighted.
7. Move and size the Option button.

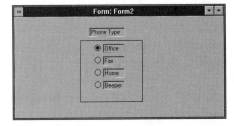

Figure 7.30 Using an option group on a form.

8. Assign a value to the button's Option Value property.

9. Repeat steps 6 through 8 for each button.

List Boxes

List boxes are a unique way to add data to a table/query or select data from a table/query. A list box displays choices in either a single column or multicolumn format, and the amount of information is limited by the predefined size of the box. It is important to remember that a list box will not accept input that is not in the underlying list. The two most common types of list boxes are:

- List boxes based on a table/query.
- List Boxes based on a value list.

The unique properties of list boxes are given in Table 7.26.

Creating a list box is a four-step process:

1. Click on the List Box tool in the toolbox.

2. Click on the selected field to bind it to the option group.

3. Drag the field onto the form. When you release the mouse, the control will be added.

4. Set the values of the properties.

The Report Form

The Report form lets the user select the report they would like to run. An advanced option of this form is that a hidden list box will appear when the

Table 7.26 Unique Properties of a List Box	
Property	Description
Name	Name of the list box.
Row source type	The type of data source
Row source	Actual table/query name
Column count	Number of fields in the list box.
Column header	Determine the display of column header names.
Column widths	Widths of each column in inches
Bound column	The column bound to the table/query.

Table 7.27 Form Property Values for the Contact Form

Property	Value
Record source	
Caption	Reports
Default view	Single Form
Scroll bars	Neither
Record selectors	No
Navigation buttons	No

Phone History Report option is selected. The user then selects a contact name from the list box, and the report is executed.

To create a Report form:

1. Open a new blank form.
2. Set the form properties to the values listed in Table 7.27.
3. Add Form Header and Footer sections.
4. Set the Visible property of the Form Header section to No.
5. Expand the size of the Detail section to 7" wide by 3.5" high.
6. Expand the height of the Footer section to .5" high.
7. Use the Option Group tool to build an option group containing all the report choices. Start the option group at .5" from the left and .25" from the top. Size the option group 2.75" wide by 3" high.
8. Select the Option Button tool and add an option button at .5" from the left of the option group border.
9. Select the Option Button control and give it a value of 1 in the Option Value property.
10. Set the Caption property of the associated label control to Sorted By Contact Last Name.
11. Repeat steps 6 through 9 for each option button listed in Table 7.28. Refer to Figure 7.31 for a comparison.
12. Appropriately space the option buttons and their corresponding labels using either the drag and drop methods, the property value method, or the Format → VerticalSpacing command.
13. Use the List Box tool to create a list box.

Table 7.28 Option Button Controls for the Report Form		
Option Button	**Option Value**	**Label Caption**
2	2	Sorted By Contact Postal Code
3	3	Sorted By Contact State
4	4	Sorted By Contact Lead Source
5	5	Sorted By Contact Relationship
6	6	Not Contacted In 30 Days
7	7	Not Contacted In 60 Days
8	8	Contact Today
9	9	Contact Tomorrow
10	10	Mail Labels
11	11	Phone Log History By Client

14. Set the values of the list box's properties to those in Table 7.29.
15. Move the associated label so that it that starts .25" down from the top and 4.12" from the left. The label should be 2.25" wide and .25" high.
16. Set the Caption property to Client Last Name.
17. Create three command buttons in the Form footer section.
18. Set the values of the three button properties to those listed in Table 7.30.
19. Set the colors and attributes listed in Table 7.31.
20. Save the form as frmReport.
21. Select the Form tool from the toolbar. The Reports form in Figure 7.32 will be displayed.

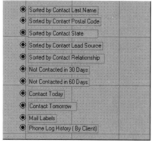

Figure 7.31 The Report Selection form option group in Design

Table 7.29 Properties of the Report Form List Box Control

Control	Property	Value
Name list box	Name	lstRepName
	Source Object	frm PhoneType sub
	Left	4.12"
	Top	.5"
	Width	2.25"
	Height	2.75"
	Visible	Yes
	Name	RepName
	Row Source Type	Table/Query
	Row Source	Select [Name] From [qryreplstname];
	Column Count	1
	Column Header	No
	Column Width	1.5"
	Bound Column	1
	Visble	No
	Special Effect	Sunken
	BackColor	Medium Gray

Table 7.30 Values of the Report Form Command Button Controls

Control	Property	Value
Close button	Name	cmdExit
	Caption	&Close
	On Click	mcrfrmReport.cmdClose
	Left	.31"
	Top	.125"
	Width	1"
	Height	.25"

(continues)

Table 7.30 (*Continued*)

Control	Property	Value
Print button	Name	cmdPrint
	Caption	&Print
	On Click	mcrfrmReport.cmdPrint
	Left	1.37"
	Top	.125"
	Width	1"
	Height	.25"
Preview button	Name	cmdPreview
	Caption	Pre&view
	On Click	mcrfrmReport.cmdPreview
	Left	2.43"
	Top	.125"
	Width	1"
	Height	.25"

Toggle Buttons

A Toggle button behaves the same as an option button, in that it allows the user to make a mutually exclusive choice from a list. The only difference is in appearance. A toggle button appears pressed when selected and unpressed when not selected. It has all the properties of the option button except one: A toggle

Table 7.31 Colors for the Report Form

Section	Color	Special Effect
Header section color	Medium Gray	
Detail section color	Medium Gray	
Footer section color	Medium Gray	
Command button color	Medium Gray	Raised
Label color	Medium Gray	
List box color	White Sunken	

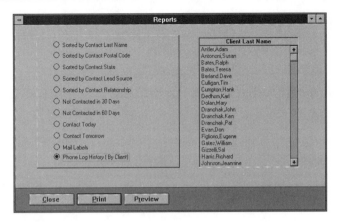

Figure 7.32 The Reports form in Form view.

button can have a caption or a picture on it. Toggle buttons also are created in four steps:

1. Select the Toggle button tool.
2. Move the cursor over the option group. The option group becomes highlighted.
3. Click and drag to draw the toggle button control.
4. Set the toggle button's properties.

Adding Pictures to Toggle and Command Buttons

As noted, toggle and command buttons have a Picture property. The Picture Builder, shown in Figure 7.33, allows the user to select a picture from the list or from a separate file. Clicking on the Picture property and then clicking on the Build button will bring up the Picture Builder menu.

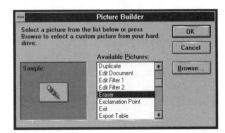

Figure 7.33 The Picture Builder.

To add a picture to a toggle or command button:

1. Select the Picture property of the button.
2. Select the Build button. The Builder will appear.
3. Select a picture from the Available pictures list box.
4. Select OK.

The Main Form

The Main form lets the user select contacts and choose which other forms they would like to view.

To build the Main form:

1. Open a new blank form with the Record Source property set to qryContactName.
2. Add Form Header and Footer sections.
3. Reduce the height of the Header section to .5" by dragging the lower border of the section upward.
4. Increase the size of the Detail section to 4" wide by 4" high.
5. Increase the height of the Footer section to .5".
6. Create five command buttons in the Form Header section.
7. Set the values of the properties of the command buttons to those listed in Table 7.32.

Table 7.32 Properties of the WinContact Main Form Command Buttons		
Control	**Property**	**Value**
Contact button	Name	cmdContact
	Caption	Contacts
	Picture	Person
	On Click	mcrfrmMain1.Contacts
	Left	.0"
	Top	.0"
	Width	.4"
	Height	.4"

(continues)

Table 7.32 (*Continued*)

Control	Property	Value
Add Contact button	Name	cmdAddContact
	Caption	AddContact
	Picture	Plus symbol
	On Click	mcrfrmReport.cmdAddContact
	Left	.4"
	Top	.0"
	Width	.4"
	Height	.4"
Reports button	Name	cmdReport
	Caption	Cascading Reports
	Picture	Books
	On Click	mcrfrmMain1.cmdReport
	Left	.8"
	Top	0"
	Width	.4"
	Height	.4"
System Maintenance button	Name	cmdSysMaint
	Caption	SysMaint
	Picture	Wrench
	On Click	mcrfrmMain1.cmdSysMaint
	Left	1.2"
	Top	0"
	Width	.4"
	Height	.25"
Phone Log button	Name	cmdPhoneLog
	Caption	Phone Log
	Picture	Phone1
	On Click	mcrfrmMain1.cmdPhoneLog
	Left	1.6"
	Top	0"
	Width	.4"
	Height	.4"

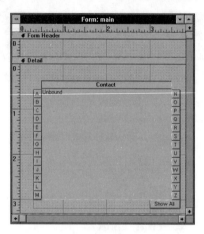

Figure 7.34 Toggle buttons on the Main form.

8. Use the Option Group tool to build an option group that will hold all the letters of the alphabet. Start the option group at .5" from the left and .25" from the top. Size the option group 3.5" wide by 3" high.

9. Click on the Toggle button tool.

10. Place a toggle button in the upper left corner of the option group border. Size it to .2" wide by .2" high.

11. Copy and paste the toggle button 26 times, placing each button down the side of the option group, directly underneath one another. Make sure that there are 13 on the left side and 13 on the right side, as illustrated in Figure 7.34.

12. Place a toggle button in the lower right corner of the option group border. Size it to .7" wide by .2" high.

13. Set the values of the toggle buttons on the left side of the option group to the values listed in Table 7.33.

14. Set the values of the toggle buttons on the right side of the option group to the values listed in Table 7.34.

15. Create a list box using the values in Table 7.35. There is no Row Source property, because it will be set dynamically.

16. Move the associated label so that it starts .25" from the top and .5" from the left. Size the label so that it is 3" wide and .25" high.

17. Set the label's Caption property to Contacts.

Table 7.33 Values for the Left Option Buttons of the WinContact Main Form

Name	Caption	On Mouse Down
A	A	mcrfrmMain1.Filter_A
B	B	mcrfrmMain1.Filter_B
C	C	mcrfrmMain1.Filter_C
D	D	mcrfrmMain1.Filter_D
E	E	mcrfrmMain1.Filter_E
F	F	mcrfrmMain1.Filter_F
G	G	mcrfrmMain1.Filter_G
H	H	mcrfrmMain1.Filter_H
I	I	mcrfrmMain1.Filter_I
J	J	mcrfrmMain1.Filter_J
K	K	mcrfrmMain1.Filter_K
L	L	mcrfrmMain1.Filter_L
M	M	mcrfrmMain1.Filter_M

Table 7.34 Values for the Right Option Buttons of the Wincontact Main Form

Name	Caption	On Mouse Down
N	N	mcrfrmMain1.Filter_N
O	O	mcrfrmMain1.Filter_O
P	P	mcrfrmMain1.Filter_P
Q	Q	mcrfrmMain1.Filter_Q
R	R	mcrfrmMain1.Filter_R
S	S	mcrfrmMain1.Filter_S
T	T	mcrfrmMain1.Filter_T
U	U	mcrfrmMain1.Filter_U
V	V	mcrfrmMain1.Filter_V
W	W	mcrfrmMain1.Filter_W
X	X	mcrfrmMain1.Filter_X
Y	Y	mcrfrmMain1.Filter_Y
Z	Z	mcrfrmMain1.Filter_Z
Show All	Show All	mcrfrmMain1.Filter_All

Table 7.35 Property Values for List Box in WinContact Main Form

Property	Value
Name	lstContact
Row source type	Table/Query
Row source	
Column count	3
Column header	No
Column width	Left.5"
Top	.5"
Width	3"
Height	2.5"
Bound column	
Visible	No
Special effect	Sunken

18. Create two command buttons in the Form Footer section.
19. Set the values of the properties of the command buttons to those listed in Table 7.36.

Table 7.36 Properties of the WinContact Main Form Command Buttons

Control	Property	Value
Exit button	Name	cmdExit
	Caption	E&xit
	On Click	mcrfrmMain1.cmdExit
	Left	.0"
	Top	.0"
	Width	1"
	Height	.25"
Help button	Name	cmdHelp
	Caption	&Help
	On Click	mcrfrmMain1.cmdHelp
	Left	1.6"
	Top	0"
	Width	1"
	Height	.25"

Table 7.37 Colors for the WinContact Main Form		
Section	Color	Special Effects
Detail section color	Medium Gray	
Footer section color	Medium Gray	
Command button color	Medium Gray	Raised
Label color	Medium Gray	
List box color	White	Sunken

20. Select the colors and attributes listed in Table 7.37 from the Color Palette tool.

21. Save the form as frmMain1.

22. Select the Form tool from the toolbar. The Main form, illustrated in Figure 7.35, will be displayed.

Utilizing Combo Boxes

Combo boxes are exactly like list boxes with these two additional capabilities:

- Users can update them interactively.
- They can reduce space taken up on the form when not selected.

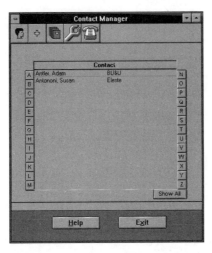

Figure 7.35 The completed main form.

There are several controls on the Contacts form that can take advantage of the combo boxes:

- Company
- Prefix
- State
- Relationship
- Lead Source

To finish the Contacts form:

1. Open frmContact in Design mode.
2. Create three command buttons in the Form Header section.
3. Set the values of the properties of the command buttons to those listed in Table 7.38.

Table 7.38 Properties of the Contacts Form Command Buttons Form Header section

Control	Property	Value
Reports button	Name	cmdReport
	Caption	Report
	Picture	Books
	On Click	mcrfrmContacts.cmdReport
	Left	0"
	Top	0"
	Width	.4"
	Height	.4"
Print Form button	Name	cmdPrint
	Caption	Print Form
	Picture	Printer
	On Click	mcrfrmContacts.cmdPrint
	Left	.4"
	Top	0"
	Width	.4"
	Height	.25"

(continues)

Table 7.38 (*Continued*)

Control	Property	Value
Phone Log button	Name	cmdPhoneLog
	Caption	Phone Log
	Picture	Phone1
	On Click	mcrfrmContacts.cmdPhoneLog
	Left	.8"
	Top	0"
	Width	.4"
	Height	.4"

4. Delete the following text boxes from the form: Company Name, Prefix, State Relationship, and LeadSource.

5. Use the Combo Box tool to create five combo boxes.

6. Set the values of the properties of the command buttons to those listed in Table 7.39.

Table 7.39 Properties of the Contacts Form Combo Boxes

Control	Property	Value
Company combo	Name	cmbCompany
	Control Source	Company
	Row Source Type	Table/Query
	Row Source	Select[Company],[ContactID] From[Contacts]
	Column Count	2
	ColumnWidth	1", 0"
	Bound Column	1
	Left	.78"
	Top	.07"
	Width	.96"
	Height	.167"

(continues)

Table 7.39 (*Continued*)

Control	Property	Value
Prefix combo	Name	cmbPrefix
	Control Source	Prefix
	Row Source Type	Value List
	Row Source	Mr;Mrs;Ms;Dr
	Column Count	1
	Bound Column	1
	Left	.23"
	Top	.58"
	Width	.4"
	Height	.167"
State combo	Name	cmbState
	Control Source	State
	Row Source Type	Table/Query
	Row Source	Select STATE_ABRE from STATES order by STATE_ABRE
	Column Count	1
	Column, Widths	.5"
	Bound Column	1
	Left	.91"
	Top	2.2"
	Width	.44"
	Height	.167"
Relationship combo	Name	cmbRelationship
	Control Source	Relationship
	Row Source	TypeTable/Query
	Row Source	Select [RelationshipID],[Relationship] From[RELATIONSHIP]
	Column Count	2
	Column, Widths	0"; .625"
	Bound Column	1
	Left	1.5"
	Top	2.8"

Table 7.39 (*Continued*)

Control	Property	Value
	Width	.84"
	Height	.167"
Lead Source combo	Name	cmbLeadSource
	Control Source	LeadSource
	Row Source Type	Table/Query
	Row Source	LEAD_SOURCE
	Column Count	2
	Column, Widths	0";.625"
	Bound Column	1
	Left	.12"
	Top	3"
	Width	1.3"
	Height	.167"

7. In the Detail section, use the Subform/Subreport tool to create a subform that is 3" wide by 1" high starting 3.375" from the left and .25" from the top.

8. Set the values of the subform's properties to those listed in Table 7.40.

9. In the Detail section, use the Subform/Subreport tool to create a subform that is 3" wide by .62" high starting 3.375" from the left and 1.55" from the top.

10. Set the values of the subform properties to those listed in Table 7.41.

11. Drag and drop the Notes field into the Detail section.

Table 7.40 Property Values of the Phone Subform

Property	Value
Name	SubPhone
Source object	SubFrmPhone
Link child fields	ContactID
Link master fields	ContactID

Table 7.41 Property Values of the E-mail Subform

Property	Value
Name	EMail
Source object	frmEMailSub
Link child fields	ContactID
Link master fields	ContactID

12. Size the field to 3.1" wide by 1.1" high., starting 2.56" from the top and 3.375" from the left.

13. Drag the Notes label over the Notes field. Position the label 3.75" from the left and 4.22" from the top. Size the label to .13" high by 3.1" wide.

14. Set the Notes label's Special Effect property to Sunken.

15. Create two command buttons in the Form Footer section.

16. Set the values of the properties of the command buttons to those listed in Table 7.42.

Table 7.42 Properties of the Build Email Subform Command Buttons

Control	Property	Value
OK button	Name	cmdOk
	Caption	&Ok
	On Click	mcrfrmContact.cmdOk
	Left	3.51"
	Top	.125"
	Width	1"
	Height	.25"
Help button	Name	cmdHelp
	Caption	&Help
	On Click	mcrfrmContact.cmdHelp
	Left	1.48"
	Top	.125"
	Width	1"
	Height	.25"

Table 7.43 Colors for the Contacts Form		
Section	Color	Special Effect
Detail section color	Medium Gray	
Footer section color	Medium Gray	
Command button color	Medium Gray	Raised
Label color	Medium Gray	
Combo box color	White	Sunken

17. Set the colors and attributes listed in Table 7.43.

18. Save the form.

19. Test the form after completing the subforms. The completed Contacts form is illustrated in Figure 7.36.

The Contact E-Mail Subform

The Contact E-mail subform is used to display the E-mail addresses and services a contact has. A subform is used because there is a one-to-many relationship between contacts and E-mail services. The number of services a contact can have also varies; some may have one, while others may have five. The use of a subform allows for maximum flexibility in this variable.

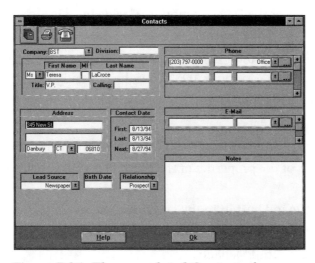

Figure 7.36 The completed Contacts form.

Table 7.44 Properties of the E-Mail Subform Combo Boxes		
Control	Property	Value
Service combo	Name	1stEMailService
	Control Source	Service
	Row Source Type	Table/Query
	Row Source	E_MAIL_SERVICE
	Column Count	2
	ColumnWidth	0"; 1"
	Bound Column	1
	Left	1.62"
	Top	.06"
	Width	.96"
	Height	.167"
	Special Effect	Sunken

To build the Contact E-mail subform:

1. Open a new blank form.
2. Set the Default View property of the form to Continuous.
3. Reduce the size of the Detail section to 3" wide by .35" high.
4. Set the Detail section's background color property to Medium Gray.
5. Drag and drop the Address field into the Detail section. Make it 1.45" wide by .18" high. Position it .093" from the left and .06" from the top.
6. Set the Address text box control's Special Effect property to Sunken.
7. Delete the Address label.
8. Use the Combo Box tool to create a combo box in the Detail section.
9. Set the values of the properties of the combo box to those listed in Table 7.44.
10. Create a command button in the Detail section.
11. Set the button's properties to those listed in Table 7.45.
12. Save the form as frmEMailSub.

Table 7.45 Build Mail Command Button Properties

Property	Value
Name	cmdBuildMailType
Caption	...
Left	2.57"
Top	.047"
Width	.285"
Height	.20"
On Click	mcrfrmContacts.cmdBuildService

13. Select the Form tool from the toolbar. The Build E-mail Service form, in Figure 7.37, will be displayed.

14. Close the form.

The Contact Phone Subform

The Contact Phone subform is used to display the phone numbers, extensions, and phone types for a contact. The subform also provides flexibility by allowing a contact to have a variety of phone numbers associated with him or her.

To build the Contact Phone subform:

1. Open a new blank form based on the PHONE table.

2. Reduce the size of the Detail section to 3" wide by .35" high.

Figure 7.37 The completed Build E-mail subform.

3. Set the form's Default View property to Continuous forms.

4. Set the form's background color to Medium Gray.

5. Drag and drop the Number field into the Detail section. Make it .92" wide by .167" high. Position it .093" from the left and .06" from the top.

6. Set the Number text box control Special Effect property to Sunken.

7. Delete the Number label.

8. Assign to the Input mask property of the Number text box the following expression:

```
!\(999")"000\-0000;;""
```

9. Drag and drop the Extension field into the Detail section. Make it .39" wide by .18" high. Position it 1.12" from the left and .06" from the top.

10. Set the Extension text box control Special Effect property to Sunken.

11. Delete the Extension label.

12. Use the Combo Box tool to create combo boxes.

13. Set the values of the properties of the combo boxes to those listed in Table 7.46.

14. Create a command button in the Detail section.

Table 7.46 Properties of the Contacts Form Combo Boxes		
Control	**Property**	**Value**
Type combo	Name	lstPhoneType
	Control Source	Type
	Row Source Type	Table/Query
	Row Source	PHONE_TYPE
	Column Count	2
	Column, Widths	0"; 1"
	Bound Column	1
	Left	1.62"
	Top	.06"
	Width	.96"
	Height	.167"
	Special Effect	Sunken

Table 7.47 Build Phone Button

Property	Value
Name	cmdBuildPhoneType
Caption	...
Left	2.57"
Top	.047"
Width	.285"
Height	.20"
On Click	mcrfrmContacts.cmdBuildPhone

Figure 7.38 The completed Build Phone Type form.

15. Set the button's properties to those listed in Table 7.47.

16. Save the form as frmPhoneSub.

17. Select the Form tool from the toolbar. The Build Phone Type form, which is illustrated in Figure 7.38, will be displayed.

Congratulations! You have now completed all of the forms.

Chapter 8

Reports

In traditional applications development, one of the most time-consuming aspects was report creation. Third- and forth-generation languages required development teams to work with users to "spec" reports on paper. This was a very laborious task because each character had to be accurately positioned in the report record, and the process had to be repeated for each report in the application. And, because reports often go through an iterative process of design, every time a change was required, all the characters had to be remapped to the report.

Microsoft Access uses a different approach. By providing the user with a graphical interface, the user can place and format information right on the screen. Chapter 7 introduced the concept of direct manipulation, which reduces the time it takes to develop reports, and increases user satisfaction with the result because changes can take place very quickly. The user can also be present while the reports are being created and (or) modified.

This chapter discusses the features and uses of the Microsoft Access Report Wizards and Report Design window to create reports, and utilizes the WinContact application to demonstrate this. You will learn:

- What a report is.
- Why you use reports.
- The types of reports.
- How to modify reports.

- How to create a report that accepts input from a form.
- How to create a report that uses a grouping function.

What Is a Report?

Reports are utilized to provide static information to an end user. A report can be a reformat of a raw data table, a subset of a data table, or some combination of the two. Usually, it is based on some user-specified criteria. A report is often used in a situation that is not conducive to viewing the information on-line. For instance, perhaps the end user is not computer literate, or there is too much information to fit on a standard monitor, or the information is needed where a computer is not available (such as a meeting). As information processing technology improves, there may be no need for paper reports, but currently, they are still the preferred method in most business scenarios.

Types of Reports

There are five types of standard reports that can be created with Access:

- Tabular
- Single-column
- Grouping
- Mail Labels
- Summary

A tabular report, illustrated in Figure 8.1, is one of the most common reports. Each record is displayed on one report line, and sometimes, certain fields are totaled or arithmetically manipulated at the end. Because a tabular report is a condensed listing on a single line, it is easier for the user to read. Unfortunately, when the design requires for formatting a large amount of report information, the tabular report may be too restrictive, because all of the data may not fit on one line of a page. In this case, using the tabular report would cause an overflow onto the next line, and the report becomes cluttered and headings don't line up.

A single-column report (Figure 8.2) is utilized for a simple report that may have a very long record or because it looks better in a multilined single-column group. A single-column report is easy to design because proper spacing of controls is not as critical as in a tabular report; conversely, it can be hard for the user to actually use the report. Single-column reports often contain one record per page.

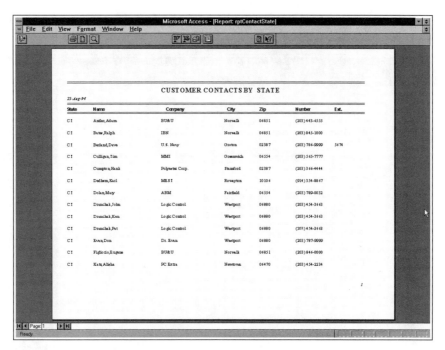

Figure 8.1   A tabular report.

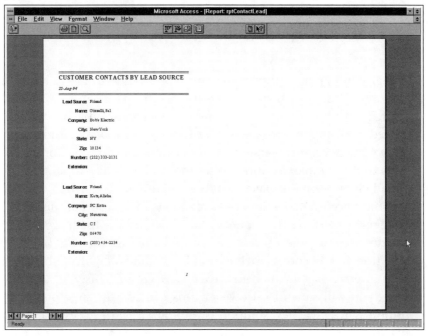

Figure 8.2   A single-column report.

287

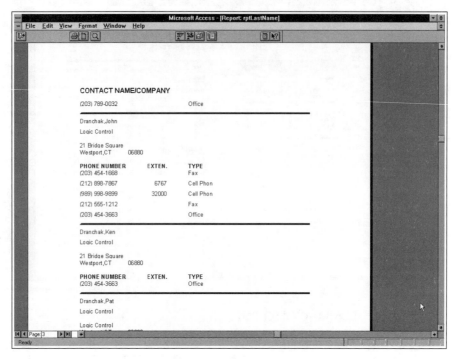

Figure 8.3 A grouping report.

A grouping report, shown in Figure 8.3, is used to group and sometimes to total sets of data with the same criteria. Grouping can also be used to "nest" related records underneath a master record. For example, transactions could be nested underneath a master account record for a bank customer. This format allows the developer some additional flexibility in report formatting, but also adds to the complexity and development time. A developer will often need to spend time resolving page-breaking requirements on this type of report. A common occurrence in grouping reports is for a group of subrecords to span a page break. As such, the parent record is left on the first page and the children on the second page. Access has several options for correcting this kind of situation, but, of course, each option has a trade-off. One of the simpler options is to insert a page break before each new group. This will satisfy most of the cases you will run into. However, this can use up large quantities of paper unnecessarily. The best solution is to program with Access Basic. Then, before placing a new report group on a page, the actual lines left on the page are

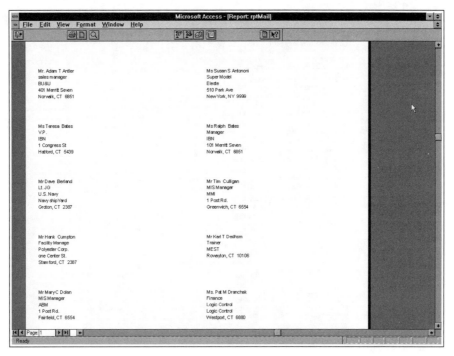

Figure 8.4 A mail label report.

analyzed via a counter, the number of records in the group are analyzed from the query, and a decision is made within the logic as to whether this group should be placed on the current page or be moved to a new page. For example, if you have a group with three records in it and two lines left on the page, it would be best to place the group on the new page.

A mail label report, a sample of which is illustrated in Figure 8.4, is used to create mailing labels and multicolumn reports. Utilizing a multicolumn design can make record comparison easier. A common example of a multicolumn design is a phone book. The Mailing Labels Report Wizard has page setup definitions that support many standard Avery labels.

A summary report, shown in Figure 8.5, provides totals for groups of records. For example, this format could be used to show a one-page executive report for the number of sales of a product in Idaho. It differs from a grouping report in that it would not display the individual grouped records on the printed report. A summary report is a type of group report.

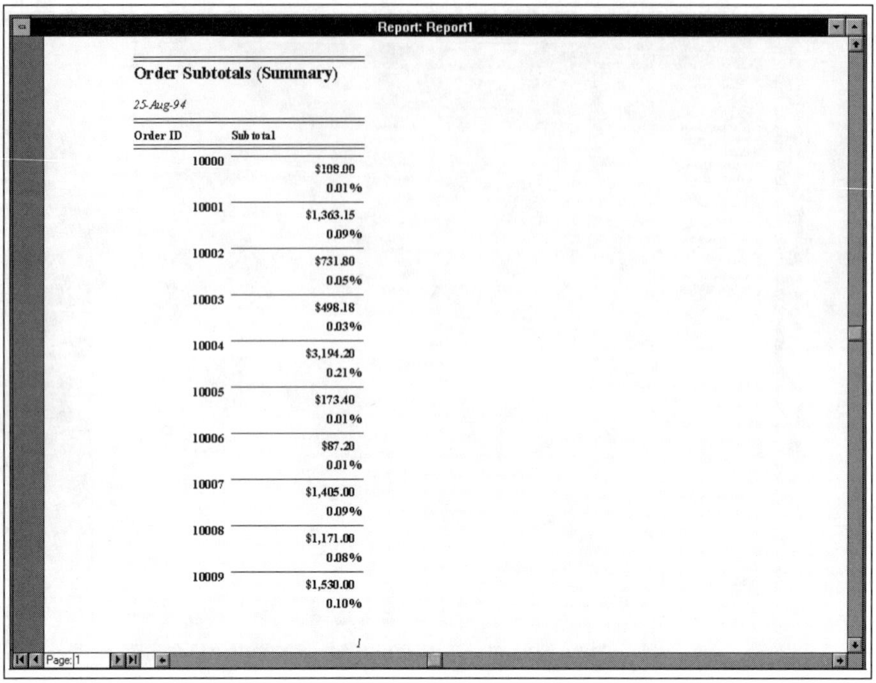
Report: Report1
Order Subtotals (Summary)
25-Aug-94
Order ID
Subtotal
10000
$108.00
0.01%
10001
$1,363.15
0.09%
10002
$731.80
0.05%
10003
$498.18
0.03%
10004
$3,194.20
0.21%
10005
$173.40
0.01%
10006
$87.20
0.01%
10007
$1,405.00
0.09%
10008
$1,171.00
0.08%
10009
$1,530.00
0.10%
1
Page: 1

Figure 8.5 A summary report.

In the WinContact application you will be creating 11 reports that utilize four out of five of these formats, which are identified in the following lists.

Tabular Reports

Customer Contact List by Zip Code

Customer Contact List by State

Customers Not Contacted in the Last 30 Days

Customers Not Contacted in the Last 60 Days

Customers Who Need Calls Today

Customers Who Need Calls Tomorrow

Single-Column Reports

Customer Contact List by Lead Source

Customer Contact List by Relationship

Grouping Reports

Customer Contacts by Last Name

Customer Contact History

Mailing Labels

Customer Mail Labels

Building Reports

The flexibility of Microsoft Access allows the user a variety of options when building a report. Simple reports can be built using the Report Wizards. Complex reports, however, must be built from scratch in the Report Design window. Both of these processes are called constructive editing, which is defined for our purposes as constructing a product from the ground up. Sometimes it can be beneficial to use a wizard to roughly format a report and then modify it in the Report Design window. This process is called deconstructive editing. Deconstructive editing provides both speed and flexibility for report creation.

In Chapter 7, good design practices were discussed in relation to creating forms. Report design follows these same general rules. LaCroce's three report design rules are:

- Place information in the report window in the order of importance.
- Group like information.
- Use multiple reports, if necessary.

Placement of report information is from left to right and top to bottom of a printed report page, with the most important or controlling information in the upper left portion of the report. Each data item is placed according to its importance. The same rule applies for placing data in a vertical manner. Additionally, information should be grouped together where relationships exist. For example, the address-related fields of a contact are generally placed together on a report. Finally, it is very important to make sure that the report contains only appropriate information. Always refer to the design specification so as not to lose sight of the objective of the particular report. A common mistake of both users and developers is to add unrelated information to an existing report because they didn't have the resources to build another report. The nature of Access precludes this happening.

As stated, Microsoft Access has a set of powerful report generators called the Report Wizards, which corresponds to the five report types: tabular, single-column, grouping, mail labels, and summary. You will be using the Report Wizards to start most of the reports that you need to create. Each report can then be modified for a more customized look by toggling into the Report Design window and using deconstructive editing.

To build a report with a Report Wizard:

1. Open a new report in Report Wizards mode.
2. Choose a table or query against which to execute the report.
3. Select the appropriate Report Wizard.
4. Select the fields to be placed in the report.
5. Select the sort order and grouping, if necessary.
6. Select the layout of the report.
7. Enter a title for the repor.t
8. Run the report.
9. Save the report.

Note that, in step 4, you must select the fields that you want displayed on the report. Each field will be displayed in the order that you place it in the list box. To place a field into the report, select a field in the Available fields list box and select the > button or double-click on the field. The field is then placed in the Field order on report list box, as illustrated in Figure 8.6. To remove a field from the report, select the field in the Field order on report list box and select the < button. The field is then placed back in the Available fields list box.

Note

To add all of the fields, use the >> button. To remove all the fields, use the << button.

To navigate through the Report Wizard, use the buttons shown on the bottom of the screen in Figure 8.6. They allow the user to go forward one screen, backward one screen, cancel the report, and finish the report.

If you selected Grouping, the Reports Wizard now asks which field(s) should be used for sorting. Select the fields in the order that you want Access to sort

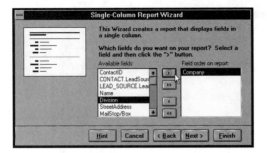

Figure 8.6 Placing a field into the Field order list box.

on. The first field selected will be the primary sort key; the second field will be the secondary sort key. This process works by sorting all the records by the primary sort key. When two or more records have the same primary sort key, they are then sorted by the secondary sort key.

The Report Wizard next gives you a choice of the type of formatting you will use for your report. You will need to select:

- A style
- Page layout as Portrait or Landscape
- Line Spacing

Lastly, the Report Wizard, as illustrated in Figure 8.7, will ask you:

- For a title.
- If you want to fit all of the fields on one page.
- If you want to open Cue Cards.
- Whether you want to run the report or see it in Design mode.

Figure 8.7 The Report Wizard final screen.

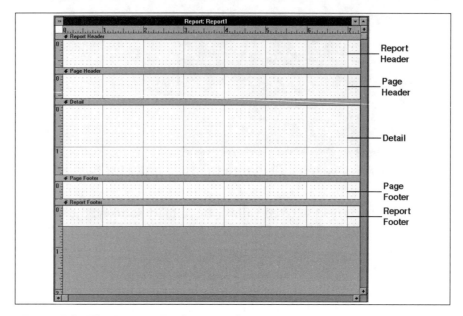

Figure 8.8 The Report Design window.

The Report Design Window

The Report Design window allows you to use Windows drag and drop capabilities to quickly build and edit reports. The first thing you will notice (see Figure 8.8) is that the actual window of the report is divided into five sections:

- Report Header
- Page Header
- Detail
- Page Footer
- Report Footer

The Report Header section appears once at the beginning of the report and usually contains the title of the report and the date. This is also the place to indicate any other types of fields that you want to appear at the beginning. The Page Header section specifies the titles/text or other objects that should appear at the top of every page. The Detail section displays the actual fields/text that will appear in each record. The Page Footer section specifies the text that will appear at the bottom of every page (including page numbers). The Report Footer section specifies the text/fields that will appear once at the end of the report.

The Report Design window also contains horizontal and vertical rulers. When you select a field and move it, a guideline on each of the corresponding rulers shifts correspondingly. This makes accurately aligning fields very easy and ensures that all fields will line up on the screen. Additionally, there are several tools that can assist in building or modifying a report. The four most common are:

- Toolbox
- Color Palette
- Property Sheet
- Field List

Hint

Turn the rulers on and off by selecting View → Ruler while in Design mode.

Chapter 7 discussed the most common implements in the toolbox for designing forms. Essentially, the report tools are exactly the same, although it would not make sense to use some of the controls, such as a combo box on a report. Microsoft has added pop-up Tool Tips for all tools to help identify them for the user. Simply move the mouse pointer over the tool in question and wait. A yellow label appears with the name of the tool. Familiarize yourself with these tools.

The Color Palette is used to set the visual properties of objects, including:

- Foreground Color
- Background Color
- Border Color
- Border Weight
- Border Style

You learned about the Property Sheet in detail in Chapter 7. Report properties are very similar to form properties. Since most reports are used just to format data in a presentable manner, you may find that you don't spend much development time on report properties. The moving and sizing functions are usually done with a mouse. Some of the most common properties of a report are shown in Table 8.1. Sections also have their own set of properties, and the

Table 8.1 Report Properties	
Property	Description
Record Source	Identifies the query or table the report is based on.
Caption	Text that appears in the title bar of the Report window.
Menu Bar	Identifies which menu options will be displayed when the report is run.
On Open	Identifies what will happen on opening the form.
On Close	Identifies what will happen on closing the form.

most common are listed in Table 8.2. As you know from Chapter 7, controls also have their own sets of properties, and Table 8.3 lists several of the most common.

Building WinContact Reports with the Report Wizards

Report Wizards will be utilized to format the following eight of the WinContact application's reports:

Customer Contact List by Zip Code
Customer Contact List by State
Customer Contact List by Lead Source
Customer Contact List by Relationship
Customers Not Contacted in the Last 60 Days
Customers Who Need Follow-Up Calls Today
Customers Who Need Follow-Up Calls Tomorrow
Customer Mailing Labels

Table 8.2 Section Properties	
Property	Description
Name	Identifies the section.
Visible	Determines whether a section is displayed.
Width	Specifies how wide the section is.
Height	Specifies how high the section is.

Table 8.3 Control Properties	
Property	**Description**
Name	Identifies the control.
Control Source	Identifies the field to which the Control is bound.
Format	Specifies how the control will be formatted.
Visible	Determines whether a control is displayed.
Width	Specifies how wide the control is.
Height	Specifies how high the control is.
Left	Identifies where the control is positioned in relation to the left border of the form.
Top	Identifies where the control is positioned in relation to the top border of the form.
Font Name	Determines font type.
Font Size	Determines font size.

The Customer Contact List by Zip Code Report

This is used to display contacts sorted by zip code and last name. The report will list contact name, company address, and phone number for each contact, and you will use a tabular Report Wizard to build it.

To build the Customer Contact List by Zip Code report:

1. Open the CONTACTS database, if it is not already open.
2. Select the Reports tab.
3. Select New. The New Report dialog box, which is illustrated in Figure 8.9, will be displayed.
4. Select qryContactZip from the Table/Query list box.

Figure 8.9 The New Report dialog box.

Figure 8.10 Screen 1 of the Tabular Report Wizard.

5. Select Report Wizards.

6. Select Tabular from the list box. The first screen of the Tabular Report Wizard, which is illustrated in Figure 8.10, will be displayed.

7. Select OK.

8. Select ZipCode from the Available fields list box.

9. Select the > button. ZipCode has now been added to the Field order on report list box.

10. Repeat steps 8 and 9 for each of the following:

> Name
> Company
> City
> State
> Number
> Extension

11. Select Next >. The second screen of the Tabular Report Wizard, shown in Figure 8.11, will be displayed.

Figure 8.11 Screen 2 of the Tabular Report Wizard.

Figure 8.12 Screen 3 of the Tabular Report Wizard.

12. Double-click on ZipCode in the Available fields list box. Notice that ZipCode has been added to the Sort order of records list box.

13. Double-click on Name in the Available fields list box.

14. Select Next >. The third screen of the Tabular Report Wizard, Figure 8.12, will be displayed.

15. Select the Landscape option button from the Layout option group.

16. Select Next >, and the fourth screen of the Tabular Report Wizard, which is illustrated in Figure 8.13, will be displayed.

17. Type {Customer Contacts by Zip Code} in the What title do you want for your report? edit box.

18. Select Finish. Access now creates the report for you and places you into the Print Preview mode. The finished report is in Figure 8.14.

19. Select File → Save.

20. Type {rptContactZip} in the Report Name edit box.

21. Select OK.

Figure 8.13 Screen 4 of the Tabular Report Wizard.

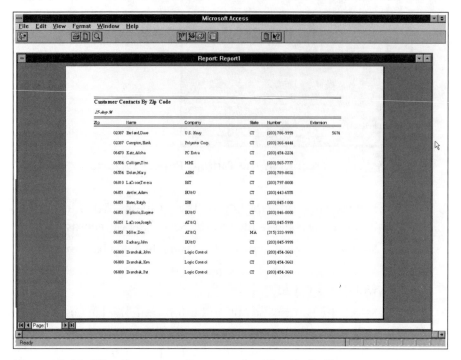

Figure 8.14 The Customer Contacts by Zip Code Report.

In the Zip Code report, you'll immediately notice that there are several errors that need correcting. First, there are "lost" zeros on the ZipCode control because Access does not store leading zeros in the table. Second, the contents of the ZipCode and Extension controls are aligned too far to the right. Finally, the ZipCode and Extension controls were totaled.

To correct the ZipCode control, you must set the value of the Format property edit box control for the ZipCode control to display leading zeros.

To correct the ZipCode control:

1. Select the Design View tool from the toolbar.

2. Select the ZipCode edit box control.

3. Select the Left Align Text button on the toolbar.

4. Select View → Properties. The Properties Sheet for ZipCode, which is illustrated in Figure 8.15, is displayed.

Figure 8.15 The Property Sheet for the ZipCode field.

5. Type five zeros in the Format property's edit box. This will place leading zeros on the report.

6. Select the Print Preview tool from the toolbar.

The second error, that the contents of the extension control were aligned too far to the right, can be corrected by following these steps:

To correct the extension control:

1. Select the Design View tool from the toolbar.

2. Select the Extension control.

3. Select the Left Align Text tool on the toolbar.

4. Select the Print Preview tool from the toolbar.

The last error that needs correcting is that the Report Wizard totals any numeric controls that are bound to a datatype and builds a summary control. These controls are found in the Report Footer section. Obviously, there is no reason for having summary controls for Zip Code or Extension, so the summary controls should be deleted here.

To delete the summary controls:

1. Select the Design View tool from the toolbar.

2. Select the ZipCode summary field.

3. Hold down the Shift key.

4. Select the Extension summary field. Notice they are both selected.

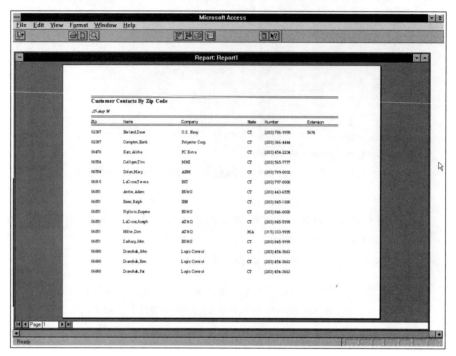

Figure 8.16 The corrected Customer Contacts by Zip Code report.

5. Press the del key.

6. Save the report as rptContactZip.

7. Toggle into Print Preview mode. The finished report is illustrated in Figure 8.16.

The Customer Contact List by State Report

This report is used to display customer contact information similar to that in the preceding report. To create the report, copy the Customer Contact by Zip Code report and implement these three simple changes:

- Change the title.
- Swap the State and ZipCode fields.
- Set as the control source for the report the qryContactState query.

Figure 8.17 The Paste As dialog box.

To build the Customer Contact List by State report:

1. In the database window, select the rptContactZip report.
2. Select Edit → Copy.
3. Select Edit → Paste. The dialog box illustrated in Figure 8.17 will be displayed.
4. Type {rptContactState}.
5. Select OK.
6. Select rptContactState in the Database window.
7. Select Design. The report is opened in Design mode.
8. Select the Title text box.
9. Drag and drop the ZipCode text box control and the Zip label control to the bottom of the Detail section.
10. Drag and drop the State text box control and State label control to occupy the position on the report where the ZipCode control used to be.
11. Move the Extension and Number text box controls to the right to make room for the ZipCode text box control.
12. Move the Extension and Number label controls to the right to make room for the Zip label control.
13. Drag and drop the ZipCode text box control and the Zip label control to the position on the report where the State text box control used to be. The report should look like Figure 8.18.
14. Select Edit → Select Report.
15. Select View Properties.
16. Set the Record Source property to qryContactState.
17. Select View → Sorting and Grouping. The Sorting and Grouping window, which is illustrated in Figure 8.19, will be displayed.

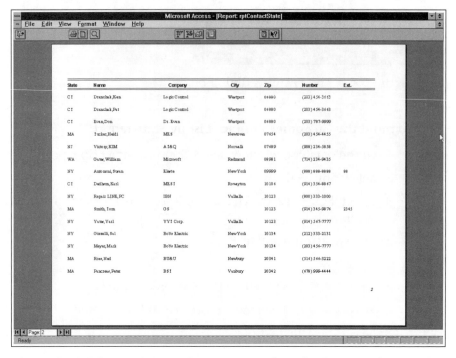

Figure 8.18 The rptContactState report after the State and ZipCode controls have been moved.

18. Replace ZipCode in the Field/Expression column with State.

19. Select File → Save.

20 Run the report. The results are shown in Figure 8.20.

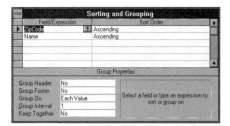

Figure 8.19 The Sorting and Grouping window.

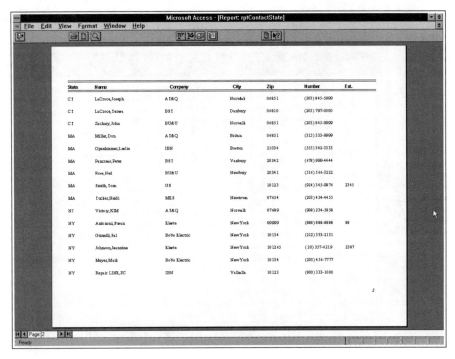

Figure 8.20 The Customer Contact by State report.

The Customers Not Contacted in the Last 30 Days Report

This report is used to display any contact whose LastContactDate field is less than the current date minus 30. The report lists the contact name and phone number and the last date contacted.

To build the Customers Not Contacted in the Last 30 Days report:

1. Select the Report tab.
2. Select New.
3. Select qryContactLastDate from the Table/Query list box.
4. Select Report Wizards.
5. Select Tabular from the list box.
6. Select OK.
7. Select LastDateContacted in the Available fields list box.

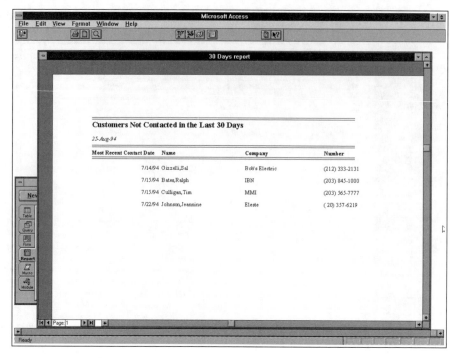

Figure 8.21 The Customers Not Contacted in the Last 30 Days report before correction.

8. Select the > button.

9. Repeat steps 7 and 8 for the Name, Company, and Number fields.

10. Select Next >.

11. Add LastDateContacted as the primary sort key and Name as the secondary sort key.

12. Select Next >.

13. Set the Page Orientation to Landscape.

14. Select Next >.

15. Name the report "Customers Not Contacted in the Last 30 Days."

16. Select Finish. Figure 8.21 illustrates the report. Note the LastDateContacted text box control is aligned too far to the right.

17. Select the Close tool.

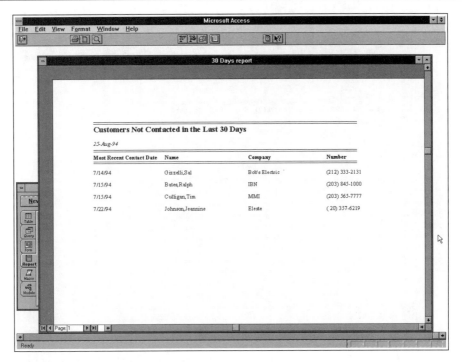

Figure 8.22 The Customers Not Contacted in the Last 30 Days report after correction.

18. Select the LastDateContacted control.
19. Select the Align Left button.
20. Save the report as rptContact30.
21. Select Print Preview to view the corrections. The finished report is illustrated in Figure 8.22.

Your Turn: Building the Customers Not Contacted in the Last 60 Days Report

The Customers Not Contacted In the Last 60 Days report, illustrated in Figure 8.23, is the same type of report as the preceding report. Create this report on your own by using a Report Wizard as demonstrated earlier or by copying rptContact30 and making the required changes. Remember to use the qryContact60 query as the report Data Source; save the report as rptContact60.

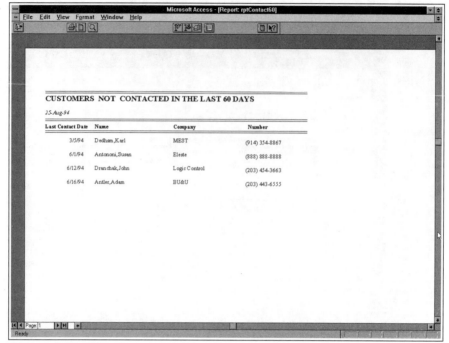

Figure 8.23 The Customers Not Contacted in the Last 60 Days

Today's Follow-Up Calls Report

This report is used to display contacts who should be called on the current date. The report is sorted by name and lists the company name and contact phone number.

To build the Customers Who Need Calls Today report:

1. Create a new tabular report using the Query Wizard, based on qryContactFollowUpDate.

2. Place the following fields into the Field order on Report list box:

    FollowUpDate
    Name
    Company
    Number

3. Sort the report by FollowUpDate and Name.

4. Name the report Today's Customer Contacts.

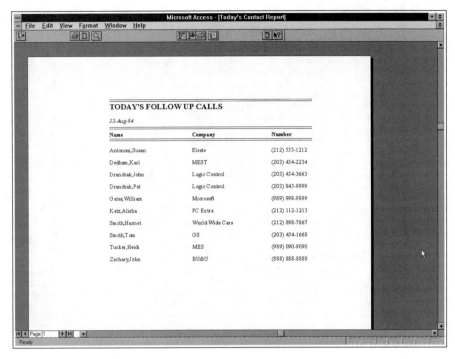

Figure 8.24 Today's Follow-Up Calls report.

5. Switch into Design mode.
6. Fix the alignment error on the FollowUpDate control using the same procedures as before.
7. Save the report as rptContactToday.
8. Toggle into Print Preview mode. The finished report is illustrated in Figure 8.24.

Your Turn: Building Tomorrow's Follow-up Calls Report

The Tomorrow's Follow-Up Calls report, illustrated in Figure 8.25, is the same type of report as the preceding example. Create this report on your own by using a Report Wizard as demonstrated earlier or by copying rptContactToday and making the required changes. Remember to use the qryContactTomorrow query as the report Data Source. Save the file as rptContactTomorrow.

You have now completed the tabular reports.

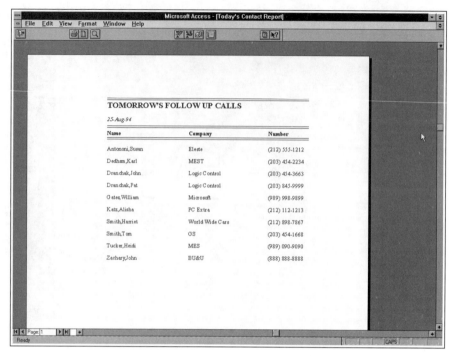

Figure 8.25 Tomorrow's Follow-Up Calls report.

The Contacts by Lead Source Report

The Contacts by Lead Source report is used to display the contact information sorted by lead source. This report is an example of a single-column format.

To build the Contacts by Lead Source report:

1. If it is not already open, open the CONTACTS database and select the Reports tab.
2. Select New.
3. Select qryContactLeadSource from the Table/Query list box.
4. Select the Report Wizard.
5. Select Single-Column from the list box.
6. Select OK. The screen changes as illustrated in Figure 8.26.
7. Double-click on the LEAD_SOURCE.LeadSource field in the list box. It will be added to the Field order on report list box.

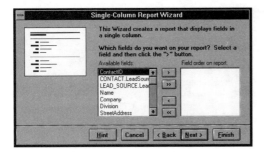

Figure 8.26 Screen 1 of the Single-Column Report Wizard.

8. Place the following fields into the Field order on report list box:

> Name
> Company
> City
> State
> Zip Code
> Number
> Extension

9. Select Next >. The screen changes, as illustrated in Figure 8.27.

10. Double-click on LeadSource in the Which fields do you want to sort by? list box.

11. Double click on Name in the Which fields do you want to sort by? list box.

12. Select Next >. The screen changes, as illustrated in Figure 8.28.

13. Accept the default layout settings.

14. Select Next >. The screen changes, as illustrated in Figure 8.29.

Figure 8.27 Screen 2 of the Single-Column Report Wizard.

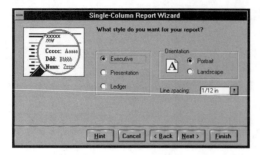

Figure 8.28 Screen 3 of the Single-Column Report Wizard.

15. Type {Customer Contacts by Lead Source} in the title edit box.

16. Select Finish.

17. Toggle into Design mode and correct the report so that it is formatted like the report in Figure 8.30.

18. Save the report as rptContactLeadSource.

Your Turn: Building the Customer Contacts List By Relationship Report

The Customer Contacts List by Relationship report, illustrated in Figure 8.31, is the same type of report as the previous example. Create this report on your own by using a Report Wizard as demonstrated earlier or by copying rptContactLeadSource and making the required changes. Remember to use the qryContactRelationship query as the report Data Source. Save the report as rptContactRelationship. You will have then completed the single-column reports.

Figure 8.29 Screen 4 of the Single-Column Report Wizard.

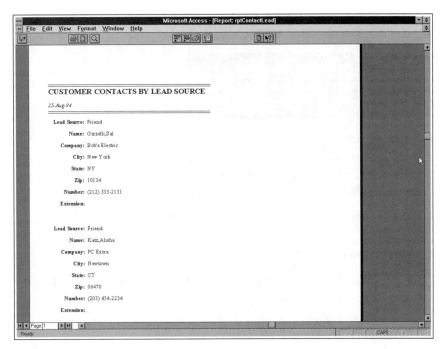

Figure 8.30 The Customer Contacts by Lead Source report.

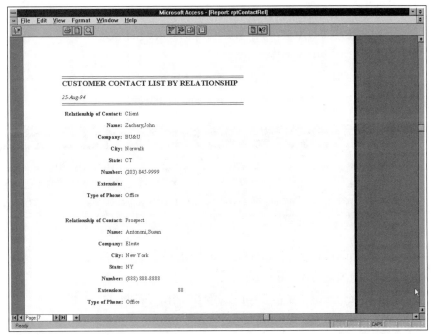

Figure 8.31 The Customer Contacts List by Relationship report.

313

Figure 8.32 Screen 1 of the Mailing Label Wizard.

The Mailing Labels Report

The Mailing Labels report is used to create contact mailing labels or multicolumn reports.

To build the Mailing Labels report:

1. If it is not already open, open the CONTACTS database and select the Reports tab.
2. Select New.
3. Select CONTACT from the Table/Query list box.
4. Select the Report Wizards
5. Select Mailing Label from the list box.
6. Select OK. The screen changes, as illustrated in Figure 8.32.

Note

Figure 8.32 shows that the Mailing Label Wizard displays a screen with all the field names and punctuation, text, and new line buttons. These additional buttons help to format a mailing label or a multicolumn label-based report.

---

7. Double-click on Prefix in the Available fields list box.
8. Select the Space button.
9. Repeat steps 7 and 8 for the following fields:

    FirstName
    MiddleInitial
    LastName

Figure 8.33 The completed mail label construction screen.

10. Select the NewLine button.

11. Repeat steps 7 and 8 for the Title field.

12. Select the NewLine button.

13. Repeat steps 7 and 8 for the Company field.

14. Select the NewLine button.

15. Repeat steps 7 and 8 for the Address field.

16. Select the Newline button.

17. Double-click on City in the Available fields list box.

18. Select the Comma button.

19. Double-click on State in the Available fields list box.

20. Select the Space button.

21. Double-click on ZipCode in the Available Fields list box. The completed mail label construction screen is illustrated in Figure 8.33.

22. Select Next >. The screen changes, as illustrated in Figure 8.34.

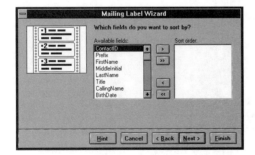

Figure 8.34 Screen 2 of the Mailing Label Wizard.

Figure 8.35   Screen 3 of the Mailing Label Wizard.

23. Set the sort order to LastName.
24. Select Next >. The screen changes, as illustrated in Figure 8.35.
25. Select Avery number 5161, which is 1" × 4", 2 across.

Note

Microsoft Access supports a variety of Avery labels in various dimensions.

26. Select Next >. The screen changes, as illustrated in Figure 8.36.
27. Accept the default font and color settings.
28. Select Next >. The screen changes, as illustrated in Figure 8.37.
29. Select See the mailing labels as they will look printed option button.
30. Select Finish. Access now creates the report for you and places you into the Print Preview mode.

Figure 8.36   Screen 4 of the Mailing Label Wizard.

Figure 8.37 Screen 5 of the Mailing Label Wizard.

31. Switch to Design mode and fix the missing lead zeros on the ZipCode.
32. Save the report as rptMail.
33. Toggle into Print Preview mode. The finished report is illustrated in Figure 8.38.

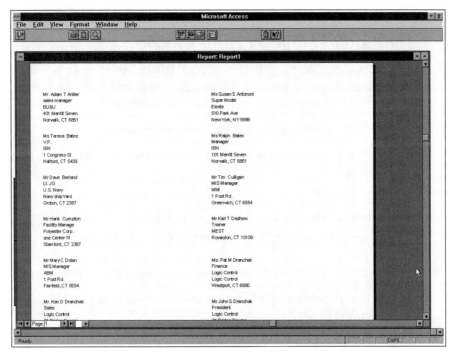

Figure 8.38 The finished Mailing Label report.

Building a Report from Scratch

Although the Report Wizards are quick and easy, they have very limited options. If the standard reports that the Wizards create are what you need, fine; if not, you need to build your reports from scratch using the Report Design window, which is demonstrated by building two reports from the WinContact application.

To build a report from scratch:

1. Create a new report based on the correct table or query.
2. Add the required sections to the report.
3. Add the required controls via drag and drop.
4. Format the report by moving and sizing the controls for consistency and setting the properties that affect each control's appearance.
5. Run the report.
6. Save the report.

The Customer Contact History Report

The Customer Contact History report is used to display a listing of phone conversations with a particular contact. This report includes the date and time of the call, the duration, and any notes from the call.

To create the Customer Contact History report:

1. If it is not already open, open the CONTACTS database and select the Reports tab.
2. Select New.
3. Select qryPhoneList from the Table/Query list box.
4. Select Blank Report. The Report Design window is displayed in Figure 8.39.

To build the Customer Contact History report Page Header section:

1. Expand the height of the Page Header section to 2.5" by dragging the bottom border.
2. Select the Label tool from the toolbox. Notice how the cursor changes.
3. Draw a Label control that is 2.4" wide and .25" high in the Page Header section by dragging from the starting point of 1.5" horizontal and .167" vertical.

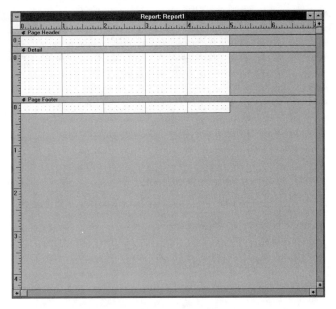

Figure 8.39 The blank Report Design window.

Note

There are two ways to place a label or text box control on a report. The first is the drag and drop method, where you "eye" the placement of the label or text box. The second is to double-click on the corresponding control tool in the toolbox. The control will be placed in the middle of the actual screen. You can then set the values of the Left, Top, Width, and Height properties in the controls property sheet. This is, of course, the more accurate of the two methods.

4. Type {Call History Profile}.

5. Press [Ctrl]-[Enter].

6. Type {For} on the second line.

7. Select the control.

8. Center the text.

9. Select the Text Box tool from the toolbox.

10. Draw a text box control in the Page Header section starting at 1.4" horizontal and .58" vertical. The text box should be 2.4" wide and .167" high.

Table 8.4 Fields for the Contact History Page Header				
Fields	Left	Top	Width	Height
Title	1.4"	.58"	2.4"	.167"
Company	1.4"	.83"	2.4"	.167"
StreetAddress	1.4"	1.08"	2.4"	.167"

11. Delete the corresponding label control.

12. Double-click on the text box. The text box Property sheet is displayed.

13. Set the Name property to txtName.

14. Set the text box Control Source property to the following expression or use the Expression Builder to do so:

```
= ([Prefix]&" "&[FirstName]&" "&[MiddleInitial]&" "&[LastName])
```

15. Close the Property sheet.

16. Select the Align Center button.

17. Select the Field List tool from the toolbar.

18. Drag and drop the fields listed in Table 8.4 from the Field List into the Page Header section, as illustrated in Figure 8.40.

19. Delete the label control for each.

20. Draw a text box control in the Page Header section starting at 1.4" horizontal and 1.41" vertical. The text box should be 2.4" wide and .167" high.

21. Repeat steps 11 through 14 for the following expression:

```
= ([City]&","&[State]&" "&Format([ZipCode],"00000"))
```

To build the Customer Contact History report Detail section:

1. Create a label control at 2.25" vertical and .25" horizontal. Make it .75" long.

2. Type {Start Time}.

3. Create a label at 2.25" vertical and 1.75" horizontal. Make it 1" long.

4. Type {Length of Call}.

5. Create a label at 2.25" vertical and 3" horizontal. Make it .5" long.

6. Type {Notes}.

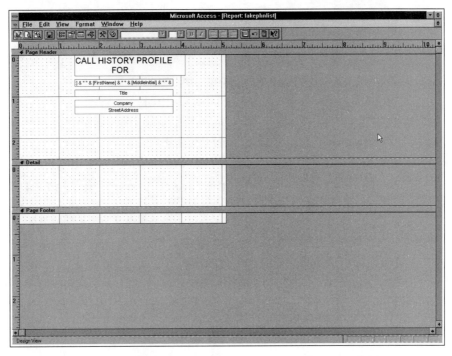

Figure 8.40 The Call History Profile report in Design mode.

7. Select the Line tool.

8. Draw a line at 2.37" vertical from .25" to 5" horizontal.

9. Select the Property sheet of the line.

10. In the Border Width property, select 3pt.

11. Display the Field List, if it is not already displayed.

12. Select the StartTime field from the Field List.

13. Drag the StartTime field into the Detail section underneath the "Start Time" label control.

14. Select the Text Box tool.

15. Add a Text Box that is .167" high underneath the "Length of Call" label control.

16. Set the value of the Name property to "txtLength."

17. Set the Control Source property to this expression:

```
=([EndTime]-[StartTime])
```

18. Set the Format property to Short Time. This will compute the difference in minutes.

19. Select the Align Left Button.

20. Select the Text Box tool from the toolbox.

21. Delete the corresponding label control.

22. Select Notes from the Field List and drag it into the Detail section underneath the Notes label control.

23. Adjust the size of the Notes field to 2" wide by 1" high.

24. Draw a line the width of the page at .1" horizontal and 2.41" vertical.

25. Set the line width to 1pt.

26. Save the report as rptPhoneList.

This report cannot be tested at this time because you have not created the macro that will help you provide the report with the required input (contact name). When you have learned to create the mcrfrmReport macro in Chapter 9, then you can use the frmReport form and select the Phone Log (by client) option from the option group. The finished report is illustrated in Figure 8.41.

The Customer List by Last Name Report

The Customer List by Last Name report is used to display the standard contact information along with all of a contact's phone numbers (fax, home, beeper). This report demonstrates the uses of grouping headers. To build this report follow these steps:

To build the Customer Contact by Last Name report:

1. Open a blank report based on the qryContactLastName query.

2. Select Format → Report Header/Footer.

3. Expand the height of the Report Header section to 1.25" by dragging the bottom border.

4. Draw a label control in the Report Header section by dragging from the starting point of 1.25" horizontal, 0" vertical, to 3.5" horizontal and 0.37" vertical.

5. Type {Customer List By Last Name}in the label control.

6. Select the control.

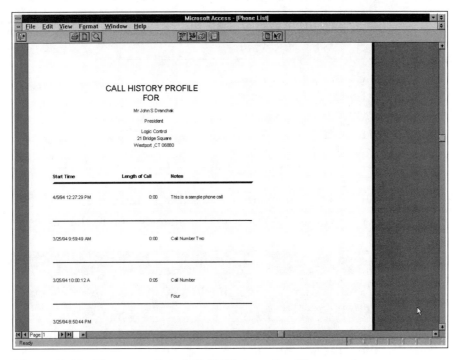

Figure 8.41 The completed Call History Profile report.

7. Select the Font Size drop-down list box and change the label control font size to 16.

8. Draw a text box control in the Report Header section by dragging from the starting point of .25" horizontal, .25" vertical, to 1.5" horizontal and .5" vertical.

9. Set the value of the Name property to txtDate.

10. Set the Control Source property to the following expression:

    =Date().

11. Delete the corresponding label control of the text box.

12. In the Page Header section, draw a label that measures .37" high by 3" wide. Start the box at .3" horizontal and .05" vertical.

13. Type {CONTACT NAME/COMPANY}.

14. Change the label control font size to 14.

15. Select the Sorting and Grouping tool.

Table 8.5 Group Properties for the Name Group	
Property	**Value**
Group Header	Yes
Group Footer	No
Group On	No
Group Interval	1
Keep Together	No

16. Click on the down arrow and select Name in the Field/Expression cell.

17. Set the Group Properties for the Name group to the values in Table 8.5.

Note
Using the grouping function allows you to create a subgroup of phone numbers for each contact.

18. Close the Sorting and Grouping window.

19. Expand the Name Header section to 1.5" high.

20. Draw a line at 0" vertical, and from .25" to 5" horizontal.

21. Set the line width to 3pts.

22. Use the Field List to add the fields in Table 8.6 into Name Header section, as illustrated in Figure 8.42.

23. Draw a text box control from .3" horizontal and .91" vertical that is 2" wide and .167" high.

24. Delete the corresponding label control for each text box control.

25. Set the Name property to "txtlocation."

26. Set the Control Source property to the following expression:

```
= ([City]&", "&[State]&" "&Format([ZipCode]"00000"))
```

27. Delete the corresponding label control for each text box control.

28. Draw a Label control at 2.25" vertical and .25" horizontal. Make the box .75" long.

29. Type {Phone Number}.

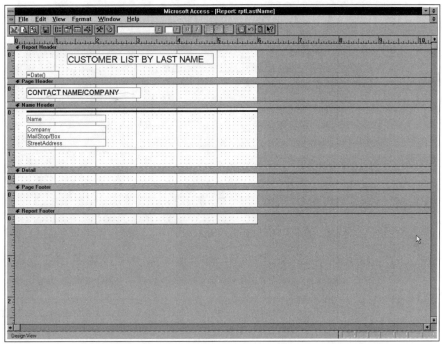

Figure 8.42   The Customer List by Last Name report in Design

30. Create a label control at 2.25" vertical and 1.75" horizontal. Make it 1" long.

31. Type {Exten}.

32. Create a label control at 2.25" vertical and 3" horizontal. Make it .5" long.

33. Type {Type}.

34. Compare the control placement in Figure 8.43 to the report you have designed to ensure that the two are similar.

To build the Detail section of the Customer List by Last Name report:

1. Display the Field List, if it is not already displayed.

2. Add the Number text box control into the Detail section below the Phone Number label control.

3. Add the Extension text box control into the Detail section below the Exten label control.

4. Add the PHONE_TYPE.Type text box control into the Detail section below the Type label control, as illustrated in Figure 8.44.

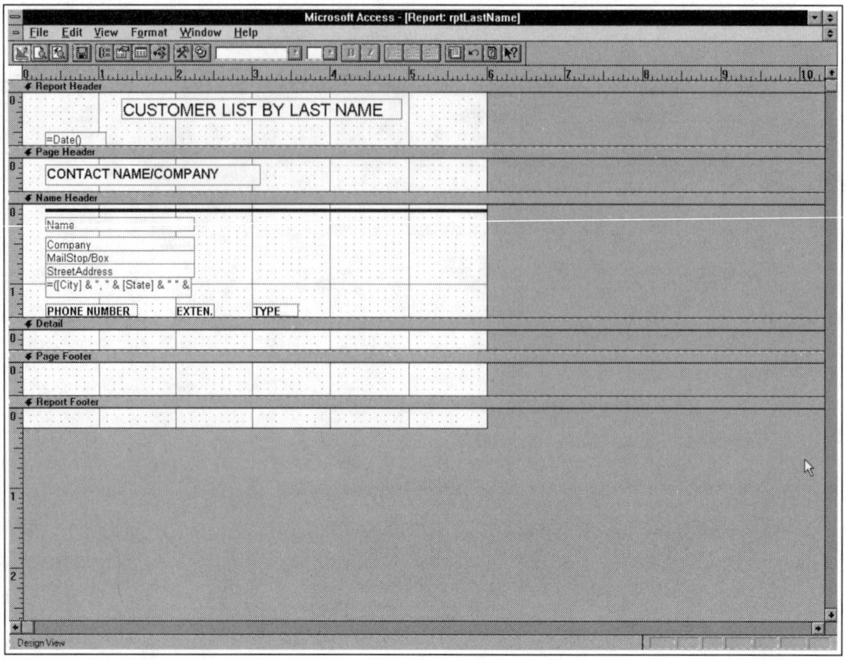

Figure 8.43 The Design view of the Customer List by Last Name Report Page Header section.

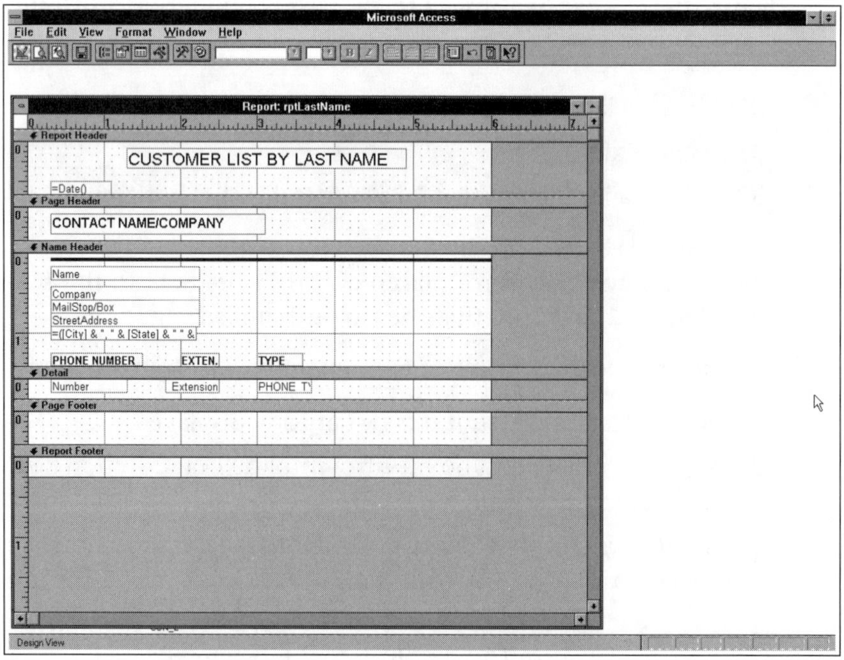

Figure 8.44 The Design view of the Customer List by Last Name

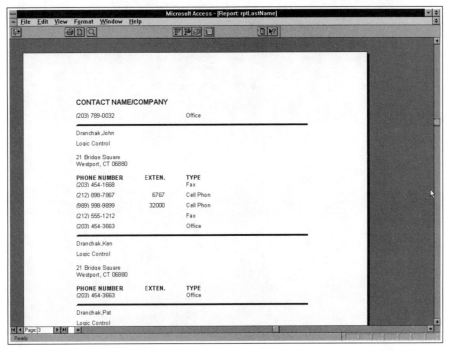

Figure 8.45 The completed Customer List by Last Name report.

5. In the Page Footer section, drag a line at 2.37" vertical from .25" to 5" horizontal.

6. Set the line's Border Width to 3pt.

7. Draw a text box .25" high by .75" wide at .25" horizontal and .167" vertical.

8. Set the Name property to txtpage.

9. Set the Control Source property to the following expression:

    ```
    =[Page]
    ```

10. Save the report as rptLastName.

11. Toggle into Print Preview mode to view the report, which is shown in Figure 8.45.

Chapter 9

Macros

While tables, queries, reports, and forms are the foundation of any Access application that involves multiple windows, macros are the glue that binds them together. This chapter discusses the basics of creating and utilizing macros. You will learn:

What a macro is.

The parts of the Macro Design window.

How to create, save, and execute a macro.

Macro actions.

What a macro group is.

How to document a macro.

How to test a macro.

What Is a Macro?

Macros have evolved from the simple keystroke recorder of the early Lotus 1-2-3 program to become an actual programming language. Lotus 1-2-3 was one of

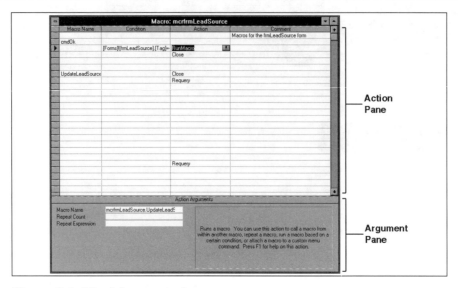

Figure 9.1 The Macro window.

the first applications that employed macros to perform repeated executions of various functions such as cut and paste. Today, macros come standard with most Microsoft software. These prepackaged commands can be combined with various arguments and conditions to control the flow of an entire application.

The Macro Window

When you enter the Macro window, which is illustrated in Figure 9.1, you are presented with a split screen. The upper portion of the screen, called the action pane, is broken into rows and columns. The lower portion of the screen is called the argument pane. The argument pane has edit boxes in which to enter specific arguments or argument clauses. These cells relate to each action in the action pane.

Understanding the Panes

The action pane of a Macro window has four columns: Macro Name, Condition, Action, and Comment. When you first open a new macro window, by default only the Action and Comment columns are displayed. To display the Macro Name column, select the Macros Names button on the toolbar or select

View → Macro Names. To display the Condition column, select the Conditions button on the toolbar or select View → Conditions. You can use the same methods to hide these columns, because they are toggle buttons.

The Macro Name column is used to assign a name to a series of macros. If you have only one macro in a macro sheet, the macro name is optional. If you would like to place more than one macro in a macro sheet, a name for each macro is required. This is called macro grouping and is described in detail later in this chapter. The Condition column is used to specify a conditional expression, which is evaluated before the row of the macro is executed. If it evaluates to true, then the row will be executed; if it evaluates to false, then the row is skipped. The action column is used to specify the actual procedure that you want to perform. There is a fixed list of macro actions that will be described later. Every time an Action is entered, the argument pane changes to reflect the specific arguments that relate to the action. To set the arguments, type or make a selection from the drop-down list box, if there is one. Many arguments also allow you to use the Expression Builder. The Comment column is used add notations to document your macros. Although it is tempting to skimp on documenting your work, remember that the amount of time it takes up front saves much more time when you or someone else needs to modify the application at a later date.

Hint

You can quickly switch between panes by pressing F6.

Conditionals

Access macros, by default, execute sequentially, from top to bottom. There are often times when it is necessary to change the flow of execution—perhaps skip over several rows of a macro. A conditional expression is one that evaluates to one of two values: true or false; there are no other possible outcomes. This is known as Boolean logic. It is possible to change the flow of execution in a macro by using the Macro Design window's Condition column. Whenever a conditional expression is placed in the Condition column, Access evaluates it before the action on the corresponding line is executed. If the conditional expression evaluates to true, the macro action will be executed. If the conditional expression evaluates to false, the line is skipped, and Access evaluates the next line of the macro. To have several actions executed in response to a conditional expression, you must repeat the conditional in every row of the macro. This is necessary because each row is evaluated independently. An alternative to repeating the full conditional expression is to use the conditional expression in the first row, and then use an ellipsis (...) in all adjacent following rows in which you wish to use the same conditional. This will make the macro code more readable, and will also cut down on the amount of work (and potential for errors) because you will only have to modify the first occurrence of the conditional, as opposed to the second or third, or however many there are. Like any expression in Access, the conditional expression can be typed manually or created using the Expression Builder. Examine the following expression:

```
[Forms]![frmContact]![LastName] = "LaCroce"
```

If this expression were placed in the Condition column of a macro, the action would only execute if the Last Name control on the Contact form contained the value LaCroce. In other words, if [Forms]![frmContact]![LastName] ="LaCroce" were true, the action would be executed; otherwise, the line would be skipped, and the next line would be evaluated.

Conditionals are used in the macros for the following forms:

- E-Mail Service
- Relationship
- Phone Type
- New Call
- Report
- Lead Source

Creating Macros

To create a macro:

1. Determine what you want to do.
2. List the necessary steps.
3. Open a macro window.
4. Select the appropriate actions and set their arguments.
5. Save the macro.
6. Test the macro.

Figure 9.2 Macro not found message box.

7. Decide how the macro will be invoked.

8. Assign the macro name to the event(s) that will be used to invoke the macro.

You can actually assign the name of a macro to an event before the macro is created, as you did in Chapter 7. If you do this, though, you must be careful to use the same names when you create the macros. If you do not, the message box illustrated in Figure 9.2 will be displayed. Another disadvantage of using this method is that the name of the macro will not show up in the event's drop-down list box.

Note
A macro must be saved before it is run. If you try to run it without saving it, Access will prompt you to do so.

Application Startup

If you create a macro and name it Autoexec, Access will automatically execute it whenever the database is opened. As such, the Autoexec macro is important for building applications because you can have certain actions executed every time the database is opened, without any intervention from the user.

Hint
To open the database without executing the Autoexec macro, hold down the Shift key while you select the OK button in the File Open dialog box.

The WinContact application is supposed to shield the user from having to know all of the intricacies of Access. Therefore, it must first hide the Database window, and then open and display the WinContact Main window.

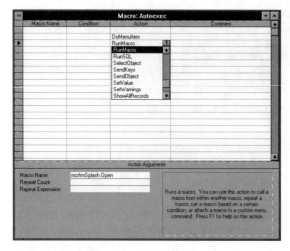

Figure 9.3 Drop-down list of actions.

To build the Autoexec macro:

1. Select the Macro tab in the Database window.

2. Select New.

3. Select the first row of the Action column. Note the arrow that appears to the right of the cell.

4. Click on the arrow. A drop-down list with all of Access's actions will be displayed, as illustrated in Figure 9.3.

5. Select the DoMenuItem action. Notice that the argument pane changes to display the arguments that correspond to the selected action, as illustrated in Figure 9.4.

6. Set the Menu Bar argument to Database.

7. Set the Menu Name argument to Window.

8. Set the Command argument to Hide.

9. Select the OpenForm action in the Action column of the next blank row.

10. Set the Form Name argument to frmMain1.

11. Select File → Save. The Save As dialog box, which is illustrated in Figure 9.5, will be displayed.

12. Type {Autoexec} in the Macro Name edit box.

13. Select OK.

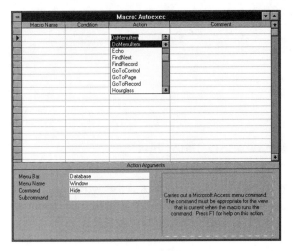

Figure 9.4 The Macro window after an action has been selected.

Now that you have built the Autoexec macro, you need to test it. In addition to assigning a macro to an event, there are five ways you can run a macro:

- Select the Run button while you are in the macro sheet.
- Select Macro → Run while you are in the macro sheet.
- Double-click on the macro in the Database window.
- Select the macro in the Database window, and then select Run.
- Select File → Run Macro from any point in Access.

If your macro sheet contains more than one macro (which will be covered later), the first four methods will only execute the first macro on the macro sheet, if it starts in the first row. To test your macros, you will most often use the File → Run Macro method since most of the macros in WinContact use macro groups. Although you can use one of these methods to test the Autoexec macro, the best way is to close the database, and then reopen it. This will cause the Autoexec macro to execute.

Figure 9.5 The Save As dialog box.

Figure 9.6 The Unhide Window dialog box.

After you test the Autoexec macro, the Database window is hidden. Before you can continue working on the application, you will have to reveal it because the Database window is the "control center" of Access.

To unhide the Database window:

1. Select Window → Unhide. The dialog box illustrated in Figure 9.6 will be displayed.
2. Double-click on Database: CONTACT in the Window list box.

Macro Actions

A macro action is a predefined executable procedure within Access. All actions require one or more arguments, that give Access detailed information about the process is to be performed. When using the OpenForm action, for example, you can specify:

- The form to open.
- The viewing mode.
- The filter to apply, if you want to use one.
- A conditional expression, if you want to use one.
- The data mode.
- The window mode.

When you select an action from the drop-down list in the Action column, the argument pane changes to display the corresponding arguments. You then set the required arguments to the values that are necessary for completeing the process. Table 9.1 lists some of the most common macro actions and definitions. For a complete description of all macro actions and their syntax, refer to the Access on-line help system.

Table 9.1: Common Macro Actions	
Action	**Description**
AddMenu	Creates a menu bar for a form or report.
ApplyFilter	Filters the data, based on some criteria.
Beep	Issues a beep on execution.
CancelEvent	Stops the execution of an event.
Close	Closes an object.
CopyObject	Creates another copy of an object.
DoMenuItem	Executes a standard Access menu command.
Echo	Updates the screen while a macro is executing.
FindNext	Finds the next record containing specified criteria.
FindRecord	Finds a specific record.
GoToControl	Sets focus to a specified control.
GoToPage	Selects first control on a specified page on a form.
GoToRecord	Selects a specified record and makes it the current record.
Hourglass	Displays an hourglass cursor.
Maximize	Causes a form or report to grow to maximum screen size.
Minimize	Reduces the current window to an icon.
MoveSize	Moves or changes the size of a window.
MsgBox	Displays a message box on the screen.
OpenForm	Opens a form.
OpenQuery	Opens a query.
OpenReport	Opens a report.
OpenTable	Opens a table.
PrintQuit	Prints a report and then closes the Report window.
SetValue	Sets the value of a property.
StopMacro	Stops execution of the running macro.

Macro Groups

Macro groups are used to group related macros, in the same macro sheet. It is common practice to organize macros so that all the macros for a given form or report are placed together in the same macro sheet. For example, each button on a form will have its own macro associated with it. In addition, there might be a macro that executes when the OnOpen event occurs. Using the WinContact Main window as an example, there are 35 macros associated with this form. If you were to create a separate macro sheet for each macro, you would need 35 just for this one window. Instead, you can place each of these macros in a single macro sheet, simply by giving each macro a name within the macro sheet. This makes it easier for the developer to keep track of all the macros that relate to one form. This is done by specifying a name in the Macro Name column of the macro sheet. When you want to refer to a macro within a macro group, you use the following syntax:

```
MacroSheetName.MacroName
```

Notice the period between the macro sheet name and the macro name. If you placed a macro called cmdOK on a macro sheet named mcrfrmMainForm, then you would refer to it elsewhere in your application as:

```
mcrfrmMainForm.cmdOK
```

Note

To create custom menus in Access, you must use macro groups, a topic covered in Chapter 10.

To create a macro group:

1. Open a macro sheet (new or existing).
2. Type a unique a name in the Macro Name column.
3. Add the required actions and set their arguments.
4. Repeat steps 2 and 3 for each additional macro that will be in the macro group.

Hint

Although not required, placing a blank line between each macro will make you macro sheet easier to understand.

Figure 9.7 The WinContact Main window.

The WinContact Main Window Macro

As just stated, the WinContact window, shown in Figure 9.7, has 35 buttons, each of which requires a macro. As such, it is a prime candidate for macro groups. The WinContact main window also has 28 toggle buttons that surround the Contacts list box. When a user selects one of the buttons, the list box is updated to show those last names that begin with the letter of the button that was selected. If the Show All button is selected, all of the contacts will be shown. To build the macro that will display all contacts when the Show All button is pushed, follow the steps shown here.

To build the macro that will show all contacts:

1. Select the Macro tab in the Database window.
2. Select New.
3. Select the first row of the Macro Name column.
4. Type {Filter_All}.
5. Select the SetValue action in the Action column.
6. Set the Item argument to the following expression:

   ```
   [Forms]![frmMain1]![lstContact].[RowSource]
   ```

7. Set the Expression argument to qryContactName_All.
8. Save the macro sheet as mcmfrmMain1.

Your Turn: Building the Macros for the Contact Buttons

You need to create a macro for every letter of the alphabet to correspond with each button. Do this by repeating the process just detailed, within the same macro sheet, and changing the name of the macro and the name of the query the macro calls. Remember to use correct naming conventions. Don't close the macro when you're done because you will be entering additional macros.

OnOpen Event Because the list box in the WinContact Main window is not bound, it is necessary to fill it with data when the form is first opened. Since you just created a macro that will display all contacts, just call the mcrfrmMain1.Filter_All macro, which will do the work. To build the macro that will populate the list box when the WinContact window is first opened, follow the steps shown here.

To build the macro for the WinContact window's OnOpen event:

1. Type {OnOpen}in the Macro Name column of the next blank row.
2. Select the RunMacro action in the Action column.
3. Set the macro name argument to mcrfrmMain1.Filter_All.
4. Select the GoToControl action in the Action column of the next blank row.
5. Set the Control Name argument to lstContact. This action will set the focus to the list box in the center of the window.
6. Save the macro.

When you refer to this macro in the OnOpen event for frmMain1, do so as mcrfrmMain1.OnOpen. This tells Access to go to the mcrfrmMain1 macro group and execute the OnOpen macro.

Contact Button When the Contact command button is clicked, two things should happen:

- The WinContact window should be hidden.
- The Contacts form should be opened.

When the Contacts form is opened, it should contain the contact that was selected in the Main window.

To build the macro for the Contact command button on the WinContact window:

1. Type {cmdContact} in the Macro Name column of the next blank row.

2. Select the SetValue action in the Action column.

3. Set the Item argument to the following expression:

```
[Forms]![frmMain1].[Visible]
```

Note

The Visible property is used to determine whether the form is displayed or hidden.

4. Set the Expression argument to False.

5. Select the OpenForm action in the Action column of the next blank row.

6. Set the Form Name argument to frmContact.

7. Set the Where Condition argument to the following expression:

```
[ContactId]=[Forms]![frmMain1]![lstContact]
```

8. Save the macro.

New Contact Button   When the Add Contact command button is clicked, two things should happen:

- The WinContact window should be hidden.
- The Contacts form should be opened.

When the Contacts form is opened, it should be in Data Entry mode.

To build the macro for the AddContact command button on the WinContact window:

1. Type {cmdAddContact} in the Macro Name column of the next blank row.

2. Select the SetValue action in the Action column.

3. Set the Item argument to the following expression:

```
[Forms]![frmMain1].[Visible]
```

4. Set the Expression argument to False.

5. Select the OpenForm action in the Action column of the next blank row.

6. Set the Form Name argument to frmContact.

7. Set the Data Mode argument to Add.

8. Save the macro.

Report Button When the Report command button is selected, these two things should happen:

- The WinContact window should be hidden.
- The Report form should be opened.

Because the Report form can be opened from more than one place in the application, it is necessary to track which form the button that called the macro was on because the macro hides the calling form, and has to unhide the correct form when the Report form is closed. This is done by setting the value of the Tag property, and later reading the value back.

To build the macro for the Report command button on the WinContact window:

1. Type {cmdReport} in the Macro Name column of the next blank row.

2. Select the SetValue action in the Action column.

3. Set the Item argument to the following expression:

```
[Forms]![frmMain1].[Visible]
```

4. Set the Expression argument to False.

5. Select the OpenForm action in the Action column of the next blank row.

6. Set the Form Name argument to frmReport.

7. Select the SetValue action in the Action column.

8. Set the Item argument to the following expression:

```
[Forms]![frmReport].[Tag]
```

Note
The Tag property is used to identify which form invoked frmReport.

9. Set the Expression argument to Main.

10. Select the MoveSize action in the Action column of the next blank row.

11. Set the Width argument to 4.

Phone Log Button When the Phone Log command button is selected, two things should happen:

- The WinContact window should be hidden.
- The Phone Log form should be opened.

When the Phone Log form is opened, it should correspond to the contact that was selected in the Main window. Like the Report form, because the Phone Log form can be opened from more than one place in the application, it is necessary to track which form the macro was invoked from. This is done by setting the value of the Tag property, and later reading the value back.

To build the macro for the Phone Log command button on the WinContact window:

1. Type {cmdPhoneLog} in the Macro Name column of the next blank row.

2. Select the SetValue action in the Action column.

3. Set the Item argument to the following expression:

   ```
   [Forms]![frmMain1].[Visible]
   ```

4. Set the Expression argument to False.

5. Select the OpenForm action in the Action column of the next blank row.

6. Set the Form Name argument to frmNewCall.

7. Set the Data Mode argument to Add.

8. Select the SetValue action in the Action column of the next blank row.

9. Set the Item argument to the following expression:

   ```
   [Forms]![frmNewCall]![txtContactId]
   ```

10. Set the Expression argument to the following expression:

    ```
    [Forms]![frmMain1]![lstContact]
    ```

11. Select the SetValue action in the Action column of the next blank row.

12. Set the Item argument to the following expression:

    ```
    [Forms]![frmNewCall].[Tag]
    ```

13. Set the Expression argument to Main.

System Maintenance Button   When the System Maintenance command button is selected, two things should happen:

- The WinContact window should be hidden.
- The System Maintenance form should be opened.

To build the macro for the System Maintenance command button on the WinContact window:

1. Type {cmdSysMaint} in the Macro Name column of the next blank row.
2. Select the SetValue action in the Action column.
3. Set the Item argument to the following expression:

   ```
   [Forms]![frmMain1].[Visible]
   ```

4. Set the Expression argument to False.
5. Select the OpenForm action in the Action column of the next blank row.
6. Set the Form Name argument to frmSysMaint.

Exit Button   When the Exit command button is selected, WinContact and Access should be closed. This can be done in one step with the Quit action.

To build the macro for the Exit command button on the WinContact window:

1. Type {cmdExit} in the Macro Name column of the next blank row.
2. Select the Quit action in the Action column of the next blank row.

The Contacts Form

The Contacts form, which is illustrated in Figure 9.8, has several command buttons that require macros. These macros will:

- Open the Report form.
- Print the Contacts form.
- Open the Phone Log for the current contact.
- Close the Contacts form and return to the WinContact Main window.

OK Button   When the OK button is selected, the Contacts form should be closed, and then the WinContact Main window should be unhidden.

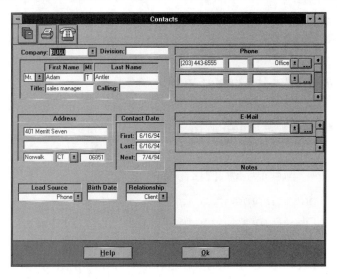

Figure 9.8 The Contacts form.

To build the macro for the OK button on the Contacts form:

1. Open a new macro sheet.
2. Type {cmdOK} in the first row of the Macro Name column.
3. Select the Close action in the Action column.
4. Set the Object Type argument to Form.
5. Set the Object Name argument to frmContact.
6. Select the SetValue action in the Action column of the next blank row.
7. Set the Item argument to the following expression:

   ```
   [Forms]![frmMain1].[Visible]
   ```

8. Set the Expression argument to True.
9. Save the macro as mcrfrmContacts.

Report Button   When the Report command button is selected, two things should happen:

- The Contact window should be hidden.
- The Report form should be opened.

As explained earlier, the Report form can be opened from more than one place in the application. The requirements for this macro are the same as when it is called form the WinContact form.

To build the macro for the Report button:

1. In a blank row, type {cmdReport} in the Macro Name column.
2. Select the SetValue action in the Action column.
3. Set the Item argument to the following expression:

   `[Forms]![frmContact].[Visible]`

4. Set the Expression property to False.
5. Select the OpenForm action in the Action column of the next blank row.
6. Set the Form Name argument to frmReport.
7. Select the SetValue action in the Action column of the next blank row.
8. Set the Item argument to the following expression:

   `[Forms]![frmReport].[Tag]`

9. Set the Expression argument to Contact.
10. Select the MoveSize action in the Action column of the next blank row.
11. Set the Width argument to 4.

Phone Log Button   When the Phone Log command button is selected, two things should happen:

- The Contact window should be hidden.
- The Phone Log form should be opened.

As explained earlier, the Phone Log form also can be opened from more than one place in the application. The requirements for this macro are the same as when it is called form the WinContact form.

To build the macro for the Phone Log button:

1. In a blank row, type {cmdPhoneLog} in the Macro Name column.
2. Select the SetValue action in the Action column.
3. Set the Item argument to the following expression:

   `[Forms]![frmContact].[Visible]`

4. Set the Expression property to False.

5. Select the OpenForm action in the Action column of the next blank row.

6. Set the Form Name argument to frmNewCall.

7. Set the Data argument to Add.

8. Select the SetValue action in the Action column of the next blank row.

9. Set the Item argument to the following expression:

```
[Forms]![frmNewCall![txtContactId]
```

10. Set the Expression argument to the following expression:

```
[Forms]![frmContact]![ContactID]
```

11. Select the SetValue action in the Action column of the next blank row.

12. Set the Item argument to the following expression:

```
[Forms]![frmNewCall].[Tag]
```

13. Set the Expression argument to Contact.

Print Button   When the Print command button is selected, the Print Preview screen is opened, and the Contact forms is printed.

To build the macro for the Print button:

1. In a blank row, type {cmdPrint} in the Macro Name column.

2. Select the DoMenuItem action in the Action column.

3. Set the Menu Bar argument to Form.

4. Set the Menu Name argument to File.

5. Set the Command argument to Print Preview.

Phone Type Button   When the Phone Type button is selected, the PHONE-_TYPE table appears, which allows the user to make modifications to the phone type.

To build the macro for the Phone Type button:

1. In a blank row, type {cmdBuildPhoneLog} in the Macro Name column.

2. Select the OpenForm action in the Action column.

3. Set the Form Name argument to frmPhoneType.

4. Select the SetValue action in the Action column of the next blank row.

5. Set the Item argument to the following expression:

```
[Forms]![frmPhoneType].[Tag]
```

6. Set the Expression argument to -1.

E-Mail Service Button   When the E-Mail Service button is selected, the EMail-_SERVICE table appears, which allows the user to make modifications to the e-mail services.

To build the macro for the E-Mail Service button:

1. In a blank row, type {cmdBuildService} in the Macro Name column.
2. Select the OpenForm action in the Action column.
3. Set the Form Name argument to frmEMailService.
4. Select the SetValue action in the Action column of the next blank row.
5. Set the Item argument to the following expression:

```
[Forms]![frmEMailService].[Tag]
```

6. Set the Expression argument to -1.

The System Maintenance Form

The System Maintenance form, which is illustrated in Figure 9.9, has several command buttons that require macros. These macros will:

- Open the Lead Source form.
- Open the Phone Type form.
- Open the E-Mail Service form.
- Open the Relationship form.
- Close the System Maintenance form and return to the Main window.

OK Button   When the OK command button is selected, two things should happen:

- The System Maintenance window should be closed.
- The Wincontact window should be unhidden.

Figure 9.9   The System Maintenance form.

To build the macro for the OK button:

1. In a blank row, type {cmdOK} in the Macro Name column.

2. Select the Close action in the Action column.

3. Set the Object Type argument to Form.

4. Set the Object Name argument to frmSysMaint.

5. Select the SetValue action in the Action column of the next blank row.

6. Set the Item argument to the following expression:

   `[Forms]![frmMain1].[Visible]`

7. Set the Expression argument to True.

Lead Sources Button   When the Lead Sources command button is selected, the Lead Sources window will be opened with the LEAD_SOURCES table available for modification.

To build the macro for the Lead Sources button:

1. In a blank row, type {cmdLeadSources} in the Macro Name column.

2. Select the OpenForm action in the Action column.

3. Set the Form Name argument to frmLeadSource.

Relationship Button   When the Relationship command button is selected, the Relationship window will be opened with the RELATIONSHIPS table available for modification.

To build the macro for the Relationship button:

1. In a blank row, type {cmdRelationships} in the Macro Name column.
2. Select the OpenForm action in the Action column.
3. Set the Form Name argument to frmRelationship.

Phone Type Button   When the Phone Type command button is selected, the Phone Type window will be opened with the PHONE_TYPE table available for modification.

To build the macro for the Phone Type button:

1. In a blank row, type {cmdPhoneType} in the Macro Name column.
2. Select the OpenForm action in the Action column.
3. Set the Form Name argument to frmPhoneType.

E-Mail Service Button   When the E-Mail Service command button is selected, the E-mail Service window will be opened with the EMAIL_SERVICES table available for modification.

To build the macro for the E-Mail Service button:

1. In a blank row, type {cmdEMailService} in the Macro Name column.
2. Select the OpenForm action in the Action column.
3. Set the Form Name argument to frmEmailService.

The Relationship Form

The Relationship form, which is illustrated in Figure 9.10, is used to update the RELATIONSHIP table.

Figure 9.10 The Relationship form.

Figure 9.11 The E-Mail Service form.

OK Button   When the OK button is selected, the Relationship form should be closed.

To build the macro for the OK button:

1. In a blank row, type {cmdOK} in the Macro Name column.
2. Select the Close action in the Action column of the next blank row.
3. Set the Object Type argument to Form.
4. Set the Object Name argument to frmRelationship.
5. Select the StopMacro action in the Action column of the next blank row.

The E-Mail Service Form

The E-Mail Service form, shown in Figure 9.11, can be opened from more than one place in the application. Therefore, it is necessary to track which form invoked the macro because the macro hides the calling form, and has to unhide the correct form when the E-Mail Service form is closed. This is done by setting the value of the Tag property, and later reading the value back.

OK Button   When the OK button is selected, the E-Mail Service form should be closed, and the window that it was called from should be unhidden.

To build the macro for the OK button:

1. In a blank row, type {cmdOK} in the Macro Name column.
2. In the Condition column, use the Expression Builder to build the following condition:

```
[Forms]![frmEmailService].[Tag]=-1.
```

3. Select RunMacro in the Action column.

4. Set the Macro Name argument to mcrfrmEmailService.UpdateMailService.

5. Select the Close action in the Action column of the next blank row.

6. Set the Object Type argument to Form.

7. Set the Object Name argument to frmEMailService.

8. Select the StopMacro action in the Action column of the next blank row.

Update E-Mail Service List Box   The Update E-Mail Service macro is called from the macro that is executed when the OK command button is executed (cmdOK). After the E-MAIL SERVICE table is updated from the E-Mail Service form, you must requery the E-Mail Service list box (lstEMailService) on the Contacts form to reflect the changes because Access executes the query to fill a list box on a form when the form is first opened. As a result, if you add a record to the underlying table, it will not be seen in the list box. When you use the Requery action on a control, the query is refreshed. Remember that this macro is only called from the cmdOK macro if the condition is met. To build the macro that will update the E-Mail Service list box on the E-Mail Service form (which is a subform displayed on the Contacts form), follow these steps.

To build the Update E-Mail Service macro:

1. In a blank row, type {UpdateMailService} in the Macro Name column.

2. Select the Close action in the Action column.

3. Set the Object Type argument to Form.

4. Set the Object Name argument to frmEMailService.

5. Select the Requery action in the Action column of the next blank row.

6. Set the Control Name argument to lstEMailService.

The Phone Type Update Form

The Phone Type form (Figure 9.12) is similar to the E-Mail Service form. It too can be called from multiple forms and, therefore, it is necessary to keep track of where it was invoked.

OK Button   When the OK button is selected, the Phone Type form should be closed, and the window that it was called from should be unhidden.

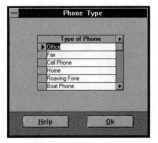

Figure 9.12 The Phone Type form.

To build the macro for the OK button:

1. In a blank row, type {cmdOK} in the Macro Name column.
2. In the Condition column, use the Expression Builder to build the following condition:

   `[Forms]![frmPhoneType].[Tag]=-1.`

3. Select RunMacro in the Action column.
4. Set the Macro Name argument to mcrfrmPhoneType.UpdatePhoneType.
5. Select the Close action in the Action column of the next blank row.
6. Set the Object Type argument to Form.
7. Set the Object Name argument to frmPhoneType.
8. Select the StopMacro action in the Action column of the next blank row.

Update Phone Type List Box   The Update Phone Type macro is similar to the update E-Mail Service macro. It too uses the requery action to display the updated list box. To build the macro that will update the Phone Type list box on the form (which is a subform displayed on the Contacts form), use the following procedure.

To build the Update Phone Type macro:

1. In a blank row, type {UpdatePhoneType} in the Macro Name column.
2. Select the Close action in the Action column.
3. Set the Object Type argument to Form.
4. Set the Object Name argument to frmPhoneType.
5. Select the Requery action in the Action column of the next blank row.
6. Set the Control Name argument to lstPhoneType.

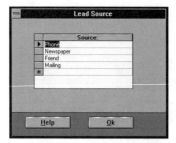

Figure 9.13 The Lead Source form.

The Lead Source Form

The Lead Source form, shown in Figure 9.13, is used to update the LEAD_SOURCE table.

OK Button   When the OK button is selected, the Lead Source form should be closed.

To build the macro for the OK button:

1. In a blank row, type {cmdOK} in the Macro Name column.
2. Select the Close action in the Action column of the next blank row.
3. Set the Object Type argument to Form.
4. Set the Object Name argument to frmLeadSource.
5. Select the StopMacro action in the Action column of the next blank row.

The Call Log Form Macro

The Call Log form, illustrated in Figure 9.14, has several command buttons that require macros. These macros will:

- Open the Call History form.
- Set the start time of a call.
- Set the end time of a call.
- Close the New Call form and return to the Main window.

OK Button   The OK button is used to close the New Call form and return to the previous form. When the OK button is selected, the following should occur:

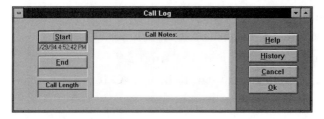

Figure 9.14 The Call Log form.

- The New Call Form should be hidden.
- The form that invoked the New Call form will be identified (WinContact Main or Contacts) and become unhidden.
- The New Call form will be closed.

To build the macro for the OK button:

1. In a blank row, type {cmdOK} in the Macro Name column.
2. Select the SetValue action in the Action column.
3. Set the Item argument to the following expression:

   ```
   [Forms]![frmNewCall].[Visible]
   ```

4. Set the Expression argument to False.
5. In the Condition column of the next blank line, enter the following expression:

   ```
   [Forms]![frmNewCall].Tag="Main"
   ```

6. Select the SetValue action in the Action column of the next blank row.
7. Set the Item argument to the following expression:

   ```
   [Forms]![frmMain1].[Visible]
   ```

8. Set the Expression argument to True.
9. In the Condition column of the next blank line, enter the following expression:

   ```
   [Forms]![frmNewCall].Tag="Contact"
   ```

10. Select the SetValue action in the Action column of the next blank row.
11. Set the Item argument to the following expression:

    ```
    [Forms]![frmContact].[Visible]
    ```

12. Set the Expression argument to True.

13. Select the Close action in the Action column.

14. Set the Object Type argument to Form.

15. Set the Object Name argument to frmNewCall.

Start Time Button The Start Time button sets the StartTime field to the current date and time. The Now(HL) function is used for this.

To build the macro for the Start Time button:

1. In a blank row, type {cmdStartTime} in the Macro Name column.

2. Select the SetValue action in the Action column.

3. Set the Item argument to the following expression:

```
[Forms]![frmNewCall]![txtStartTime]
```

4. Set the Expression argument to Now(HL).

End Time Button The End Time button sets the EndTime field to the current date and time. The Now(HL) function is used for this.

To build the macro for the End Time button:

1. In a blank row, type {cmdEndTime} in the Macro Name column.

2. Select the SetValue action in the Action column.

3. Set the Item argument to the following expression:

```
[Forms]![frmNewCall]![txtEndTime]
```

4. Set the Expression argument to Now(HL).

Call History Button The Call History button opens the Call Log form for a selected contact.

To build the macro for the Call History button:

1. In a blank row, type {cmdHistory} in the Macro Name column.

2. Select the OpenForm action in the Action column.

3. Set the Form Name argument to frmCallLog.

4. Set the Where argument to the following expression:

```
[ContactID]=[Forms]![frmContact]![ContactID]
```

Cancel Button   The Cancel button is used to cancel the Add event, close the form, and return to the previous form. When the Cancel button is selected the following should occur:

- The Add event is canceled.
- The New Call Form will be hidden.
- The form that invoked the New Call form will be identified (WinContact Main or Contact) become and unhidden.
- The New Call form will be closed.

To build the macro for the Cancel button:

1. In a blank row, type cmdCancel in the Macro Name column.
2. Select the CancelEvent action in the Action column.
3. Select the Close action in the Action column of the next blank row.
4. Select the SetValue action in the Action column of the next blank row.
5. Set the Item argument to the following expression:

   ```
   [Forms]![frmMain1].[Visible]
   ```

6. Set the Expression argument to True.

The Reports Form

The Report form, which is illustrated in Figure 9.15, is used to provide the user with a choice of reports, which can be printed or previewed. Macros, when used

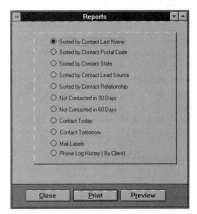

Figure 9.15 The Reports form.

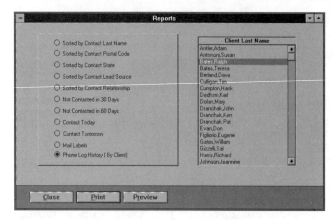

Figure 9.16 The Reports form with list box.

with option groups on forms, can execute a variety or reports from one form. The Reports macro is an example of this. Each option button has its own macro. In Chapter 7, a value was assigned to each button on the report. This macro will use conditionals to test for and execute a chosen commmand. In addition, the Phone Log option button requires another box to be displayed when the button receives focus. This list box, which is illustrated in Figure 9.16, contains the contact names. which will be used as input for the report.

Print Button   When the Print button is selected, the proper report will be identified and printed.

To build the macro for the Print button:

1. In a blank row, type {cmdPrint} in the Macro Name column.
2. Set the Condition argument to the following expression:

   ```
   [report to print]=1
   ```

3. Select the OpenReport action in the Action column of the next blank row.
4. Set the Report Name argument to rptLstName.
5. Set the View argument to Print.
6. In the Condition column of the next blank line, enter the following expression:

   ```
   [report to print]=2
   ```

7. Select the OpenReport action in the Action column.

8. Set the Report Name argument to rptContactZip.

9. Set the View argument to Print.

10. In the Condition column of the next blank line, enter the following expression:

    ```
    [report to print]=3
    ```

11. Select the OpenReport action in the Action column.

12. Set the Report Name argument to rptContactState.

13. Set the View argument to Print.

14. In the Condition column of the next blank line, enter the following expression:

    ```
    [report to print]=4
    ```

15. Select the OpenReport action in the Action column.

16. Set the Report Name argument to rptContactLeadSource.

17. Set the View argument to Print.

18. Enter the following expression in the Condition cell:

    ```
    [report to print]=5
    ```

19. Select the OpenReport action in the Action column.

20. Set the Report Name argument to rptContactRelationship.

21. Set the View argument to Print.

22. In the Condition column of the next blank line, enter the following expression:

    ```
    [report to print]=6
    ```

23. Select the OpenReport action in the Action column.

24. Set the Report Name argument to rptContact30.

25. Set the View argument to Print.

26. In the Condition column of the next blank line, enter the following expression:

    ```
    [report to print]=7
    ```

27. Select the OpenReport action in the Action column.

28. Set the Report Name argument to rptContact60.

29. Set the View argument to Print.

30. In the Condition column of the next blank line, enter the following expression:

    `[report to print]=8`

31. Select the OpenReport action in the Action column.

32. Set the Report Name argument to rptContactToday.

33. Set the View argument to Print.

34. In the Condition column of the next blank line, enter the following expression:

    `[report to print]=9`

35. Select the OpenReport action in the Action column.

36. Set the Report Name argument to rptContactTommorrow.

37. Set the View argument to Print.

38. In the Condition column of the next blank line, enter the following expression:

    `[report to print]=10`

39. Select the OpenReport action in the Action column.

40. Set the Report Name argument to rptMail.

41. Set the View argument to Print.

42. In the Condition column of the next blank line, enter the following expression:

    `[report to print]=11`

43. Select the RunMacro action in the Action column.

44. Set the Macro Name argument to mcrfrmReport.mcrPrintPhoneHist.

The finished macro is shown in Figure 9.17.

Your Turn: Building the Print Preview Macro

Now it's your turn to build the macro for the Print Preview button. Functionally, it works just like the macro for the Print button, but instead of opening reports in Print mode, they will be opened in Print Preview mode. Build the new macro by copying the cmdPrint macro (within the same macro sheet), changing the

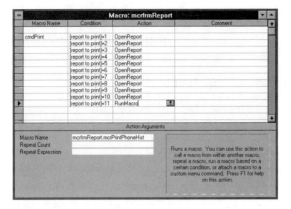

Figure 9.17 The finished cmdPrint macro.

view argument for all of the Open Report actions, and then renaming it to cmdPreview.

Close Button   When the Close button is selected, the following occur:

- The Report form is hidden.
- The form that invoked the Repot form is unhidden.
- The Report form is closed.

To build the macro for the Close button:

1. In a blank row, type {cmdClose} in the Macro Name column.
2. Select the SetValue action in the Action column.
3. Set the Item argument to the following expression:

   ```
   [Forms]![frmReport].[Visible]
   ```

4. Set the Expression argument to False.
5. In the Condition column of the next blank line, enter the following expression:

   ```
   [Forms]![frmReport].Tag="Main"
   ```

6. Select the SetValue action in the Action column.
7. Set the Item argument to the following expression:

   ```
   [Forms]![frmMain1].[Visible]
   ```

8. Set the Expression argument to True.

9. In the Condition column of the next blank line, enter the following expression:

```
[Forms]![frmReport].Tag="Contact"
```

10. Select the SetValue action in the Action column.

11. Set the Item argument to the following expression:

```
[Forms]![frmContact].[Visible]
```

12. Set the Expression argument to True.

13. Select the Close action in the Action column of the next blank row.

14. Set the Object Type argument to Form.

15. Set the Object Name argument to frmReport.

Phone Log History Option Button   When the Phone Log History option button is selected, the report form will be enlarged and a list box of contact names opened for selection.

To build the macro for the Phone Log History button:

1. In a blank row, type {optPhoneLogHistory} in the Macro Name column.

2. Select the MoveSize action in the Action column.

3. Set the Width argument to 7".

4. Select the SetValue action in the Action column of the next blank row.

5. Set the Item argument to the following expression:

```
[Forms]![frmReport]![ClientLastName].[Visible]
```

6. Set the Expression argument to True.

7. Select the SetValue action in the Action column of the next blank row.

8. Set the Item argument to the following expression:

```
[Forms]![frmReport]![RepName].[Visible]
```

9. Set the Expression argument to True.

Phone History Report   When the Phone History macro is invoked, the macro checks to make sure a contact was selected. If one has been, then the report is printed; if one has not been selected, a message is displayed.

To build the macro for the Phone History option button:

1. In a blank row, type {optPhoneLogHist} in the Macro Name column.

2. In the Condition column, enter the following expression:

```
[Forms]![frmReport]![RepName] is not Null
```

3. Select the OpenReport action in the Action column.

4. Set the Report Name argument to rptPhoneList.

5. Set the View argument to Print.

6. In the Condition column of the next blank line, enter the following expression:

```
[Forms]![frmReport]![RepName] is Null
```

7. Select the MsgBox action in the Action column.

8. Set the Message argument to You Must Select a contact Before printing a Report!

Your Turn: Building the Print Preview Phone History Report Macro

Now it's your turn to build the macro that will display the Phone History report in Print Preview mode. Functionally, it works just like the macro that prints the Phone History report, but instead of opening the report in Print mode, it opens in Print Preview mode. Build the new macro by copying the mcrPrintPhoneHist cmdPrint macro (within the same macro sheet), changing the view argument for the Open Report action, and then renaming it to mcrPrintPreviewPhoneHist.

Testing Macros

Many of the macros in the WinContact application read and write values of properties from other objects, such as reports and forms. In order for these references to work, the objects must be loaded into memory. If the object is not loaded into memory, you will get an error message. The only way to test a macro is to have the associated forms, reports, and queries available.

If your macro crashes for some other reason, Access will display an error message that tells you where the error occurred. At this point, it is recommended that you go back and run the macro in Single-Step mode. Single-step mode allows your to step through you macro one line at a time, and to see what to value the

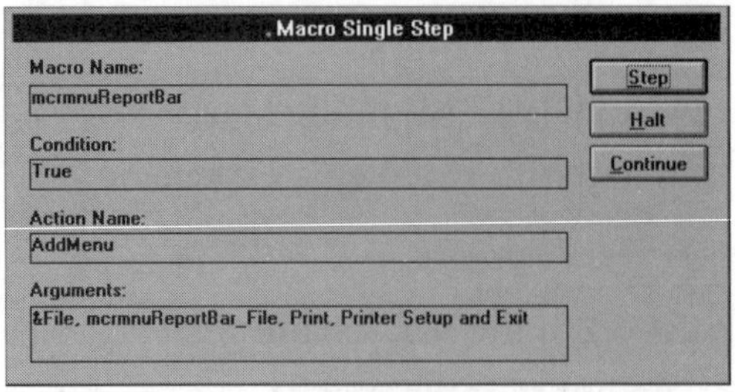

Figure 9.18 Single-Step mode for testing macros.

condition column evaluated. To toggle into Single-Step mode, select the Single-Step button on the toolbar. The next time you run your macro, you will be in Single-Step mode. The Macro Single-Step dialog is shown in Figure 9.18.

Chapter 10

Using Macros to Modify the User Interface

Recall from Chapter 3 that menus consist of three logical components: menu bars, drop-down menus, and menu items. Custom menus are implemented in Access by creating several interrelated macros. For each menu bar in the application, you will need a macro, which in essence contains a list of all of the individual drop-down menus that the bar will contain. Each item is added to the list using the AddMenu action. For each drop-down menu, a macro group (with a single macro in the group for every item on the menu) will need to be created. Each item that appears on the menu is identified by a macro name. Within the macro will be specified the action(s) that are to be executed when the item is selected. More often than not, the RunMacro action is used to run a macro that has already been created. There are two ways in Access to create the macros necessary for your custom menus in your application with the Menu Builder Add-In, or you can manually create the menu macros.

The Menu Builder Add-In is a good way to learn how the underlying macros are structured. Creating the macros from scratch requires a little more thought, but can actually be faster than the Macro Builder once you've gained some experience. It is also common to use the Menu Builder to build the skeleton macros, and then to manually modify them.

365

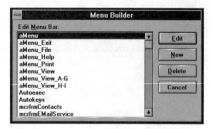

Figure 10.1 The first screen of the Menu Builder.

The Menu Builder Add-In

The Menu Builder Add-In tool graphically creates menus that shield the user fom the underlying macro structure. The best way to get a feel for the Menu Builder is to simply walk through it.

To walk through the Menu Builder Add-In:

1. Select File → Add-Ins → Menu Builder. The dialog box illustrated in Figure 10.1 will be displayed.

2. Select New. The dialog box in Figure 10.2 will be displayed. Leave the default selection of <Empty Menu Bar>.

Hint

You can also start the Menu Builder from Design mode. When you select the form's Menu Bar property, a Build button appears. Selecting the Build button at this point will open the Menu Builder, either at the second screen (if you are creating a new menu bar) or at the third screen (if you are editing an existing menu bar).

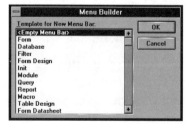

Figure 10.2 The second screen of the Menu Builder.

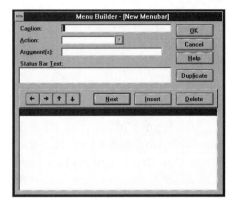

Figure 10.3 The third screen of the Menu Builder.

3. Select OK. The dialog box in Figure 10.3 will be displayed. This is referred to as the Menu Builder Construction window.

Note

Both forms and reports have a Menu Bar property. From this point on, whenever the term form is used in relation to the Menu Bar property, report can also be used.

The menu builder Construction window consists of 16 components:

- Caption edit box
- Action combo box
- Argument(s) edit box
- Status Bar Text edit box
- Indent one level button
- Outdent one level button
- Move item up one row button
- Move item down one row button
- Next item button
- Insert item button
- Delete item button
- OK command button

- Cancel command button
- Help command button
- Duplicate command button
- Menu Outline

The Caption edit box is used to specify the name of either the drop-down menu, submenu, or the menu item. If the item is flush left, it will be a drop-down menu. If it anything other than flush left, it will be an item on the drop-down menu that precedes it or a submenu. The Action combo box is used to select which macro action will be executed when the menu item is selected. The only three actions that can be specified using the Menu Builder are DoMenuItem, RunCode, and RunMacro. None of the other macro actions available in the Action drop-down list in the Macro Design window is available (although you can still use them if you create the macro manually or modify it later manually). The Argument(s) edit box is used to specify values for the arguments that correspond to the macro action that is selected in the Action combo box. If the DoMenuItem action is selected, a builder button appears next to the Argument(s) text box. Selecting this builder will display a dialog box that sets the corresponding arguments from the drop-down lists. Selecting either the Run-Code or RunMacro actions requires typing the name of the procedure or macro into the Argument(s) edit box. The Status Bar Text text box is used to specify the status bar text that will be displayed when the menu or menu item is selected.

The Indent one level button is used to indent the selected item one level. As stated earlier, if an item is flush left (no indentation), it will be a drop-down menu. If the selected item is indented one increment, it will be an item on the drop-down menu specified in a previous row. If an item has one or more indents and has additional items directly below it with another level of indentation, the item will be a submenu. The first menu item cannot be indented. If it is, when you try to exit the Macro Builder, the message box illustrated in Figure 10.4 will be displayed.

Figure 10.4 The indentation message box.

The Outdent one level button is used to move the selected item one indent to the left. The Move item up one row button is used to move the selected item up one row in the Menu Outline. The Move item down one row button is used to move the selected item down one row in the Menu Outline. The next item button is used to select the next item down in the Menu Outline. The Insert item button inserts a blank row for another item, above the current item. The Delete item button deletes the selected item.

The OK command button closes the Menu Builder and displays a message box that prompts you for a name under which to save the macro. The Cancel command button closes the Menu Builder without saving any of the changes. The Help command button displays help on the Menu Builder. The Duplicate command button saves the current menu bar's macros under another name. It behaves like the Save As command that is common in Windows applications.

The Menu Outline displays a graphical representation of the menu's structure, and allows you to select items for definition. As described earlier, any item that is flush left is a menu; any item that is indented is either a menu item or a submenu. The following is an example:

First drop-down menu

First item on first drop-down menu
Second item on first drop-down menu
Third item on first drop-down menu

Second drop-down menu

First item on second drop-down menu
Second item on second drop-down menu
Third item on second drop-down menu

Third drop-down menu

First item on third drop-down menu
Second item on third drop-down menu
Third item on third drop-down menu

To build custom menus using the Menu Builder:

1. Identify the drop-down menus that are needed for the menu bar.
2. Identify the items for each of the menus.
3. Invoke the Menu Builder and create a new menu bar.

4. Type text that will appear on the menu bar for the drop-down menu in the Caption edit box. Notice that when the Caption text box loses focus, the item is added to the lower portion of the dialog box.

5. Type the text that will appear in the status bar when the menu is selected in the Status Bar Text edit box.

6. Select Next to move to the next line in the Menu Outline.

7. Select the Indent button.

8. Add the caption for the first item that will appear on the menu created in the previous step(s) in the Caption edit box.

9. Select the desired action from the Action combo box.

10. Set the required argument(s) in the Argument(s) edit box that correspond to the action selected in step 9.

11. Type the corresponding status bar text.

12. Repeat steps 6 through 11 for every additional item on the first menu, omitting step 7 (indenting the item).

13. Select Next.

14. Select the Outdent button.

15. Repeat steps 2 through 14 for every additional menu that is required.

16. Select OK. The dialog box illustrated in Figure 10.5 will be displayed.

17. Type the name of the menu bar name in the Menu Bar Name edit box. Remember to follow the standard naming conventions.

18. Select OK.

As soon as you select OK, the Menu Builder creates the required macros. One macro will be created for the menu bar itself, and a macro will be created for each drop-down menu and submenu. The macro for the menu bar will have the name you gave it in the Save As dialog box, and will contain AddMenu actions that call each of the macros that correspond to the menus.

Figure 10.5 Menu Bar Name Save As dialog box.

Figure 10.6 Invalid actions message box for the Menu Builder.

If the Menu Builder was invoked via a Build button while in Form Design mode, Access automatically sets the Menu Bar property of the form to the name specified in the Menu Builder's Save As dialog box. If the Menu Builder was invoked via the File → Add-Ins → Menu Builder command, the Menu Bar property must be manually set for the form(s) that will use the menu.

The message box shown in Figure 10.6 will be displayed if the Menu Builder is used to edit a menu that uses any action other than DoMenuItem, RunCode, or RunMacro. Selecting OK will return you to the screen from which the Menu Builder was invoked.

Manually Creating Menu Macros

Manually creating menu macros can allow more flexibility than the Menu Builder, because any macro actions, not just DoMenuItem, RunCode, and RunMacro, can be used directly. Manually creating menu macros is a 12-step process:

1. Identify the drop-down menus that are needed for the menu bar.
2. Identify the items for each of the menus.
3. Create a macro sheet for the menu bar.
4. Use an AddMenu action for each menu to specify which macro contains the menus.
5. Save the macro sheet.
6. Open a new macro sheet.
7. Type the name of the menu item in the Macro Name column.
8. Set the actions and arguments that are required for the menu item.
9. Repeat steps 7 and 8 for each additional item.
10. Close the macro sheet and save it under the name that you specified in the corresponding AddMenu action.

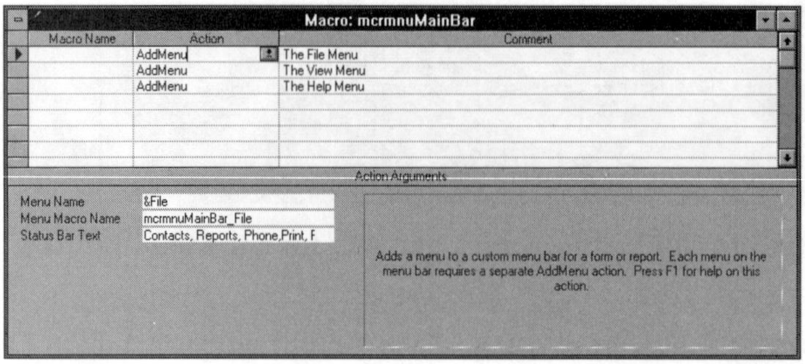

Figure 10.7 **The macro sheet for the WinContact Main window menu bar.**

11. Repeat steps 6 through 10 for every additional menu on the menu bar.

12. Assign the name of the menu bar macro to the form's Menu Bar property.

Figure 10.7 shows the macro for the WinContact Main window menu bar. Figure 10.8 illustrates the macro for its File menu.

Separator bars are created by typing a hyphen in the Macro Name column, and leaving the Action column blank. Status bar text is created by typing text in the Comment column.

Creating the Menus for WinContact

WinContact Main Window

The WinContact Main window has command and toggle buttons that allow the user to:

- Edit a contact.
- Add a contact.
- Print and print preview standard reports.
- Work with the phone log.
- Select which contacts to display in the Contact list box.
- Perform system maintenance.
- Exit WinContact.

For consistency, the custom menu for this form should include the same functionality. This functionality is easy to create by using the RunMacro action

Figure 10.8   The macro sheet for the WinContact Main window File menu.

and specifying the macros that were already created for each of the buttons. In addition to this functionality, to be consistent with the Windows interface guidelines, the menus also need to be able to:

- Display help on the Windows Help system.
- Display the table of contents for Help.
- Display an About screen.

To accomplish these tasks, the menu bar will contain three drop-down menus: File, View, and Help. The File menu, which is illustrated in Figure 10.9, will contain seven items (actually nine, including the separator bars), which correspond to all of the command buttons, except for Help. Each item will use a RunMacro action to execute the macro that corresponds to each of the command buttons on the form.

The View menu, which is illustrated in Figure 10.10, is where the user will select which contacts to view in the Contact list box. Since there are 27 toggle

Figure 10.9   The File menu.

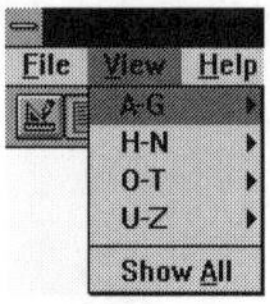

Figure 10.10 The View menu.

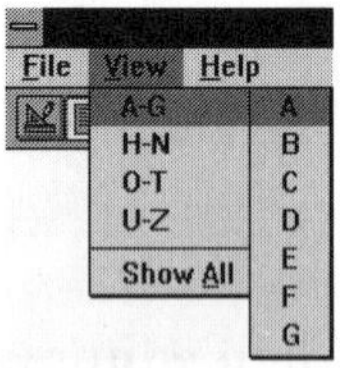

Figure 10.11 The A–G submenu.

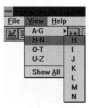

Figure 10.12 The H–N submenu.

Figure 10.13 The O–T submenu.

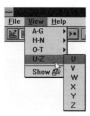

Figure 10.14 The U–Z submenu.

Figure 10.15 The Help menu.

buttons, your first thought might be to use a drop-down menu with an item that corresponded to each button. But a much more effective use of the interface would to be to provide four cascading menus (submenus), which will allow the user to select only certain letters, and an item that will show all. Figures 10.11 through 10.14 illustrate each of the submenus. When one of the items on a submenu is selected, the macro for the corresponding toggle button will be executed.

The Help menu, which is illustrated in Figure 10.15, is where the user will access help. Since a Windows Help file is not created in this book, a "dummy" message box is displayed for each of these items. You can either modify this message box to be more informative, or create a Windows Help file. The Access Developers Toolkit or some other help authoring tool that includes the Windows Help Compiler (such as the WexTech Systems Doc-To-Help) is required to do this. Since there are no corresponding macros, you will not be able to use the RunMacro action as in the other two macros. Instead, you will use the MsgBox action.

Now that the menu requirements for this form have been defined, it is time to implement the design. Because the Menu Builder does not support the MsgBox action, the macro that corresponds to the Help menu will have to be manually modified after everything else is completed.

To build the menu bar and the File menu for the WinContact Main window:

1. Open frmMain1 in Design mode.
2. Display the Property sheet, if it isn't already visible.
3. Select the Menu Bar property .
4. Select the Build button to the right of the Menu Bar property. The second Menu Builder dialog box will be displayed. Note that <Empty Menu Bar> is selected.
5. Select OK. The Construction window is displayed.
6. Type {&File} in the Caption text box.

7. Type {Contacts, reports, phone log, print, printer setup and exit} in the Status Bar Text edit box.

8. Select Next to move to the next line in the lower portion of the dialog.

9. Select the Indent button.

10. Type {&Edit Contact} in the Caption text box.

11. Type {View or Edit a contact} in the Status Bar Text edit box.

12. Select RunMacro in the Action combo box.

13. Type {mcrfrmMain1.cmdContact} in the Argument(s) edit box.

14. Select Next to move to the next line in the lower portion of the dialog.

15. Type {&Add Contact} in the Caption text box.

16. Type {Add a contact} in the Status Bar Text edit box.

17. Select RunMacro in the Action combo box.

18. Type {mcrfrmMain1.cmdAddContact} in the Argument(s) edit box.

19. Select Next to move to the next line in the lower portion of the dialog.

20. Type {-} in the Caption text box.

21. Select Next to move to the next line in the lower portion of the dialog.

22. Type {&Reports...} in the Caption text box.

23. Type {Print or Print Preview standard reports} in the Status Bar Text edit box.

24. Select RunMacro in the Action combo box.

25. Type {mcrfrmMain1.cmdReport} in the Argument(s) edit box.

26. Select Next.

27. Type {Phone &Log...} in the Caption text box.

28. Type {View or Edit the phone log} in the Status Bar Text edit box.

29. Select RunMacro in the Action combo box.

30. Type {mcrfrmMain1.cmdPhoneLog} in the Argument(s) edit box.

31. Select Next.

32. Type {System &Maintenance...} in the Caption text box.

33. Type {Perform system maintenance} in the Status Bar Text edit box.

34. Select RunMacro in the Action combo box.

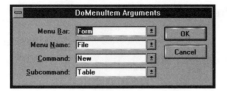

Figure 10.16 The DoMenuItem Arguments dialog box.

35. Type {mcrfrmMain1.cmdSysMaint} in the Argument(s) edit box.

36. Select Next.

37. Type {-} in the Caption text box.

38. Select Next.

39. Type {Print &Setup...} in the Caption text box.

40. Type {Change printer settings} in the Status Bar Text edit box.

41. Select DoMenuItem in the Action combo box.

42. Select the Build button next to the Argument(s) text box. The dialog box illustrated in Figure 10.16 will be displayed.

43. Select Report from the Menu Bar combo box.

44. Select Print Setup... from the Command combo box.

45. Select OK. The arguments are automatically pasted into the Argument(s) text box.

46. Select Next.

47. Type {-} in the Caption text box.

48. Select Next.

49. Type {E&xit} in the Caption text box.

50. Type {Exit WinContact} in the Status Bar Text edit box.

51. Select DoMenuItem in the Action combo box.

52. Select the Build button next to the Argument(s) text box.

53. Select Database from the Menu Bar combo box.

54. Select Exit... from the Command combo box.

55. Select OK.

56. Select Next.

To build the View menu for the WinContact Main window:

1. Select the Outdent button.
2. Type {&View} in the Caption text box.
3. Type {Filter Phone List} in the Status Bar Text edit box.
4. Select Next.
5. Select the Indent button.
6. Type {A-G} in the Caption text box.
7. Type {Display all contacts that have last names that start with a, b, c, d, e, f, or g} in the Status Bar Text edit box.
8. Select Next.
9. Select the Indent button.
10. Type {A} in the Caption text box.
11. Select RunMacro in the Action combo box.
12. Type {mcrfrmMain1.Filter_A} in the Argument(s) edit box.
13. Select Next.
14. Repeat steps 10 through 13 for the B, C, D, E, F, and G items.
15. Select the Outdent button.
16. Repeat steps 6 though 14 for the H–N submenu and each of its items.
17. Select the Outdent button.
18. Repeat steps 6 though 14 for the O–T submenu and each of its items.
19. Select the Outdent button.
20. Repeat steps 6 though 14 for the U–Z submenu and each of its items.
21. Type {Show &All} in the Caption text box.
22. Type {Display all contacts} in the Status Bar Text edit box.
23. Select RunMacro in the Action combo box.
24. Type {mcrfrmMain1.Filter_All} in the Argument(s) edit box.
25. Select Next.

To build the Help menu for the WinContact Main window:

1. Select the Outdent button.
2. Type {&Help} in the Caption text box.
3. Type {Help and information about WinContact} in the Status Bar Text edit box.
4. Select Next.

5. Select the Indent button.

6. Type {&Help on Help} in the Caption text box.

7. Type {Display Help on using Windows Help} in the Status Bar Text edit box.

8. Select Next.

9. Type {&Contents} in the Caption text box.

10. Type {Display Help Table of Contents} in the Status Bar Text edit box.

11. Select Next.

12. Type {-} in the Caption text box.

13. Select Next.

14. Type {&About} in the Caption text box.

15. Type {Display information about WinContact} in the Status Bar Text edit box.

16. Select OK.

17. Type {mcrmnufrmMainBar} in the Menu Bar Name edit box.

18. Select OK. You will be returned to the Form Design window for frmMain1. Note that the Menu Bar property has been set to mcrmnufrmMainBar.

19. Save the form.

20. Close the form's Design window.

21. Select the Macro tab in the Database window.

22. Open mcrmnufrmMainBar_Help in Design mode. This is the macro sheet that the Menu Builder created for the Help menu.

23. Replace the DoMenuItem action in all three of the macros with the MsgBox action, using the arguments listed in Table 10.1.

24. Close the Macro Design window and save the changes.

25. Open the WinContact Main window to test the new menus.

Table 10.1 Argument Values for the Help Menu Message Boxes	
Argument	**Value**
Message	No Help Created!
Beep	Yes
Type	Information
Title	WinContact

The Contacts Form

The Contacts form has command buttons that allow the user to open the Report form, print the Contacts form, and open the Phone Log for the current contact. The custom menu for this form should include these functions. Like the WinContact Main window, a Help menu should also be included. Instead of re-creating the Help menu for every menu bar, each of the additional menu bars will just call mcrmnuMainBar_Help. Additionally, a user should be able to:

- Change printer settings.
- Cut, copy, and paste data to and from the Windows clipboard.

The menu bar for the Contacts form, which is illustrated in Figure 10.17, will contain three menus. The File menu is illustrated in Figure 10.18, the Edit menu in Figure 10.19, and the Help menu in Figure 10.20.

Figure 10.17 The Contacts form.

Figure 10.18 The Contacts File menu.

Figure 10.19 The Contacts Edit menu.

Figure 10.20 The Contacts Help menu.

Row	Action	Argument	Value
Table 10.2 Values for the AddMenu Actions			
2	AddMenu	Menu Name	&Edit
		Menu Macro Name	mcrmnuContactBar_Edit
		Status Bar Text	Cut
3	AddMenu	Menu Name	&Help
		Menu Macro Name	mcrmnuMainBar_Help
		Status Bar Text	Help and information about this application

To build the menu bar for the Contacts form:

1. Open a new macro sheet.
2. Select the AddMenu action in the Action column of the first row.
3. Set the Menu Name argument to &File.
4. Set the Menu Macro Name argument to mcrmnuContactBar_File.
5. Set the Status Bar Text argument to Contacts, Reports Phone, Print, Printer Setup, and Exit.
6. Repeat steps 2 through 5 in the next two rows, using the values listed in Table 10.2.
7. Save the macro sheet as mcrmnuContactBar.
8. Close the Macro window.

To build the File menu for the Contacts Form:

1. Open a new macro sheet.
2. Type {&Reports} in the Macro Name column of the first row.
3. Select the RunMacro action in the Action column.
4. Type {Print or Print Preview standard reports} in the Comment column.
5. Set the Macro Name argument to mcrfrmContacts.cmdReport.
6. Type {Phone &Log} in the Macro Name column of the next blank row.
7. Select the RunMacro action in the Action column.
8. Type {Phone Log} in the Comment column.
9. Set the Macro Name argument to mcrfrmContacts.cmdPhoneLog.

10. Type {-} in the Macro Name column of the next blank row.

11. Type {&Print} in the Macro Name column of the next blank row.

12. Select the DoMenuItem action in the Action column.

13. Set the Menu Name argument to File.

14. Set the Command argument to Print Preview.

15. Type {P&rint Setup} in the Macro Name column of the next blank row.

16. Select the DoMenuItem action in the Action column.

17. Set the Menu Name argument to File.

18. Set the Command argument to Print Setup.

19. Save the macro sheet as mcrmnuContactBar_File.

To build the Edit menu for the Contacts Form:

1. Open a new macro sheet.

2. Type {Cu&t} in the Macro Name column of the first row.

3. Select the DoMenuItem action in the Action column.

4. Set the Menu Name argument to Edit.

5. Set the Command argument to Cut.

6. Type {&Copy} in the Macro Name column of the next blank row.

7. Select the DoMenuItem action in the Action column.

8. Set the Menu Name argument to Edit.

9. Set the Command argument to Copy.

10. Type {&Paste} in the Macro Name column of the next blank row.

11. Select the DoMenuItem action in the Action column.

12. Set the Menu Name argument to Edit.

13. Set the Command argument to Paste.

14. Save the macro sheet as mcrmnuContactBar_Edit.

To assign the Contacts form menu bar to the Contacts form:

1. Open frmContact in Design view.

2. Display the Property sheet if it is not already visible.

3. Set the Menu Bar property to mcrmnuContactBar.

4. Save and close the form.

5. Open the form to test the new menus.

Figure 10.21 The System Maintenance menu bar.

Figure 10.22 The System Maintenance File menu.

Figure 10.23 The System Maintenance Help menu.

Your Turn: Building the System Maintenance Form Menus

The System Maintenance form requires menus that correspond to each of the form's four main command buttons, as well as the standard Help menu. Figure 10.21 illustrates the menu bar, Figure 10.22 the File menu, and Figure 10.23 the Help menu. Using your choice of methods, build the macros necessary for the System Maintenance form's menus, and then assign the menu bar to the form.

Hint

An easy way to create these menus is to copy some of the macros that you have already created and modify them as required.

Your Turn: Building the New Call Form Menus

The New Call form requires menus that will display call history, start the call timer, and stop the call timer, as well as the standard Help menu. Figure 10.24 illustrates the menu bar, Figure 10.25 the File menu, and Figure 10.26 the Help menu. Using the your choice of methods, build the macros necessary for the New Call form's menus, and then assign the menu bar to the form.

Figure 10.24 The New Call menu bar.

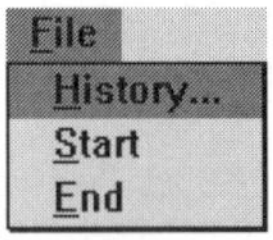

Figure 10.25 The New Call File menu.

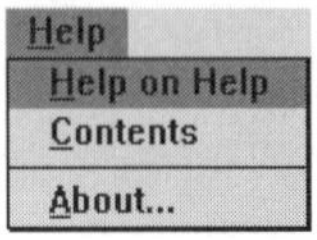

Figure 10.26 The New Call Help menu.

Figure 10.27 The Report menu bar.

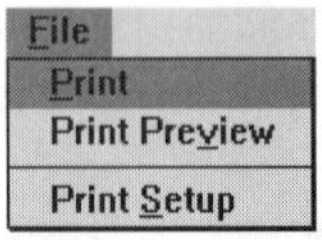

Figure 10.28 The Report File menu.

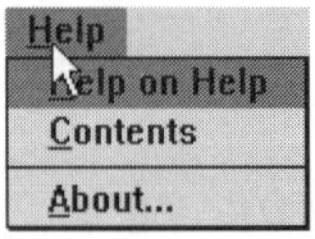

Figure 10.29 The Report Help menu.

Your Turn: Building the Phone Log Form Menus

Since the Phone Log form has no command buttons on it, it does not require a custom menu bar. By default, if you do not specify a custom menu bar, the Access Form menu will be displayed. Because this is inconsistent with shielding the user from the intricacies of Access, you should assign the New Call form's menu bar to the Phone Log form.

Your Turn: Building the Report Form Menus

The Report form requires menus that correspond to Print and Preview command buttons, as well as the standard Help menu. In addition, a menu command to change printer settings should be made available on the File menu. Figure 10.27 illustrates the menu bar, Figure 10.28 the File menu, and Figure 10.29 the Help menu. Using your choice of methods, build the macros necessary for the Report form's menus, and then assign the menu bar to the form.

Index

Free Companion Disk!

That's right, you can get a **FREE*** companion disk for **Building Access 2.0 Applications Using Point and Click Programming** by filling out the coupon below (or making a copy of it, if you don't want to cut your book up!), and enclosing $9.95 to cover shipping and handling.

-----------------------------✂-----------------------------

First Name	Last Name	Area Code/Telephone
Company	Title	
Street	P.O. Box	
City	State	ZIP

BAA

Please make check payable to Logic Control

Send to: Logic Control
21 Bridge Square
Westport, CT 06880

Who Is Logic Control?

Logic Control is a Microsoft Training Channel Partner and Consulting Channel Partner that specializes in the development of missions critical and client/server applications, developer education, and on-line help systems.

Mission Statement

Logic Control's mission is to provide creative business solutions using leading-edge technologies. Logic Control does this by offering:

➤ Developer Education

➤ Custom Software Development

➤ Technology Mentoring

Authorized Technical Education Center

Developer Education

To help you meet your software education needs, Logic Control offers:

➤ **A State-of-the-Art Training Facility:** One 66 Mhz 486DX2 workstation with a 17" monitor for each student.

➤ **Small Classes:** Maximum class size is limited to ten students.

➤ **Faculty with Real-World Experience:** All Logic Control faculty are actively involved in custom software development projects, and come from a variety of business disciplines.

➤ **Faculty Certification:** All Logic Control faculty are certified by Microsoft to deliver Microsoft University courseware.

➤ **Developer Oriented Curriculum:** Offerings include Logic Control and Microsoft University courses on:

➤ Microsoft/Sybase SQL Server

➤ Microsoft Visual Basic

➤ Microsoft Windows NT

➤ Microsoft Windows NT Advanced Server

➤ Microsoft Access

➤ Microsoft Excel

➤ Microsoft Word

➤ Microsoft Mail

➤ Microsoft Visual C++

➤ Information Modelling

➤ Relational Database Design

➤ User Interface Design

➤ **Convenient Location:** Logic Control's facilities are located in beautiful Westport, CT, on the shores of the Saugatuck River, between the Merritt Parkway and I-95, and are within walking distance of the Westport Metro North train station. This location makes our facility easy to reach from New York City, Westchester, and Connecticut.

Software Development

Logic Control has real-world experience in building custom solutions based on the products found in Microsoft Office. OLE, DDE, MAPI, and ODBC are the foundation technologies which are part of solutions that we have delivered to clients in recent engagements.

Technology Mentoring

By providing software development, and education services, Logic Control is in a unique position to help you take control of your environment, and harness new technology for the benefit of your organization.

21 Bridge Square, Westport, CT 06880
203•454•3663